D0921265

FARTHER SHORES

Exploring how near-death, kundalini and mystical experiences can transform ordinary lives

YVONNE KASON, M.D.

Author's Choice Press
iUniverse, Inc.
New York   Bloomington

Farther Shores
Exploring How Near-Death, Kundalini and Mystical Experiences Can Transform
Ordinary Lives

Copyright © 1994, 2000, 2008 by Yvonne Kason

Author's Choice Press
an imprint of iUniverse

iUniverse books may be ordered through booksellers or by contacting:

iUniverse
1663 Liberty Drive
Bloomington, IN 47403
www.iuniverse.com
1-800-Authors (1-800-288-4677)

Because of the dynamic nature of the Internet, any Web addresses or links contained in this
book may have changed since publication and may no longer be valid.

The views expressed in this work are solely those of the author and do not necessarily reflect
the views of the publisher, and the publisher hereby disclaims any responsibility for them.

ISBN: 978-0-595-53396-1

Library of Congress Control Number: 2008942348

Printed in the United States of America

Dedicated to the memory of Pandit Gopi Krishna
1903–1984

A Light in the Darkness

Contents

Acknowledgments

I wish to thank Bob Grant and Brian Clegg, who risked their lives to rescue me, Sally, and Gerry—saving our lives after the plane crash in 1979. I also wish to thank Gerald Kruschenske, who skillfully piloted the falling plane, avoiding deadly trees to bring us down onto the semi-frozen lake. I wish to acknowledge and honor the memory of Jean Peters, who lost her life in that fateful crash.

I wish to thank Jason Hintermeister and John Bradley for their love, patience, and support as I focused intensely on the revisions and updates needed to create *Farther Shores* from its earlier version.

I also thank Rolf Hintermeister, for his support and the hundreds of hours he spent babysitting our son Jason years ago so that I could work relatively uninterrupted on the completion of the first manuscript. Keeping my then three-year-old son away from "helping mommy with her book" was a formidable task, one I much appreciated.

I thank Phyllis Bruce for her vision and support throughout the journey of unfoldment of *Farther Shores*.

I am deeply grateful to Gopi Krishna, who introduced me and many others in the West to the reality of mystical experiences and kundalini awakening happening in the world.

Finally, I wish to thank the many patients, colleagues, and friends who shared the stories of their spiritually transformative experiences with me, and thereby ultimately made this book possible.

Author's Note

The personal case histories and stories included in this book are based on actual experiences, as they were described to me by patients, colleagues, and friends. In order to protect the anonymity and confidentiality of the persons involved, I have paraphrased the stories and have changed some small details and identifying features. When individuals wished to have their identities revealed, I have left their stories in their own words.

Introduction

Many people around the world are having mystical experiences. I know this first hand—I had a life-changing mystical experience in an airplane crash in 1979. My "near-death experience" (NDE) propelled me, as a medical doctor and a psychotherapist, to research mystical and paranormal experiences. I wanted to discover what was known by medicine, psychology, and spiritual traditions about mystical experiences and to share this awareness with others.

Farther Shores is the product of 20 years of inner and outer research. Over these years, hundreds of people have shared the stories of their Spiritually Transformative Experiences (STEs) with me: their mystical experiences, near-death experiences, spiritual energy or kundalini episodes, inspired creative experiences, and psychic awakenings. I've studied my own inner spiritual experiences over this time as well, researched the scholarly literature, exchanged insights with other consciousness researchers, and spoken with teachers of both Eastern and Western spiritual traditions.

With time, more and more people have come forward to speak to me as a doctor and psychotherapist, until my medical practice has become mainly focused on assessing and counseling people who are having STEs. My patients tell me of long-term STE after-effects—how an STE often seems to herald the beginning of a long-term process of spiritual transformation of consciousness. As you will read, this long-term process of psychological purification and spiritual refinement is known of in various spiritual traditions, where it has been called the "mystical path" or "kundalini process." I am grateful to the Higher Power for blessing my life with a kundalini awakening in 1976, while I was completing medical school, and a near-death experience in 1979, while I was completing my Family Practice residency. My NDE prepared me for my ultimate specialty—transpersonal psychology. I am also grateful that my medical practice evolved into a bridge between medicine, psychology, and spirituality—between body, mind, and spirit.

Unfortunately, until now, Western medicine, psychology, and society as a whole have been quite uninformed about mystical experiences and their prevalence among people today. At the time of my NDE in 1979, even good friends and medical colleagues invalidated my experience and speculated that my NDE was a "dream" or an "electrolyte imbalance." I knew this could not be true of an experience that was intensely positive. I knew my experience was real, and spiritual in nature. This societal lack of understanding launched me on a personal quest to learn more about mystical experiences and to help other people deal with similar life-changing events.

In *Farther Shores* I'm sharing the conclusions from my quest—a framework that I have found helpful in understanding STEs and long-term spiritual transformation, a framework called the modern kundalini model. This model is based on a blend of Gopi Krishna's contemporary interpretation of ancient yogic concepts with the insights of myself and other consciousness researchers, and it provides a framework that bridges Eastern and Western thought, as well as medicine and spirituality. It is the best framework I have found to understand STEs and their common after-effects—the biological, psychological, and spiritual symptoms of long-term spiritual transformation of consciousness.

This book is a guide for those people having STEs and undergoing long-term spiritual transformation. I hope that by reading *Farther Shores* they will realize that they are not alone, that their STEs are real and are also being experienced by many people today, and that STEs have been known for millennia in the mystical traditions of the world's major faiths. I offer such individuals some practical guidelines for navigating many years of what is often a tumultuous spiritual transformation, requiring intense psycho-spiritual housecleaning.

Farther Shores is also a guide for health care professionals and spiritual counselors to whom STE experiencers may turn for help. My hope is to give professionals a preliminary framework for understanding STEs and the transformation process, so they can better assess and assist their clients.

Finally, I hope this synthesis of my 20 years of clinical work and research will stimulate the research of others. Large numbers of people are having STEs and undergoing spiritual transformation. I think it essential that more research be done to better understand these experiences, and to learn how best to assist persons having them, so they are not mislabeled, mistreated, or pathologized.

I hope that every reader comes away with one clear message: We are loved. Many mystics live in the world today—doctors, lawyers, teachers, artists, business people, homemakers—people from all walks of life. These modern mystics are those who have been blessed with a glimpse of the infinite, unconditional love of the Higher Power. With near-death, spiritual energy/kundalini, and mystical experiences, the veil that normally clouds our perception temporarily lifts, and we get a brief, clear glimpse of farther shores. We reawaken to the Truth . . . that we are all loved, all the time, whether we are aware of it or not.

Section 1

Spiritually Transformative Experiences

CHAPTER 1

My Own Near-Death
Experience

Each person's life journey is unique. Still, certain types of remarkable experiences are shared by a great many people at different times along the way. These experiences often seem to punctuate the spiritual journey we all share and have a powerful effect on the individual. If there is any one thing common to them, it is that they bring about personal change, particularly when the onset of one—or many—of these experiences is sudden or dramatic. Such an experience often challenges a person's entire world view and, as a result, their ideas, values, priorities, and beliefs change. They think, feel, and see the world differently. I often hear people say after one of these experiences that their perception of reality—and their whole personality—has been transformed and propelled in a far more spiritual direction. For this reason I have come to call them Spiritually Transformative Experiences.

I speak from experience. When I was twenty-six years old I had a Near-Death Experience that would change my life forever. My childhood was fairly ordinary. My father and mother were both European immigrants who came to Canada to seek a better life after the brutality of World War II. I was born and raised—along with a sister and two brothers—in the pleasant, upper-middle-class suburbs of Toronto. Like many people who find themselves involved in the process of spiritual transformation, I was interested in spiritual matters as a child. Raised a Christian, I participated in Sunday School and, as a teenager, in the church choir of my local United Church of Canada. I believed in a God both because I had been taught to do so and because the belief gave me hope that the world—and humankind—might somehow survive its history of senseless violence and repeated wars.

Because I was considered "gifted," I was placed in a special school program. One benefit of this was that I developed a tremendous love of reading. In high school during the late 1960s, I was introduced to the writings of Alan Watts and Timothy Leary and became fascinated with their discussions of the so-called mystical states of consciousness that could be glimpsed through the use of hallucinogenic drugs such as LSD. But it quickly became clear to me that people should be able to reach these mystical states—if they did indeed represent some type of union with the divine—without the use of drugs. This thought led me, like many others of my generation, to the study of the Eastern philosophies, meditation, and yoga. This search continued throughout university and medical school.

During this time I practiced yoga intermittently and began to read books on positive thinking and a wide range of spiritual practices. Early in life I had developed a strong inner conviction that the best road in life was one of moderation and balance, and I sought out teachings that reflected this attitude. When I was in my early twenties, and practicing meditation, I had an initial experience with consciousness-altering that I was not to understand fully until later in life. In my last year of medical school I began to meditate daily and use creative visualization and positive affirmations. To this day I am convinced that these practices helped me survive a plane crash in 1979. The mystical experience I had during the airplane crash marked the beginning of a profound spiritual transformation in my own life.

The Plane Crash

In the spring of 1979, as part of my medical residency in family practice at the University of Toronto, I was assigned for one month to a small, rural hospital in Sioux Lookout that provided service for a number of isolated Native villages in remote, isolated areas of Northern Ontario. On March 27, my supervising physician designated me to accompany a Native woman, Jean Marie Peters, who had measles encephalitis, on a medical air evacuation from Sioux Lookout to Winnipeg, Manitoba. She needed the more specialized medical facilities there to treat her rapidly deteriorating condition.

During the flight, I was required to supervise her care, giving her the intravenous drugs needed to stabilize her condition and manually pumping a breathing bag, at regular intervals, that would send oxygen directly into her lungs through an airway tube that was inserted through her mouth.

The plane, a six-seat, twin-engine Piper Aztec, was packed. The patient was strapped onto a stretcher directly behind the pilot's seat where two of the original six seats had been, with the oxygen tank wedged behind the seat normally used by a co-pilot. Sally Irwin, a nurse who had also been assigned to the flight, and I were seated beside the patient.

When the plane lifted off the runway, I was so busy tending the patient that I didn't notice a heavy snowstorm had begun. But by the time we had flown for thirty or forty minutes and were about twenty miles from Kenora, a town on Lake of the Woods, the storm had become a near-blizzard. Suddenly, I noticed a change in the sound of the twin propellers. I looked up and saw that the right propeller had then stopped. The pilot, Gerald Kruschenske, was vigorously pushing buttons and pulling levers. Something was obviously wrong. Shouting over the roar of the engine, I asked what was going on. He shouted back that everything was all right. About ten seconds later I was reassured when the right propeller started again. Everything seemed to be back to normal, and I returned my attention to the patient.

A few minutes later the left propeller started sputtering. Looking up, I saw that the right propeller was still working but the left propeller had stopped. Alarmed, I shouted again at Gerry to find out what was happening, but he didn't answer. He was desperately pushing buttons, pulling levers, and pumping handles in an attempt to restart the left engine. I noticed we were flying quite low over the trees and hills. Unbeknownst to the nurse Sally and me, Gerry had been in radio contact with the Kenora airport for some time and was trying to make an emergency landing there. He had already made one attempt, but, flying with only one engine in the howling wind, he couldn't maneuver the plane into proper position. The airport then tried to direct him to a landing strip on the frozen lake. Through the raging snow, he saw what he thought was the landing strip and made an attempt to come down, but again he couldn't get the plane into proper position. As he fought to pull the sluggish plane up again and take another try at the landing, he saw a hill near the edge of the lake and realized instantly that the plane would never clear it. Taking his only option, he cut the sputtering right engine and headed down, praying the ice would hold.

Although Sally and I realized something was wrong, I had no idea how desperate the situation was—until I looked out the window and saw the second propeller die. Both engines were gone.

"Oh my God," I thought, "we're going to crash!" A wave of intense fear and panic overtook me. "God, help! I'm going to die!"

Then, as quickly as the panic had overtaken me, I was suddenly flooded with a feeling of calm. I heard an inner voice comforting me. Verses from the Bible—verses that I didn't know by heart and wasn't consciously trying to remember—flowed through my mind, as if they were being poured into my consciousness by some other force: "Be still, and know that I am God." "God is our refuge and our strength, of what shall we be afraid!" "I am with you, now and always." As the words penetrated my soul, I was suddenly overwhelmed with a sense of peace, love, and the presence of God. I was no longer afraid. My mind was still. I knew that God was there, and I knew with absolute certainty something

I had never known before: There was absolutely nothing to fear in death. I felt enveloped and protected by God.

As the plane tumbled towards the ground, I turned again to tending the patient Jean. She had regained consciousness and was frightened by the terrible turbulence and the atmosphere of tension in the plane. Her eyes looked into mine, pleading for help. Filled with the peace, calm, and bliss that had somehow come upon me, I was able to reassure her. "Everything will be all right," I comforted her, somehow knowing this to be true whether we lived or died. Just then Sally suggested that we turn off the oxygen tank. Agreeing, I turned off the tank and freed Jean so she could breathe on her own and then continued to calmly reassure her with absolute conviction: I knew that, no matter what happened, everything was proceeding according to some divine plan and that there was nothing to fear.

Gerry managed to steer the engineless plane and skid onto the ice—but just as the plane touched down, he saw that the lake was only partially frozen and the plane was headed towards a huge stretch of open water. Knowing the plane would never stop in time, he forced its nose down into the ice. It dug in and, by some miracle, the plane stopped just at the edge of the ice.

But as soon as the full weight of the plane settled, the ice began to break and the plane started to sink into the freezing water. Gerry jumped out of his door, stood on the left wing, and started radioing an emergency message.

Meanwhile, icy water was filling the floor of the plane, and I was struggling without success to open the door on the right. The water rose. I shouted to Gerry but he was still frantically trying to radio for help. The freezing water was pouring deeper and deeper into the plane. Although I was still in a mystical, peaceful state, I knew we urgently needed to get out of the plane. I turned to Sally: "Help me lift the stretcher and we'll float it out." Again I shouted to Gerry. Dropping the radio, he grabbed the door handle, found it was jammed, and banged with his fist until he finally managed to force it open. I stepped out through the door onto the right wing of the plane and found myself up to the groin in freezing lake water. Though I pulled with all my might at the patient's stretcher, I could not get it out of the door. I called to Gerry for help. Just as I did, he shouted that the plane was going down! I grabbed Sally out from behind the stretcher and, together, we desperately tried to pull Jean, floating, strapped to her stretcher, out of the door. But it was impossible. Then I remembered that the stretcher had been loaded through the cargo hatch at the back, and that there was simply no way to get it out of the door. Before we could even think about trying to unstrap her, the plane tilted radically, nose dived, and sank. There was no way to dive after Jean; the plane had sunk without a trace into the pitch-black water.

Gerry, Sally, and I were suddenly floating in freezing water about 200 yards from an island. Open water with a strong, swiftly moving current separated us from the shore. Behind us the rest of the lake appeared to be frozen, but we had no way of judging the thickness of the ice. Later, I learned that we had landed on Lake of the Woods at a place called Devil's Gap that never froze because of the strength of the current.

As I kicked and struggled to keep my head above the water, I quickly began to tire. My bulky arctic parka was dragging me down, and my insulated boots were starting to feel like lead weights. When I tried to take off the parka, I discovered my hands were so close to frozen that I had lost my sense of touch and couldn't manipulate the zipper. I knew we had to get out of the water, fast. I looked across the black, icy water and heard a voice in my head say, "Swim to shore!"

But my rational mind interjected with words ingrained since childhood about water safety: "Never try to swim to shore!" "It's always further than it seems." "You'll drown if you try!" Gerry shouted, "Try to get on the ice!" I swam towards it and tried to climb on. Each time I attempted to kick and pull myself up, the chunks beneath my arms would break off and sink. Again and again I tried, becoming more exhausted with each attempt. The voice in my head told me again to swim to shore. "The ice is too thin," I shouted to Gerry and Sally, who were still struggling to get onto it. Later I learned that Sally couldn't swim.

Finally, the inner voice became so loud as it repeated "swim to shore" that I surrendered to it, turned from the ice, and began swimming through the fast-moving open water towards the island. It was a long and difficult swim.

As I struggled through the frigid water, I suddenly heard a low-pitched whooshing noise, something like the rushing of a large bird's wings. Without warning, I felt my consciousness rise above the water and found myself looking down at my body struggling through the water. It seemed as if my being had expanded and filled a much larger space than it ever had before. The sense of peace and calm I had been feeling intensified, and a sense of unconditional universal love flowed through me. I was surrounded by light. The world around seemed lighter and brighter; as if the sun were brightly shining in spite of the snow and the dark, overcast sky.

I felt like I was being embraced by a universal, loving, and omnipotent intelligence. This was not an intellectual knowledge; it was a certainty that went to the very core of my being. The presence of this loving intelligence enveloped and overwhelmed me. It was the most profoundly beautiful, blissful experience I have ever had in my life. I knew that everything was unfolding as it should.

From above, I watched with detachment and curiosity as my physical body swam to shore. I seemed to flit between being aware of what was happening to my physical body and being totally absorbed in this blissful mental state. As my body struggled towards the island, it sank twice from sheer exhaustion and the weight of my waterlogged clothes. Each time it went under, icy lake water filled my lungs. As I watched from above, I saw myself sputter, cough, and struggle back to the surface. Just when my body was completely exhausted, my consciousness seemed to slip momentarily back into my body, and I found myself looking towards the shore. It was only twenty feet away, but there was a strong current pulling me to the right and I could swim no farther. But I was still in that beautiful, peaceful state of mind, and I knew with absolute certainty that death held nothing to fear. I felt only a vague intellectual curiosity and can remember thinking, "Oh, I see, I am meant to die here in the life play I'm acting in just now."

Blissfully, I surrendered to the divine and the thought of death. But just as I was about to go down for the third and last time, I saw—once again, through my eyes—that a tall, fallen pine tree lay in the water, extending out from the shore. The tree was to my right, and the current was rapidly carrying me towards it. Suddenly I realized that if I could swim just two more strokes, the current would carry me right into the tip of the tree. The tree looked like a rescuing hand that was beckoning and reaching out to me.

Somehow I was granted the strength to swim those last two strokes. When my frozen hand struck the fallen tree, I felt no sensation at all. I looked down at my completely numb hand, saw that it was bright red, and felt surprised. My rational, medically trained mind pierced my blissful state of consciousness, telling me my hand should be white if it was frozen, since blood vessels constrict to save body heat. Later I learned that, in the latter stages of freezing, the body loses the ability to constrict blood vessels and the white hands become red. Death usually comes fairly quickly after this if the body isn't warmed.

Mechanically, I pulled myself along the tree to shore and climbed over some piles of ice onto the island. I turned to the lake and shouted to Gerry and Sally to swim to shore. "You can make it!" I urged them. Gerry by that time had helped Sally grab a piece of frozen wood and ice that was keeping her afloat. It wouldn't hold them both, so he turned and started swimming to shore. He made it in and crawled to my side. The lake was silent. The nurse had stopped crying for help. I believed that she, like Jean, must have drowned.

Still floating between paranormal and normal consciousness, I asked Gerry if he knew how to light a fire without matches. He didn't. Deathly cold, I started vomiting repeatedly. The desire to go to sleep was almost overwhelming, but my inner voice kept screaming "No!" Somehow I knew that— even though my consciousness was floating out of my body— I must not let my physical body fall asleep. If I did, I wouldn't wake up again. Instinctively, I crouched into a full squat and tucked my frozen fingers into my armpits to try to warm them. I told Gerry to do the same. The bitter, freezing cold was beyond description. Then I felt my consciousness start to move further away from my physical body again. I knew that we could not survive long in the snowstorm, the subzero weather, and our wet, nearly frozen clothes. We were freezing to death. My consciousness hovered above my freezing body in light and love.

Rescue and Spiritual Awakening

We almost certainly wouldn't have been rescued in time if it hadn't been for an amazing series of coincidences. The snowstorm was so severe and the terrain so hilly that our final distress signal could only have been picked up by a plane flying almost directly overhead. Just at the critical moment one was. An Air Canada flight, on its way from Edmonton to Ottawa, picked up the signal and radioed our crash location to the airport in Kenora.

Still, we were a long way from rescue. We had crashed in a remote region. Because of the mix of ice and open water, the island was not accessible by either boat or snowmobile. Nothing but a helicopter could reach us, and normally none were located in the region. But, by chance, one was being ferried that day from Edmonton to Val d'Or, Quebec, by a pilot named Brian Clegg. Concerned by the snowstorm, Brian had hoped to land at Kenora Airport but had been forced to come down at a small Ontario Ministry of Natural Resources base about five miles from where our plane had crashed.

When Brian had first landed, he had gone into the base and met with a Ministry staff pilot, Bob Grant, who had also been grounded by the storm. As they were talking, the phone rang: Kenora Airport was relaying a message from the pilot of a twin-engine Aztec that was flying in the area and having serious engine trouble.

Brian Clegg sensed that his helicopter might be needed. He rushed out, began removing its protective weather covering, and turned on his radio. He, too, heard the relayed message from the Air Canada jet and immediately started his engines. He called to

Bob Grant and, without any thought for their own safety, the two headed into the storm.

As they flew, Kenora Airport directed them to the general area of the crash. The two pilots searched frantically for the large pieces of wreckage they thought would be visible on the ice or among the trees, but hampered by the snowstorm, they could not see Gerry and me huddled under the trees on the island or Sally floating like a human icicle clinging to a piece of ice-caked wood in the lake. After making a rapid sweep of the area and finding nothing, they decided to take a closer look at Devil's Gap, where they thought they might have seen something floating in the open water. Coming down low, they spied a seat cushion—then they spotted Sally, who was unconscious.

Brian hovered the helicopter a few feet above her in the icy water, while Bob climbed out and, hanging on to a strut, tried to pull her rigid, ice-covered form out of the water. Again and again she slid from his grasp. When all else failed, Brian tried to balance the helicopter right on the water, a dangerous maneuver since the least shift in weight could cause the helicopter to crash. Fearlessly Bob—a non-swimmer—straddled the skid, dangled his legs in the icy water, and managed to grasp Sally and, eventually, get one of her hands around the skid. With Sally hanging and Bob pressing her hand onto the skid, the helicopter carried them to a spot where the ice was thick enough to hold Sally's weight. Then, as the helicopter hovered a few feet above the ice, Bob balanced on the skid and tried in vain to push all of her rigid, frozen body through the doorway and onto the seat. Finally, he managed to wedge in all but her legs. Using his body to brace her in, Bob stood outside the helicopter on the ice-caked skid while they flew to Kenora Hospital.

About twenty minutes later the two men returned to the island. They found us, but couldn't find a place to land. The island was covered with trees and bordered by fast-moving water. They were on the verge of despair when they noticed a small inlet where the water was protected enough to have frozen solid. Brian managed to land the helicopter, with its rear propeller dangling over the water, on this small piece of ice.

Our rescuers gestured to us to come to the helicopter. Gerry was able to stumble to the helicopter, but I was only semi-conscious and unable to walk. Without hesitation, Bob jumped out and—not knowing if the ice could support the additional weight—came to get me. He carried and pulled me over a hill, across the ice, and into the helicopter. Once in the helicopter, I lost consciousness.

When we arrived at Kenora Hospital, the helicopter landed on the hospital's driveway. My consciousness was once again floating above my body. I was taken out of the helicopter, placed on a stretcher, and wheeled into the hospital. I still felt completely at peace and had no fear of what seemed to be my impending death. As I watched from above, a nurse covered me and my wet, frozen clothes with a thin, loosely woven cotton hospital blanket. Another nurse tried to take my temperature and was puzzled that she couldn't get a temperature reading. My body temperature was so low the thermometer could not measure it! As I watched I felt myself start to float further and further away from my body. I knew that I was dying, and I was at peace.

Suddenly I heard a voice say, "Boy, could I use a hot bath!" Hovering above, I was surprised to realize the voice had come from my own physical body. Later I discovered that rewarming the body by submersion in hot water had recently come to be considered an excellent emergency treatment for advanced hypothermia. However, I hadn't been taught this in medical school—and I have no idea why or how my body uttered these words.

Thinking I was regaining consciousness and making a brave attempt at humor, the nurses laughed. Like me, they were untrained in treating hypothermia. But then one nurse grew serious and suggested that the hot water might help revive us. The nurses wheeled our stretchers to the physiotherapy department, pulled off our ice-encrusted clothes, and slid our frozen bodies into the whirlpools.

As I was submerged in the hot, swirling water, I felt my consciousness abruptly shrinking from its expanded state and pulled through the top of my head back down into my body. The sensation was similar to what I imagine a genie might feel when it is forcibly sucked back into its tiny bottle. I heard a whoosh, felt a downward pulling sensation, and was suddenly aware of being totally back in my body again. I rubbed my numb hands along my legs and my arms in the hot water, and exclaimed with joy, "I'm back! I'm going to live!" And I knew that it was true.

Even though I was quite ill—with severe frostbite on my face, neck, and hands and a wrenching cough from the dirty lake water I had aspirated—I felt wonderful emotionally. I was overwhelmed with joy at being given another chance at life and awed by the spiritual impact of my experience. Peace flowed over me.

That night, Sally and I were put in the same room. She also seemed to be strangely blissful and at peace. At one point she turned to me and said, "I don't know why it happened, Yvonne, but we have both been saved. Maybe we are going to do something important in our lives." I just smiled in agreement. I sensed that she, too, must have had some sort of intense spiritual experience.

In May of that year Brian Clegg and Bob Grant were publicly acknowledged by the government of Ontario for their courage and, in September, the Governor General of Canada awarded them both the Star of Courage, one of Canada's highest awards for civilian valor. Two months later they received an international award for outstanding valor—a Silver Medal from the Andrew Carnegie Hero Fund Commission. And, when an inquest on the accident was held, our pilot, Gerald Kruschenske, received a commendation for the quick thinking and skill that undoubtedly kept us from all dying when the plane first went down.

The day after the crash, I was released from Kenora Hospital. I returned to Toronto but was unable to work for about four weeks. The frostbite on my hands was so severe that I couldn't even hold a pen or fork and I had absolutely no feeling in my fingertips. This meant I couldn't use my hands to examine patients at work. For a while I coughed and was feverish, but eventually my lungs managed to clear the bits of residue from the lake water that I had inhaled.

The month I had off work helped me recuperate physically but, more important, gave me time to begin to integrate the overwhelming emotional and spiritual impact of the experience into my daily life.

For some time I remained in a state of awe. I wept with joy at the thought of being alive and at having been given a second chance. When I looked at the world, a rapturous love flooded out of me towards everyone and everything. During those weeks, wonder filled my life. Any song that mentioned love, life, children, parents, animals, or righting any type of social injustice made me weep and often triggered feelings of bliss. I felt a powerful, personal connection to a totally loving Higher Power, what I call God, and I knew that every other person on the planet was connected to God in the same way.

Using terms from my Christian upbringing, I could have said that I had experienced the grace of God—and had been blessed with a miracle. Still, I had no idea what to call what had happened to me. I talked excitedly to many of my friends and medical colleagues about floating out of my body, the light, being in some type of mystical state, and feeling as if I had been in the presence of the loving power behind the universe—glimpsing God. No one could offer me an acceptable explanation. Some of my physician friends said it was a hallucination brought on by low blood sugar, an electrolyte imbalance, or the effect of cold on the brain. Only one person—a physician who was also a devout Christian—gave me an acceptable explanation: He called it, simply, a mystical experience. When I spoke of my experience from then on, I said I'd had a mystical experience while I was near death. Now I know that what I underwent that day was a Near-Death Experience.

The Transformational Impact

I soon became aware that the experience was affecting other areas of my life and having a profound transformational effect on me. I realized it was time to come to grips with and heal some of the unresolved psychological issues in my life. At the same time, suppressed childhood memories began to surface spontaneously. One involved my father: He and I had been feuding since I was a child, and we hadn't spoken for about two years. In a moment of clarity shortly after my experience, I realized much of the anger I had directed at him stemmed from witnessing a heated argument between my mother and him when I was a child. As the memory resurfaced, I realized how traumatic the experience had been for me and that I had been angry at him from that moment on.

Immediately I telephoned my father, told him I loved him for the first time, and asked if we could talk. We had a truly meaningful discussion about how my parents' marital difficulties had negatively influenced our father–daughter relationship. Somehow, the intense love and clarity that stayed with me in the weeks after my mystical experience enabled me to effortlessly let go of my resentment. The anger I had harbored towards my father for 21 years seemed to evaporate, and he and I made peace. Then I went to the rest of my family, one by one, and told them how much I loved them.

A transformation also seemed to occur in my emotional maturity and strength. With this new-found maturity I seemed to be able to see things more clearly than before, and I became aware of another piece of psychological business that needed to be resolved. At the time of the plane crash, I belonged to a small meditation group where I had learned some useful meditation techniques and important ideas. But after the crash I realized that the leader of the group had become increasingly abusive and dysfunctional and that he was becoming self-inflated and deceitful to maintain an aura of superiority. It was as if a veil that had been clouding my sight was lifted.

With my new strength and spiritual conviction, I was able to confront the leader. Gently, I tried to tell him that a spiritual group led by someone who lied could not possibly last. I asked him to admit his lies, to apologize, and to try to make a fresh start. He refused. I left the group feeling clearer emotionally than I ever had in my life.

The months of transformation that occurred after my Near-Death Experience left me feeling psychologically strong, clear, and centered. I felt tremendous inner strength and the courage to speak honestly. The experience still remains a source of tremendous inspiration some 20 years later. More important, it began a process of personal transformation that has continued to this day.

When I finally returned to work, I had regained much of the feeling in my fingertips and I felt physically and emotionally well—but I still didn't know I had had a Near-Death Experience, and I certainly didn't know an NDE could leave one's mind open to psychic input. Imagine my shock when, about two months after the plane wreck, I had my first psychic experience.

My Psychic Awakening

After work one evening, I was driving to visit my friend Susan. As I was stopped at a red light, a vivid, bright, and almost glowing image popped into my mind's eye: a brain coated in pus. The image was so clear I was stunned.

I was certain the picture I saw represented meningitis—an infection of the surface lining of the brain. I was also sure that it was Susan's brain. Initially, bewildered by the experience, I decided not to mention it to anyone. But, when I arrived at Susan's house, I asked her how she was feeling. She told me she had been suffering from a severe, unusual headache—a classic symptom of meningitis—for several hours. I didn't want to alarm her, but, just to make sure, I asked her about other common symptoms of meningitis. Even though she didn't have any of them, the image of the horrible pus-covered brain haunted me, and I felt I had to say something. Hesitantly, I told her about the vision and what I thought it represented. She thought for a moment and then asked how she could tell if her headache did indicate early meningitis. I explained that, in meningitis, the initial headache worsens, a fever and stiff neck develop, and vomiting often ensues. We agreed that, in the event these symptoms developed, she would go to the local emergency department and explain that a friend who was a doctor had suggested she be tested for meningitis.

Later that evening, Susan became increasingly ill. When she went to emergency, the doctors did a spinal tap and confirmed that she had a rare, often-fatal type of meningitis. The early diagnosis allowed the doctors to treat her successfully, and she was able to return home in two weeks.

Although I didn't realize it at the time, I now know that the image I saw in the car that day was a type of psychic experience known as a clairvoyant vision. It was a symbol that represented a physical reality that I could not possibly have known about. As amazed as I was by this experience, I was reluctant to mention it to others—especially other doctors—for many years. I was afraid that I would be disbelieved or ridiculed, even though I knew in my heart how real and powerful the vision had been.

Over the years I learned a great deal more about psychic experiences, but only when I met Dr. Kenneth Ring, the eminent NDE researcher and author, did I learn that scientific research existed to show that many people who have NDEs have similar psychic awakenings.

In addition to triggering an acceleration in my own spiritual process, my NDE intensified my desire to discover more about mystical and paranormal phenomena and how they relate to both personal transformation and long-term spiritual transformation of consciousness. As you will see in the following chapters, my search led me to the teachings of spiritual masters and the writings of great scholars and scientists. Eventually, it also led to working in my clinical practice with people who are undergoing Spiritually Transformative Experiences, helping them heal and grow on their spiritual journeys. Looking back, I can see that my Near-Death Experience accelerated my own spiritual journey. Since the NDE, I have been blessed with other mystical and paranormal experiences, and a number of phenomena associated with other types of Spiritually Transformative Experiences are now part of my daily life. But I have no grandiosity about this. Through my research and clinical work, I know that the same thing is happening to thousands, perhaps even millions, of people of all ages around the world today.

The process of spiritual transformation is never completely

smooth. Indeed, at times it can be extremely difficult. But it is possible to minimize and deal effectively with the difficulties and, in the process, increase your own potential for spiritual transformation. This is particularly true if you understand the process you are going through, begin to see how it relates to the larger picture, and start to use the many strategies for promoting a healthy transformative process that are described in detail in the following pages. We can, in short, safely reach the shore that awaits us on the other side of the sometimes rough and stormy waters.

CHAPTER 2

Spiritually Transformative Experiences

Over the years, in the process of trying to better understand my own Near-Death Experience, I began to gather a great deal of information on what I have come to call Spiritually Transformative Experiences (STEs): Mystical Experiences, Near-Death Experiences, Psychic Experiences, Spontaneous Inspired Creativity, and Spiritual Energy/Kundalini Episodes. In the following pages, I am going to consider each of these categories and look at how they have affected some of my patients, my friends, and even myself. I'll also take a closer look at how extremely intense or very dramatic STEs may be mistaken for—or possibly contribute to—some types of mental or emotional problems. In addition, I'll examine the techniques that have helped people integrate their spiritual experiences into their daily lives and deal with the tremendous change and upheaval they often cause. Beyond this, I'll explore the long-term process of spiritual transformation itself.

After years of study and research I have come to think that STEs are part of a transformation and expansion of consciousness in which we become intermittently capable of perceiving other levels of reality, including what we might consider mystical or paranormal dimensions. STEs appear to be signs that this transformation may be accelerating.

Spiritually Transformative Experiences can differ greatly in intensity. Some are relatively mild; others, which I call STE peaks or STEPs, are extremely powerful. A STEP is a discrete, time-limited episode that is intensely absorbing or even overwhelming. STEP seems a particularly appropriate name: when people have one of these experiences they often take a major step along the spiritual journey.

Sometimes the changes in our consciousness are gradual, allowing us time to adjust our view of reality slowly and thoughtfully. But often—for a number of reasons I will explain later—they seem to occur abruptly or rapidly. They can cause reality as we once knew it to shift before our very eyes. They can challenge our thinking on almost every subject, cause a major shift in our world views, and force us to question much of what we have based our lives on.

When this happens we need to know we are not alone. We need to know that these experiences are normal and while in some ways uniquely our own, are also universal. Great scholars and thinkers have, in fact, been writing about such experiences for centuries.

Mystical Experiences

References to mystical experience—the transcending of the self and the union with the divine—abound in all the world's major religions. Many can be found in the Bible. In the New Testament, there is the classic story of St. Paul on the road to Damascus, where he was blinded for three days by a white light from heaven and converted to Christianity (Galatians 1:15–16). The Catholic canon is filled with saints who spoke candidly of their union with the divine. In *The Interior Castle*, St. Teresa of Avila writes that the soul, when in this union, is "utterly dead to the things of the world, and lives solely in God. . . ."

Psychic Awakening

References to Psychic Awakenings are more common in the great religious traditions than one might expect. In Buddhism, psychic abilities are called iddhis or wonderful gifts. Although their development is considered a natural part of the spiritual journey, seekers are taught to turn away from them so that they are not distracted from their true goal, enlightenment or union with the Absolute. Hindu yogis call these powers siddhis and view them much as the Buddhists do. In early Christianity, references to the gifts of tongues, prophecy, and healing were common and, although many modern Christians tend to think of them as evidence of miracles from earlier days, St. Paul and the Apostles spoke of them as simple realities for those who had been baptized in the Holy Spirit.

Near-Death Experiences

Numerous Christian authorities accept the reality of Near-Death Experiences—and many feel the stories told by Near-Death Experiencers give added credence to the concept of life after death. The scholar and Anglican priest Tom Harpur writes in *Life After Death*, "I now believe that the near-universal, ancient human belief in personal survival after death is the result of . . . experiences of contact with another reality [i.e., Near-Death Experiences]. . . ." Harpur also finds it interesting that Near-Death Experiencers, regardless of their religion, describe scenes that are remarkably similar to the descriptions of the Bardo—the Buddhist between-life state—that are found in *The Tibetan Book of the Dead*.

Spontaneous Inspired Creativity and Genius

At first glance, Spontaneous Inspired Creativity and Genius might seem to have little to do with world religions; however, they have been experienced by many saints and spiritual masters. St. Francis of Assisi wrote beautiful, inspired poetry and songs. The little-educated nun, St. Hildegaard of Bingen, spontaneously wrote poetry, composed music, and painted beautiful pictures. Lal Ded, the most beloved yogini and saint of Kashmir, wrote poetry that transformed the Kashmiri language. And the poetic writings of many Sufi saints—including Rumi and Rabiah—are considered great literary works.

Spiritual Energy/Kundalini Episodes

Spiritual energy experiences are well described in the yogic tradition, known as the awakening of kundalini, a latent, spiritual energy in the human body. When this energy is awakened people experience a sensation of energy rushing up the body, traveling upwards from the base of the spine to the brain. Associated with inner light, heat, and inner sounds, it can bring about paranormal states of perception and, ultimately, mystical union. The awakening of kundalini, which will be explained in detail later in this chapter, is a phenomenon associated with yoga and Hinduism, but similar spiritual energy processes are described in other religions, in particular Taoism, Tibetan Buddhism, Christian mysticism, Judaism, Sufism, and shamanism.

Spiritual Energy Cross-Culturally

From these examples it is clear that Spiritually Transformative Experiences are well known in the major religions. Many of the mystical and esoteric traditions within these religions go even farther: They allude to a spiritual energy or force that seems to trigger—or underlie—all the types of transformative experiences. The common premise within all the traditions is that this spiritual energy or force, once active within an individual, is associated with new development of the STEs.

This energy or force is almost always symbolized by light or fire. In the Hindu yogic tradition, it is called kundalini; in Tibetan Buddhism, it is candali or Dumo fire. Chayim Barton, in his Ph.D. dissertation thesis, directly compares kundalini to the Tibetan Buddhist concept of igniting the inner fire, the "gtum mo" (Dumo). Citing *Tibetan Yoga* by W.Y. Evans-Wentz and John Blofeld's *The Tantric Mysticism of Tibet*, he states that in Vajrayana Buddhism in the Yoga of Psychic Heat ". . . the goal is to cause an extraordinary psycho/physical force known as the inner fire (Tibetan: gtum mo), (Sanskrit: kundalini) to ignite within one's body . . . The energies are then concentrated into the central channel (Tibetan: itsa dbu ma), (Sanskrit: shushumna nadi) where they become a force to open the psychic centers (Sanskrit: chakras) and catalyze mystical states of perception."

In Taoism, kundalini is a higher spiritual aspect of chi or the Circulation of Light. Dr. Phillip Lansky and Dr. Shen Yu, two experts in Taoist Chi Kung, propose that the esoteric techniques of "Bone marrow Chi Kung" are advanced practices aimed to create energy movement and, thereby, spiritual transformation of consciousness equivalent to kundalini awakening. Dr. Bonnie Greenwell concludes in *Energies of Transformation* that the Taoist equivalent to kundalini is the "Circulation of Light" where the mind guides the energy upwards to penetrate the "crucible of the creative" or the third eye between the eyebrows. Dr. Greenwell goes on to document many other cross-cultural references to a spiritually transformative energy like kundalini—in Eskimo shamans, Hopi Indian traditions, !Kung Bushmen of Africa, Jewish Kabbala, Gnostic gospels, and in alchemy.

Kundalini is also well known in the Sufi tradition, according to Irina Tweedie in *The Chasm of Fire*. Her teacher, a Sufi master, is quoted as saying: "It is of no importance if you believe in the existence of kundalini or not: kundalini is. Kundalini is not sex-impulse alone; but sex power forms part of kundalini. As a rule the energy at the base of the spine is more or less dormant. By our system it is awakened gently . . . One has to know how to take it up and take it down again through all the chakras . . .

When it reaches the heart chakra: it means peace, bliss, states of expanded consciousness."

In the German Kabbalistic tradition of Judaism, the mystic seeks to transform his or her soul by uniting with the divine light and fire known as Shekinah, the female aspect of God. Kundalini was also known to the Kabbalistic writers of Genesis according to Carlo Suares in "The Cipher of Genesis—The Original code of the Qabala as applied to the Scriptures," cited by Swami Kripananda in Dr. Stan Grof's *Ancient Wisdom and Modern Science*. Of the serpent in the Garden of Eden, Suares claims that "in certain [traditions] his name is Kundalini. He is the resurrection of Aleph, the principle of all that is and all that is not . . . The mission of the serpent is to plunge them [Adam and Eve] into evolution. When Esha [Eve] is questioned . . . she does not reply, as the translations assert 'The serpent beguiled me.' What she says is that the serpent blends his earthly fire with her lost heavenly fire, which comes to life again."

Further, a number of Christian theologians have recently written works showing the parallels between kundalini awakening in the Eastern traditions and the concept of the Holy Spirit in the West. In 1991, Philip St. Romaine, a spiritual counselor who is Associate Director of the Spiritual Life Center in Wichita, Kansas, published a particularly lucid and informative book on the subject called *Kundalini Energy and Christian Spirituality: A Pathway to Growth and Healing*. St. Romaine believes that some types of experiences of the Holy Spirit are kundalini experiences.

In my own reading of Christian mystical literature, I have found many descriptions similar to yogic descriptions of kundalini awakenings. These are most clearly described in the writings of Charles Fillmore, the American mystic whose teachings were instrumental in the founding of the Unity Church. A book published by the Unity School of Christianity claims, "Prayer and meditation may awaken the fire energy (Kundalini) of the Holy Spirit. This energy is the great purifier of Spirit which begins a subtle inner process which ultimately leads to a state of union with the Christ. As the result of this awakening, you may experience physical sensations of rocking, shaking, or automatic

breathing (pranayama) . . . There may be burning sensations as
the fire of the Holy Spirit purifies the energy centers in the body
. . . There may be distinct sensations in the chakras as purified
energy moves through to open them to the higher energies of the
self."

Recently I received a letter from a medical doctor in New
Zealand who has extensive training in psychiatry and a Ph.D.
in experimental psychology. Writing to me about her own
STEs, she described herself as a very active Christian and said,
"I have realized that some of the experiences I have had can be
interpreted both as 'Holy Spirit' . . . and as 'Kundalini Awakening.'" The many cross-cultural references to spiritual energy
phenomena similar to the yogic descriptions of kundalini are
also noted by Rosemary Guiley in *Harper's Encyclopedia of
Mystical and Paranormal Experience.* She states, "The rise of
the powerful Kundalini energy . . . is reported cross-culturally.
Christian mystics, such as St. Therese (1873-1897) . . . sometimes experienced the heat, energy, spontaneous body movements and pain characteristic of a yogic Kundalini awakening.
The same phenomenon is reported among the !Kung bushmen
of Africa, and in Sufism, Taoism, Buddhism, and Shamanism.
In a nonreligious context, Kundalini awakening is called a
'spiritual emergence' or 'spiritual emergency.'"

It is not the purpose of this book to attempt a detailed comparison of different religious traditions' views on spiritual
energy. However, I think it is important to realize—as strange as
it may seem to us at first—that the belief in the existence of some
type of transformative spiritual force has been around for centuries and has appeared in many cultures. When I talk about this
transformative spiritual force I will often refer to it as spiritual
energy or kundalini.

Understanding Kundalini

Although the term "kundalini" may sound foreign to the Western ear, I have chosen to use it for two reasons. First, it comes from the yogic tradition, and today almost everyone—regardless of their religious background or spiritual orientation—has some familiarity with and respect for yoga. Second, the descriptions of spiritual transformative energy and its workings are more detailed and accessible in yoga than they are in some other traditions. Yoga was, at its roots, a systematic and carefully outlined practice designed to stimulate kundalini in a healthy way.

Although the role of spiritual transformative energy is discussed in detail in Chapter Eight, we need to take a closer look at the subject before we go on to the case histories of people who are having STEs today. A good place to start is to examine kundalini and its role in yoga. When most people in the West think of yoga, they think of the physical exercises or postures known as asanas. However, these are just one aspect of the yogic tradition.

The word "yoga" comes from the Sanskrit "yuj," which means "to yoke," "to harness," or "to bind together." Yoga was developed as a system of discipline that would ultimately lead the practitioner to the realization of his or her union with the divine. Although evidence exists that yoga was practiced in the Indus Valley region of India as early as 3000 B.C., the Yoga Sutras weren't compiled until 300 B.C. at the very earliest. Written by a yogi named Patanjali, they provided an eight-limbed system for reaching samadhi or union with the divine. The spiritual seeker was taught by a guru, or spiritual teacher, to assiduously follow the disciplines involved in each of the eight steps.

Kundalini is held to be the mechanism—a kind of biological–psychological–spiritual force—the active, transformative power of the Divine in our body, that makes the realization of union with the divine possible. The word "kundalini" means "coiled up" in Sanskrit and, in the ancient Tantric texts, was symbolized by a serpent that sleeps, coiled three and a half times, at the base of the spine. By following the mental, physical, and spiritual disciplines of yoga, the student prepares herself in body, mind and spirit for kundalini awakening. With the grace of the Divine, the kundalini/spiritual energy may then awaken in the prepared spiritual aspirant, and rise up the spine and pass through the chakras—the energy centers or vortices that exist along the spine and in the brain. When kundalini is fully awakened it reaches the seventh chakra, located at the crown of the head, and the yogi attains samadhi, an experience of mystical union. Usually, after a few moments, the kundalini descends again to a lower chakra, often the one at the base of the spine. With persistent spiritual practice, moral development, and refinement, a yogi may become able to maintain the kundalini at the crown chakra for increasing amounts of time, thereby attaining deeper levels of samadhi. The yogi reaches the extremely rare sahaja state, ongoing mystical union or nirvana only when the kundalini remains permanently at the crown chakra.

It is easy to place each of the five types of Spiritually Transformative Experiences within this framework. The terms "mystical experience" and "samadhi" are often used interchangeably in the yogic literature to describe various levels of union with the divine or Absolute. A great saint or mystic with a fully awakened kundalini can manifest all of the types of STEs.

Psychic experiences have their place in the framework as well. One of the four books of Patanjali's *Yoga-sutras* is devoted to the subject of siddhis or psychic abilities. The development of these abilities is considered a sign of a partial awakening of the kundalini. Many of the phenomena associated with Near-Death Experiences are also recognized in the yogic tradition and thought by some modern yogis to be associated with some degree of transient awakening of kundalini.

Development of spontaneous inspired creativity and genius are also mentioned often in the ancient yogic texts and are believed to be gifts granted to some of those who have partially awakened kundalini. For example, in *Panchastavi*, a book from circa A.D. 800 that forms part of the Shakti doctrines of India, we find these words in praise of kundalini:

Thou art also the origin of all speech and (hence) art . . .
the sphere of Thy surpassing beauty . . . becomes the
means of granting . . . the talents of a poet [to Thy devo-
tees]. . . .

Given the fact that the five Spiritually Transformative Experiences
discussed so far are recognized within the framework of yoga and
kundalini, it is not surprising that many people who are having
transformative experiences are reporting the symptoms of kundalini awakening. However, not everyone who has an STE experiences Spiritual Energy/Kundalini activation. Some yogic
traditions also describe isolated STEs happening to individuals
due to a "Chakra activation" or limited brain center activation
without any kundalini awakening. For this reason, I have added
Spiritual Energy/Kundalini Episodes to the other categories of
STEs. Throughout the book I use the term "kundalini" in a general way to refer to the spiritually transformative energy that is
given many different names in many different spiritual traditions,
but when I discuss Spiritual Energy/Kundalini Episodes I am refer-
ring to a spiritual experience in which an individual experiences
all—or several—of the traditional signs of kundalini awakening as
they are discussed in Tantric yoga. These bodily sensations are
held to be due to the Spiritual Energy/Kundalini rising to a higher
chakra than before, or due to an increase in the intensity and
amount of upward kundalini flow.

These signs include: (1) sensations of energy, heat, or light
that rush up the spine or rise through the body towards the head
and that sometimes involve intense sensations of sexual energy
or spontaneous inner orgasms; (2) a perception of inner sound
often likened to ringing, buzzing, the rushing of wings, or the
roar of a waterfall; (3) perception of intense white light or all-
pervasive luminosity; and (4) In the classical awakening of kundalini, these physical and perceptual symptoms culminate in a
profound mystical experience which can include union with the
divine, spiritual revelation, creative insight, prophetic or psychic
visions, or a profound expansion of consciousness.

From this description, it is easy to see that there are certain overlaps between Spiritual Energy/Kundalini Episodes and the other STEs. If kundalini is indeed the spiritual transformative energy, we would expect to find that STE experiencers with signs of kundalini activity tend to have more than one type of experience and recurrent or ongoing experiences. The research I'm involved in shows that this is indeed the case.

It is also important to realize that a wide range exists in the intensity—and profundity—of STEs. There is, for example, a tremendous difference between the types of mystical experiences that involve a fleeting glimpse of the oneness of all things and those in which the experiencer loses all sense of self. The great Dominican mystic Suso refers to the latter when he writes about the mystic who "disappears and loses himself in God and becomes one spirit with Him."

My clinical experience also indicates that few people have just one STE in their lifetime. Most people having one psychic experience go on to have recurrent psychic experiences, just as those with inspired creativity go on to have recurrent inspirations. However, when an individual is blessed with a kundalini awakening or a mystical experience, which is generally accompanied by a kundalini awakening, this heralds the beginning of a long-term process of spiritual transformation of consciousness punctuated with many types of STEs. Once the process of spiritual transformation has begun, it generally goes on for the rest of the experiencer's life. And, although I believe every human being is on a spiritual journey, it may be that those who are having STEs and long-term transformation are on an accelerated journey.

Before we go on, it might be a good time for me to explain why I feel it is necessary for me to share so much of myself and my experiences in this book. It should be clear by now that I believe I am going through a spiritually transformative process that began in 1976 and was accelerated by my NDE in 1979 and my ongoing kundalini activity. It should also be clear that I think thousands, perhaps hundreds of thousands or even millions, of other people are going through a similar accelerated transformation process. So I am sharing my story with the hope that I may be able to help others see their STEs as part of a healthy, natural process and a gift. I think it helps people to know that a busy, respected, professional person like me can be in the throes of spiritual transformation and be having mystical experiences, psychic episodes, classic kundalini symptoms and be experiencing intense psycho-spiritual housecleaning—and at the same time can lead a well-adjusted, happy, balanced life.

Those who seem to be on an accelerated path will not necessarily reach their ultimate spiritual goals faster than anyone else. The ancient yogis warned us that many pitfalls exist along the spiritual path and that inflated ego was often the most difficult of all to transcend. People who are being spiritually transformed will, however, find that their lives have, in general, a far more spiritual focus, that their sense of direct connection to the loving Higher Power deepens, and that they have much stronger ethical convictions, and a stronger need to embrace personal emotional healing and recovery. They may also become increasingly involved in altruistic and humanitarian endeavors.

Now that we've considered the overall spiritual transformation process, we'll look at each type of Spiritually Transformative Experience in detail and hear the stories of some people who are going through these experiences.

CHAPTER 3

Mystical Experiences

After my dramatic Near-Death Experience, I began to search for more information on the subject. I wanted to know how it was viewed by theologians from different religions, and—because of my medical training—especially by the scientific and scholarly communities.

I wasn't disappointed in my search through the world's religions. Even though in my own church I had never heard mystical experience spoken of as something that could happen to common people, I found many descriptions of the phenomenon itself in both the Old and New Testaments and the lives of the Catholic saints. In the Eastern religions I examined, I found that mystical states of consciousness were outlined in detail. In Hinduism, texts such as the Upanishads describe states of spiritual ecstasy and, ultimately, liberation in which the individual soul realizes union with Brahman or The Absolute. I found similar references to mystical experience and ultimate liberation, or nirvana, in the Buddhist teachings and works such as *The Tibetan Book of the Dead*.

My search for scientists and scholars who wrote about these experiences led me to the noted philosopher and psychologist

William James. In his classic work *The Varieties of Religious Experience*, I found stories of many average people who had experienced—just as I had—a sense of union and communion with the divine. Reading James also helped clarify my own understanding of the experience itself. He identified four main characteristics of what he called "mystical states":

> 1. *Ineffability.* Mystical experiences "defy expression"; it is essentially impossible for the experiencer to convey their importance, grandeur, or profundity to another; they have to be experienced to be fully comprehended.
> 2. *Noetic quality.* Although mystical experiences are similar to states of feeling, they are also states of knowing. The experience contains "revelations," "illuminations," and "insights into depths of truth."
> 3. *Transiency.* Except in rare cases, mystical experiences cannot be sustained for long. Even though their quality can usually only be "imperfectly reproduced in memory," they may bring about a continual development in "inner richness" in the experiencer from one recurrence to another.
> 4. *Passivity.* Although the occurrence of mystical states may be facilitated by certain practices, once the state has begun "the mystic feels as if his own will were in abeyance" or "as if he were grasped and held by a superior power." After such experiences, a profound sense of their importance remains and they "modify the inner life of the subject" between recurrences.

My search also led to the works of a number of other medical doctors and psychiatrists. One was the Swiss psychiatrist Carl Jung, who called the mystical experience an experience of the "numinous" and saw it as a powerful, positive force in the process of individuation, or the ultimate realization of self. I was fascinated to discover that he had experienced a wide range of paranormal phenomena during his lifetime, including mystical visions and a Near-Death Experience. He had also researched and lectured on kundalini.

Psychologist Abraham Maslow also wrote about mystical experiences. He called them "peak experiences" and placed them at the very top of a hierarchy of human growth and development that led to a state of health and wholeness he called "self-actualization."

An even earlier account of mystical experience was written by Richard Maurice Bucke, a Canadian psychiatrist. After having a profound mystical experience himself, Bucke began studying the lives of many religious leaders, saints, and creative geniuses. In 1902 his book *Cosmic Consciousness* developed his well-supported theory that human consciousness was evolving and that, as it did, humans were developing an increasing ability to perceive a new, vastly expanded state of consciousness. Bucke believed the human race was moving slowly, but inexorably, towards the time when everyone alive would attain what he called cosmic consciousness. Within this framework, individuals who had profound mystical experiences represented—in vastly varying degrees—harbingers of this future state. Bucke made it clear that there was a tremendous difference between someone like himself who had what he called a fleeting "taste of Brahmic splendor" and someone like Buddha who existed in a perennial state of cosmic bliss.

As I found more and more evidence that leading thinkers in theology, psychology, and psychiatry accepted the reality of mystical experience, I became less reticent to speak with my professional colleagues about my experiences. As a result, I was asked to speak on my Near-Death Experience at more professional meetings and had many patients referred to me who had had mystical or other paranormal experiences.

Over the past twenty years, I have worked professionally with and/or counseled more than 600 people who have had a wide range of STEs. Of these, most felt they had had some type of mystical experience at some point in their lives. This is not as surprising as it might seem. A 1989 Gallup poll found that one of every three Americans believed he or she had had some type of mystical experience. I believe, in fact, that every person in whom the Spiritual Energy/Kundalini is active and who is involved in a process of spiritual transformation will eventually begin to have mystical experiences. These experiences may occur spontaneously or be stimulated by certain activities such as intense heartfelt prayer, intense meditation, focused contemplation on a deity or a spiritual concept, deep soul searching, or intense yogic practices.

The people who have discussed their mystical experiences with me come from a variety of educational backgrounds, cultures, and religious traditions. In some cases, the experience takes a form that is related to the person's own cultural and religious background. In others, it seems to cut across cultures and arise out of a tradition that is foreign to the experiencer. When this happens, the experience often causes a change in religious convictions or spiritual beliefs. During my own experience, for example, I perceived God to be an omnipresent, omnipotent, universal force of love, light, and intelligence. I found this broadened my previous concept of God considerably.

Types of Mystical Experiences

Though mystical experiences take many different forms, in my clinical work I have found that they generally fall into seven main categories. Even though any one experience might contain elements from several different categories, one of the categories usually seems to stand out and be useful for identifying the experience or giving it a name—a simple process which often helps people integrate STEs into their daily lives.

Any of the following types of experience—particularly if they are especially profound—may also be accompanied by an intense experience of white light.

> 1. *Unitive experiences.* A feeling of union with God, the divine, the universal consciousness, or with the universal life force; an experience of the oneness of all

things; a feeling that one's self is united with the entire universe or connected with all creation.

2. *Ecstatic or Bliss episodes.* Experiences of profound bliss, ecstasy, all-encompassing love, awestruck wonder at the profundity of the universe, or overwhelming feelings of devotion to the Divine, all of which are often accompanied by spontaneous tears of joy.

3. *Mystical visions.* Visions of deities, saints, gurus, spiritual archetypes, or important figures from the world's religions, including Buddha, Christ, Krishna, Mohammed, Moses, and the Virgin Mary; accompanied by a powerful feeling of unconditional love, compassion, healing, and/or guidance.

4. *Expansive episodes.* A sense of dramatically expanded consciousness in which the individual point of perception seems to expand from its normal to a much greater size; the sense of expansion may stop at a few feet beyond the head or move outward until it seems to encompass the entire earth or even the cosmos.

5. *Spiritual rebirth.* A sudden, profound spiritual awakening; a spontaneous religious conversion; a dramatic reorientation of spiritual beliefs; a sense of "dying," having a shamanistic type of encounter with the dark side, or hitting bottom that is followed by a profound experience of spiritual rebirth, illumination, ecstasy, or union with divine.

6. *Illumination.* A sudden, profound insight into the nature of the universe or absolute truth; a spontaneous intellectual revelation that is beyond the bounds of normal, analytical reason and that brings with it new spiritual insight or new knowledge for humankind.

7. *Dissolution experiences.* An experience of the complete dissolution of self into the All, the Absolute, the stillness. Deep dissolution is indescribable.

A Unitive Experience

The following story was told to me by a patient whom I will call
Courtney. Born and raised in Montreal, Canada, with a weekend family home in the mountains north of the city, Courtney
had her first STE when she was a teenager.

> *Ever since I was a child, I loved to wander through the
> fields behind my country home. I loved the smells of the
> earth, the plants, and the trees. I loved the beautiful play
> of colors in nature, how they changed through the four
> seasons, and I loved to watch the colors of the sky at
> sunset, how they highlighted the mountains in different
> hues. Somehow, even as a child, I felt close to God up
> there, like I was watching his paintbrush at work.*
>
> *One autumn day, when I was twelve or thirteen, I
> went for a long leaf-watching walk along a local country
> road. At one point I came to an opening between the
> hills and suddenly an amazing vista of brilliant orange,
> scarlet, and golden leaves garlanding the rolling hills
> blazed into my full view. The sky contrasted a dazzling,
> deep-blue hue. The view was breathtaking. I gasped, and
> in my heart spontaneously cried out an inner prayer:
> "Oh! Thank you God!"*
>
> *With this prayer, I suddenly noticed a change begin in
> me. The colors started to become brighter and more
> luminous. Overcome with the beauty, tears of awe rolled
> down my cheeks. Then, I began to feel as if I was
> expanding until, suddenly, I felt as if I'd merged with and
> filled the whole scene. I was one with the trees, one with
> the hills, and one with the sky. I felt totally connected
> with it all and with the love behind the Universe. I have
> no idea how long I stood there, riveted to the spot,
> merged into the beauty of God's creation.*
>
> *After some time my awareness returned to my body,
> standing on the road, my face covered in tears. Although
> that feeling of union had gone, I still felt a strong direct*

connection to the loving Higher Power. Inspired by this
experience, I went home and began to draw vigorously.
I tried to somehow capture on paper the blazing colors,
the luminosity—the God in nature that I had felt.

Being raised an Anglican, I had, before this experi-
ence, thought that God was a power to be feared, a
power who sat in judgment, ready to punish me for my
shortcomings. But after this experience, I knew this to be
incorrect. I just knew, somehow, to the core of my being
that God was a loving God, and that I and all people
were loved by him at all times.

This experience had a profound, transformative effect on Courtney. Her spiritual convictions dramatically shifted and deepened
afterwards. Although she found, unfortunately, that she could
not talk openly about this unitive mystical experience either in
her church or in her family, she remained convinced of its reality and sacredness. She continued to go to her local church, and
although she disagreed with some of the pastor's interpretations
of the Scriptures, she enjoyed the time for prayer and spiritual
contemplation. In her adult life she became very active in community service and charity activities in the church parish. Over
the years, Courtney has gone on to have other STEs, most
notably in her thirties when she began to have symptoms of Spiritual Energy/Kundalini Awakening. But she looks back on this
first experience as the one that set her on her spiritual path.

A Spiritual Rebirth

The following is an example of spiritual rebirth. The experience
occurred to Dr. G. Graham-Cumming, a highly respected, successful Canadian medical doctor who had been ordained as a minister
earlier in his career and later came to reject all religious teachings.
The experience changed the course of his life. He worked under
difficult and sometimes dangerous conditions in a number of coun-
tries. In a letter he wrote to me in 1991, he shared this story:

At age thirty I had become rather a bitter debunker of all "Faiths" and, having been theologically trained and ordained, rather a potent one. Going home one evening in May 1937, I came to a crossroads I crossed every day, habitually veering to the right although it did not really matter which way I went. Both roads took me home if by very different routes. Just as I was striding off as usual that evening, however, I was jolted to a halt as if by a physical barrier and "heard" ringing in my head like a bell, "You must choose NOW!" What I had to decide was whether I would live believing life to be purposive and significant or merely the aimless accident of evolution I professed to believe it. It dawned on me it would make a considerable difference in how I would live, but it was not a matter I cared to debate, let alone decide, just there and then. Trying to dismiss the challenge, I attempted to proceed but found myself unable to move—paralyzed by indecision, I suppose. I've no idea how long I stood there twisting and turning in my head. Eventually I elected to consider life to be purposive, if to what purpose I had no idea. I was startled to find myself exclaiming, "I will believe. Help my unbelief!" At once the paralysis holding me relaxed and I went home in some mental turmoil.

It was a bright moonlit night. I went out into the moonlight to wrestle with my mental tumult. Suddenly the moonlight seemed to start swirling round me, swathing me in opalescent veils that began to obscure vision and restrict movement. Just as I was beginning to get a bit scared, it seemed to me that someone out there was tearing away those smothering veils and I felt a great relief—but, as the last was stripped from me, I found myself in the Presence of an unseen but overwhelming Power, irresistible, undeceivable and inescapable. That was when I discovered sheer terror! My only wish was not to be, but that was denied. I was and had to face the essentiality of existing. Groveling on my knees, I cried

out, "Go away! Go away! I am evil!" But that "Voice"
like a bell rang, "Rise. I will enable you." I did, shakily,
hardly able to believe I was being accepted, even com-
missioned for service. It was shown to me that those
'veils of light' blinding and binding me symbolized my
misconceptions and imperfect scientific and religious
"knowledge," all of which had to be set aside, not denied
but set aside pending further enlightenment. Seeking
enlightenment is what I've been doing ever since . . . .

The transformative impact this experience had on Dr. Graham-
Cumming is clear. His working life was dedicated to humanitarian efforts. Although he is now retired, he remains involved in
social causes. His spiritual focus is stronger than ever, and he
often writes beautiful transcendental poetry that he receives
through inspiration.

Mystical Visions

Mystical Visions are another type of mystical experience that I
come across fairly frequently in my work. The next story is a
more "visual" type of mystical vision. It was told to me by a
man I'll call Jack. At the time of the experience, Jack was in university working on his Ph.D. He was actively involved in his
church where he sang in the choir:

We had just finished choir practice in the church base-
ment. We had been practicing the "Hallelujah Chorus,"
and I felt uplifted and serene. I went up to the chapel to
pray before I set off for home. I felt overwhelmed by Jesus'
love for humanity and by God's love for us all. Strains of
the Hallelujah Chorus still rang through my head.
  Suddenly in the middle of a heart-felt prayer, I felt the
strong urge to look up at the chapel altar. I opened my
eyes and saw, to my amazement, Jesus Christ glowing
with dazzling light standing by the altar. I knew it was

*Him. The look of love in His eyes penetrated my soul. I
heard Him say, "Come to me!" I burst into tears of joy,
and the vision of the Christ was gone.*

The vision had a great effect on Jack's life. His faith in God grew
stronger and he became certain, in a way he had never been
before, that God and Jesus are there for each and every person
who calls upon them for help.

Jack's experience provides a good example of how mystical
visions often occur. However, the way Jack reacted after the
experience is also significant: He was afraid to tell anyone—even
the people in his own church who shared his deep faith and religious convictions—what he had seen. In spite of his own
unshakable certainty that the experience had really happened, he
was afraid people wouldn't believe him or, worse, that they
would think he was insane. Even when he finally shared the
experience with me a few years after it had happened, he did so
only in strictest confidence.

Such fears are extremely common with people who have
STEs. Many mystical and other paranormal experiences are kept
secret. Although some people choose not to share their experiences for personal reasons, many others keep silent out of fear
of ridicule. One of my hopes in sharing these stories is that they
will help other STE experiencers realize that they are not alone.
As I explain in detail in Chapters Fifteen and Sixteen, they can
find appropriate, supportive people who are willing to listen.

Mystical visions, like all types of mystical experiences, can
take many forms. Although a vision, by definition, is in some
sense a visual experience, it may also involve other kinds of
"perception" of the presence of a religious or spiritual figure
including scent, sound, touch, taste, or emotion.

Visions can also cross religious and cultural boundaries.
Although Jack, who was a Christian, saw a vision that was very
much part of his tradition, this is not always the case. A Christian can have a mystical vision of Buddha, or a yogi can have one
of St. Francis. A story that illustrates this was told to me by an
extremely successful businesswoman whom I'll call Jeneane. Her

experience also illustrates, as was mentioned earlier, how the categories we are using to define mystical experience—and the categories of other STEs—are somewhat arbitrary and often overlap. This experience, for example, contains elements of a "perception" of a spiritual figure as well as elements of a type of unitive experience that represents, if not a union with the divine principle of the universe, a deep feeling of oneness with a holy or spiritual presence.

> *My experience occurred after I had been involved in yoga and meditation for a few years. I had been raised as a Roman Catholic and my faith was extremely important to me. In fact, I had become rather well known for my views on the importance the teachings of Catholicism held for those who had been raised in the tradition, and I did a great deal of public speaking on the subject.*
>
> *When I was in my mid-forties, the man I was very much in love with and had planned to marry suddenly left me for another woman. In an attempt to cope with my pain and disillusionment, I threw myself more deeply than ever into my career and began to work extremely long hours.*
>
> *One Sunday, as I came home after spending most of the day at the office, I paused on the doorstep. As I put the key in the door, a slight shift seemed to occur in my consciousness. An inner voice seemed to be telling me that I had to quit punishing myself and begin to nurture myself more. With this in mind, I walked up the stairs, poured myself a hot bath, and filled it with scented oil. As I settled into the soothing water, I began to slip into a deep meditative state.*
>
> *Quite suddenly, I perceived an image of an oriental woman. Although I didn't recognize her, I was certain that the woman was a holy person or saint of an Eastern religion. The woman radiated profound love and compassion.*
>
> *As the experience continued, I felt my consciousness meld with that of the saint's. I felt enveloped in the*

woman's love and compassion and even one with the woman herself. As this occurred, I was overwhelmed with emotion and felt my frustration, disappointment, and anger with my former fiancé begin to evaporate and fade away.

I remained in this deep state of union with the saint for about twenty minutes. When I arose from the bath, still in a meditative state, I even had a physical sensation of my own limbs moving with the supple grace and graciousness the saint had moved with.

The immediate effects of the experience stayed with me for twenty-four hours and, even when it began to fade, I felt a profound closeness to the saint and had a feeling that the woman was watching over me and protecting me. I felt a great sense of peace and realized that I was never alone.

The experience also had a tremendous spiritual and emotional healing effect. I was able to forgive my fiancé and wish him well. I was even able to reach out and emotionally embrace the woman he had left me for. I had received such a gift of grace, love, and compassion that I felt it flowing out of me and back to the world.

Some time later, Jeneane happened on an exact likeness of the holy woman from her experience and learned that the woman was a Buddhist enlightened being—or Bodhisattva—named Quon Yin. Jeneane discovered that, according to tradition, Quon Yin is said to have been "born of the tears of the Buddha" and is known as the goddess of compassion.

Saved by a Mystical Vision

Although mystical visions often occur during times of meditation and contemplation, they—like other types of paranormal experiences—can also occur after a heartfelt plea for guidance or help. The following events happened to a young woman whom

I'll call Julie, who had been raised as a Roman Catholic. At the time, she was about twenty years old and in university studying social work. Her story is an unusual and an extremely disturbing tale, but the vision that she saw had such a direct effect on her very survival that I have decided to include it.

> One evening I attended a friend's graduation and, to celebrate, went with a group of friends to a local pub after the ceremony. One of the group was a young man I had been acquainted with for a few years. After we had a couple of drinks, "Alex" offered to drive me home. Since I'd known him for a while I couldn't see any harm in the suggestion and accepted. But instead of driving me home, he parked the car behind a dark, deserted factory. When I explained I wasn't interested in "parking" and wanted to go home, he became angry. Before I could get away, he grabbed me and began to accost me, ripping my dress and forcing himself on me.
>
> As I struggled against him and shouted "No!" he became completely crazed, violently raped me, and brutalized me, even ripping hair from my body. Then, as I continued to fight, he began to scream that I was a bitch and that he was going to kill me. He reached under the seat with one hand and began to search for something, yelling about a knife. As he did, I managed to slip from his grasp and run from the car.
>
> Bleeding and wounded, I began to run through the wooded area behind the factory. I was gripped with terror, certain that Alex really would kill me if he caught me, and I tried to run as fast as I could. But the area was pitch black, and I was extremely weak. I crashed through the woods, stumbling over rocks and branches and into trees. I could hear Alex behind me, gaining on me, and I knew I had no hope of outrunning him.
>
> In utter desperation, I threw myself on the ground and began to pray to the Virgin Mary for help. Suddenly, a woman bathed in a radiant light appeared before me and

said, "Take my hand, I will help you." The light ema-
nating from the woman seemed to illuminate the dark
forest floor. The woman led me along, pointing out the
way to go, and motioning when I should duck down or
be completely silent. As the radiant woman led me out of
the woods, Alex thrashed through the trees looking for
me in vain. Once out of the woods, the woman contin-
ued to lead me through backyards and laneways, until I
suddenly realized I was very near a friend's house. The
woman then disappeared, and I ran to my friend who
took me in and helped me get the medical treatment I
desperately needed.

Totally traumatized, Julie was unable to report the rape for some time. And, tragically, because the event occurred long before "date rape" was recognized as the horrendous crime it is, Alex was not charged when she finally did report it.

Over time, Julie recovered with the help of supportive friends and family. But even though these people knew the story of the rape, she shared the story of the vision with no one. She believed in her heart that the Virgin Mary had appeared to her and saved her life, but she also believed that people would think she was crazy if she told them. Still she longed to tell someone and be reassured that the experience was not a symptom of mental illness.

Then one day Julie, who had been a patient of mine for some time, read an article in *The Toronto Star* about my Near-Death Experience. She began to hope that, because I had had a para-normal experience, I might be able to understand what had happened to her. Soon after this, while she was in my office for a routine physical, she suddenly blurted out her story. When she was finished, I explained that I knew many people who had had mystical visions and that I believed, as she did, that hers had appeared in answer to her prayers. She was immensely relieved to be able to tell someone about the vision and be reassured that she was not "crazy." Overwhelmed with emotion, she sobbed for some time.

A few years later, Alex was arrested and convicted of the rape and murder of an elderly woman whose home he had burglarized. It seems Julie's vision really did save her life.

Every person I have met who has had a mystical experience that might be classified as a STEP has been deeply moved by it. All of them have developed strong, personal convictions about the reality of a divine universal intelligence. Their experiences have been uplifting, and the memory of the moment has remained a continual source of inspiration. In a sense, mystical experiences are the "highest" type of STE. They are so alluring that many people yearn to have them again and spend the rest of their lives trying to regain that moment of transcendence. I believe this yearning is an irresistible force that is drawing us, as a race, towards a higher state of consciousness.

CHAPTER 4

Spiritual Energy/Kundalini Episodes

The signs of kundalini awakening have been described in sources that range from the ancient texts on yoga to the works of contemporary philosophers, psychologists, and psychiatrists. As described in Chapter Two, the mystical traditions of the world's major religions allude to a spiritual energy or force that can activate bodily symptoms, STEs, and long-term spiritual transformation of consciousness. My first contact with both kundalini and the awakening of kundalini came through the works of Pandit Gopi Krishna, an Indian yogi, philosopher, and scholar.* When he died in 1984, Gopi Krishna left a large body of published material on the subject of kundalini that included seventeen books and scores of essays and articles.

Gopi Krishna was born in a small Kashmiri village in 1903. He began to practice meditation when he was seventeen years old, rising every morning before dawn and meditating for three

---

* Pandit is an honorary Indian title given to some wise and particularly respected individuals.

hours. He followed this routine devotedly until one December morning, at age thirty-four, he had a profound mystical experience. Although this initial experience was temporary, for the next twelve years he alternated between states of expanded consciousness and periods of tormenting physical pain and fluctuating mental states that included anxiety and depression.

Struggling to discover what was happening to him, Gopi Krishna began to study the ancient yogic texts. Eventually, he came to the conclusion that he had awakened kundalini—but that the process had not occurred exactly as it should have. Further study of the ancient texts and modern translations such as Arthur Avalon's classic work *The Serpent Power* helped him discover how to correct what had gone wrong with his awakening and how to moderate the influences of this overwhelming energy. By the time he was forty-six, the fluctuating psychological and distressing physical sensations had receded and left him in a perennial state of expanded consciousness.

Although he had previously had no writing ability, he was suddenly able to write exquisitely beautiful poetry. This poetry came to him, through a process of inspiration, both in languages he knew and ones he had never heard or seen before. A rational, practical man, he was amazed by his new ability and began to search even more thoroughly through the yogic mystical literature to discover more about the transformative process he was experiencing. After many years of study—and objectively observing his own transformative process—he concluded that kundalini was the driving force behind the evolution of the human race to a higher level of consciousness and that its awakening created a potential for an accelerated transformation of the body and brain that could lead to states of what he called "higher consciousness."

After becoming respected around the world as one of the foremost authorities on the subject, he did much to convince the West that kundalini was a very real biological-psychological-spiritual mechanism. Although he was often urged by would-be disciples to become a guru, he refused. Instead, he spent the rest of his life writing about the evolution of consciousness and trying to convince the Eastern and Western scientific and medical communities of the importance of serious scientific research on kundalini as the biological basis for the evolution of the race to higher levels of consciousness and the paranormal states that would accompany it.

A number of contemporary Western scholars have also written about kundalini awakening. One of the most widely respected is Swiss psychiatrist, Dr. Carl Jung, whose seminars on kundalini are compiled in *The Psychology of Kundalini Yoga*. Jung's research on kundalini is considered a milestone in the bridging of Western psychology of individuation with the Eastern model of kundalini driven development of higher consciousness. A second respected kundalini scholar is Mircea Eliade, former Chair of the Department of History of Religions at the University of Chicago. In his classic work *Yoga, Immortality, and Freedom*, Eliade attempted to bring to the West some understanding of the relationship between yoga, the awakening of kundalini, and mystical states of consciousness.

Psychiatrists writing on the subject include Dr. Lee Sannella and Dr. Stanislav Grof. Dr. Sannella has become widely known for his books, in which he documented a number of cases of individuals in the United States who were experiencing kundalini awakening. Eventually, he opened a clinic in California that specializes in the assessment, support, and treatment of people undergoing this process. Dr. Sannella supported Gopi Krishna's idea that there was a biological basis for kundalini-type symptoms and worked with the late Dr. Itzhak Bentov studying the changes in the electromagnetic fields of long-time meditators and persons undergoing kundalini awakening.

Dr. Stanislav Grof and his wife Christina—a writer and former yoga teacher who has undergone her own kundalini awakening—have written a number of books on what they call "Spiritual Emergence Syndrome" and the part they believe kundalini awakening plays in the process of spiritual growth and transformation.

One of the most significant recent works on kundalini was written in 1990 by Dr. Bonnie Greenwell, a California psychologist. In *The Energies of Transformation* she reviews the works of many important yogis, examines the ideas of various schools of yoga, and details her experience as a counselor working with people who are having kundalini experiences.

The Signs of a Spiritual Energy/Kundalini Episode

Based on the ancient Tantric yoga texts and on his own experiences, Gopi Krishna outlined the main characteristics of classical kundalini experiences in a number of his works. They can be summarized as:

1. *Energy rushes.* Sensations of energy, heat, and/or light that rise up the spine or rush up through the body towards the head. The energy may feel like a rushing, flowing, trickling, exploding, jumping, vibrating, burning, piercing, or like an electrical current.

2. *Light.* The perceptions of inner light, radiating light, and/or a luminosity in the outer world; or the sensation of being engulfed in an overwhelming brilliant white light.

3. *Sound.* The perception of an inner sound—a humming or ringing—often likened to the rushing of wind, the distant roar of a waterfall, the rushing of wings, ringing of bells, the buzzing of bees, or the chirping of crickets; sometimes called the "music of the spheres."

4. *Sexual sensations.* Sensations of activity in the genital area or unusual, intense sexual arousal that is not associated with normal sexual stimulation; spontaneous orgasms that seem to be directed inward and upward rather than outward.

5. *Experiences of paranormal consciousness.* The above sensations associated, ultimately, with mystical experiences, psychic visions, or spontaneous experiences of inspired creativity or revelation.

In my work I have come across a great many people whose most dramatic and prominent STE has been what I refer to as a

Spiritual Energy/Kundalini Episode—a distinct, time-limited experience of two or more of the above signs. For many, the process begins quite suddenly, and the experience almost always represents a STEP. In these sudden, dramatic awakenings the signs experienced are pronounced. I think—as Gopi Krishna did—that all types of STEs can be experienced at various levels of the awakening of kundalini. However, in my clinical experience and research, I have found that not all people having STEs experience the signs of a Spiritual Energy/Kundalini activation. There are a number of reasons for this.

First, the awakening of kundalini and its subsequent activity occur on a continuum. According to the yogic tradition, only a small proportion of spiritual aspirants would ever awaken this spiritual energy, and of the few who do have the spiritual energy awaken, it is generally a partial awakening, so that even fewer would ever be able to hold it permanently at the crown chakra and successfully obtain "liberation."

I think of the awakening of kundalini as the first stirrings of this latent spiritual force that exists in all of us. At the other end of the continuum is the person in perennial cosmic consciousness—one of the illuminati. Such a person exists in the state of ultimate mystical union attained by the greatest mystics and spiritual masters (see Chapter Eight). Along the continuum are people who are experiencing varying degrees of ongoing kundalini activity and, consequently, varying degrees of transformation. Thus, some people may have STEs but be aware of only minor stirrings of the energy and experience very few of the classic signs.

Second, the awakening of kundalini is not always sudden and dramatic; it can occur slowly and increase gradually in activity over a long period of time. When this occurs, according to Gopi Krishna, the increase in kundalini activity—and the accompanying signs—can be so subtle that the individual does not even notice the minute and ever-increasing changes in his or her perception.

Third, a few individuals are born with an awakened kundalini. In these rare cases, the individual experiences all the classic signs of kundalini awakening but is not aware that his or her experiences are different from anyone else's—or the individual's body may be so prepared for or accustomed to the flow of this energy that he or she does not experience the bodily symptoms that tend to be so noticeable in sudden awakenings. A person born with an awakened kundalini would, however, exhibit the signs of higher consciousness at a very young age. Guru Nanak was an example of this type of awakening. According to tradition, he wrote inspirational poetry before he attended school, could discourse on spiritual questions while he was still a child, and went on to found the religion of the Sikhs.

Fourth, some people experiencing STEs do not have a Spiritual Energy/Kundalini activation. In the yogic tradition it is believed that an isolated STE may occur by divine grace or by a "Chakra opening" without any kundalini arousal. It is also thought that psychic abilities may be present from birth or developed through specific mental practices, without any kundalini activation. This perspective is supported by my clinical experience.

In my work, I have found that STEPs that take the form of Spiritual Energy/Kundalini Episodes occur most commonly in people who have been involved in intense spiritual practices such as meditation, Hatha Yoga, pranayama (breathwork), or extremely focused prayer.

A Dramatic Awakening in Kashmir

Since I had the honor of knowing Gopi Krishna personally and attending a number of his talks at scientific and scholarly symposiums, I would like to start with his story as it is recorded in his book *Kundalini: The Evolutionary Energy in Man* (recently republished in an expanded form as *Living with Kundalini: The Autobiography of Gopi Krishna*). This account has become widely recognized as one of the most comprehensive, descriptive accounts of kundalini awakening available.

> *One morning during the Christmas of 1937 I sat cross-legged in a small room in a little house on the outskirts of the town of Jammu. . . . I was meditating with my face*

towards the window on the east through which the first gray streaks of the slowly brightening dawn fell into the room. Long practice had accustomed me to sit in the same posture for hours at a time without the least discomfort, and I sat breathing slowly and rhythmically, my attention drawn towards the crown of my head, contemplating an imaginary lotus in full bloom, radiating light.

I sat steadily, unmoving and erect, my thoughts uninterruptedly centered on the shining lotus, intent on keeping my attention from wandering and bringing it back again and again whenever it moved in any other direction. The intensity of concentration interrupted my breathing; gradually it slowed down to such an extent that at times it was barely perceptible. My whole being was so engrossed in the contemplation of the lotus that for several minutes at a time I lost touch with my body and surroundings. . . .

During one such spell of intense concentration I suddenly felt a strange sensation below the base of the spine, at the place touching the seat, while I sat cross-legged on a folded blanket spread on the floor. The sensation was so extraordinary and so pleasing that my attention was forcibly drawn towards it. The moment my attention was thus unexpectedly withdrawn from the point on which it was focused, the sensation ceased. . . . Again I fixed (my attention) on the lotus, and as the image grew clear and distinct at the top of my head, again the sensation occurred. This time I tried to maintain the fixity of my attention and succeeded for a few seconds, but the sensation extending upwards grew so intense and was so extraordinary, as compared to anything I had experienced before, that in spite of myself my mind went towards it, and at that very moment it again disappeared. . . .

After a while I grew composed and was soon as deep in meditation as before. When completely immersed I again experienced the sensation, but this time, instead of allowing my mind to leave the point where I had fixed it, I maintained a rigidity of attention throughout. The sensation again extended upwards, growing in intensity, and I felt myself wavering; but with a great effort I kept my attention centered round the lotus. Suddenly, with a roar like that of a waterfall, I felt a stream of liquid light entering my brain through the spinal cord.

Entirely unprepared for such a development, I was completely taken by surprise; but regaining self-control instantaneously, I remained sitting in the same posture, keeping my mind on the point of concentration. The illumination grew brighter and brighter, the roaring louder, I experienced a rocking sensation and then felt myself slipping out of my body, entirely enveloped in a halo of light. It is impossible to describe the experience accurately. I felt the point of consciousness that was myself growing wider, surrounded by waves of light. It grew wider and wider, spreading outward while the body, normally the immediate object of its perception, appeared to have receded into the distance until I became entirely unconscious of it. I was now all consciousness, without any outline, without any idea of a corporeal appendage, without any feeling or sensation coming from the senses, immersed in a sea of light simultaneously conscious and aware of every point, spread out, as it were, in all directions without any barrier or material obstruction. I was no longer myself, or to be more accurate, no longer as I knew myself to be, a small point of awareness confined in a body, but instead was a vast circle of consciousness in which the body was but a point, bathed in light and in a state of exaltation and happiness impossible to describe.

After some time, the duration of which I could not judge, the circle began to narrow down; I felt myself contracting, becoming smaller and smaller, until I again became dimly conscious of the outline of my body, then more clearly; and as I slipped back to my old condition, I became suddenly aware of the noises in the street, felt my arms and legs and head, and once more became my narrow self in touch with body and surroundings.

My Kundalini Awakening

In retrospect, I think my first STE, which occurred in 1976, was actually a Spiritual Energy/Kundalini Episode. Initially, I did not realize what had happened to me, and I did not become aware that it was a kundalini experience until several years later, after my Near-Death Experience. Here is my story:

In October 1976, when I was twenty-three years old, I took a meditation course, and then began a daily practice of meditation. I found that meditation came easily to me, almost like second nature. I meditated for twenty to thirty minutes every weekday morning, and longer on weekends.

In December 1976, after about two months of regular meditation practice, I participated in a large group meditation session in an auditorium. While in a deep meditative state, I was visualizing myself sending love and light out from my heart to the others in the auditorium. After about ten minutes, I suddenly heard a noise like the roar of a waterfall, and simultaneously I felt my consciousness rise above my body. I felt as if my consciousness had filled with light and had now expanded from the size of my head to the size of the auditorium. I also experienced intense and powerful feelings of love and bliss. I remained in this state of expansion, light, and bliss for about twenty minutes. When the meditation ended, my consciousness contracted to its regular state, but I felt an afterglow of inner peace, radiance, deep joy, and love.

I did not talk to others about what had happened, because in my naiveté I thought it probably happened regularly to all the more experienced meditators. I did not want to reveal that it had taken me a few months to "finally" figure out how to meditate "correctly." "No wonder people like to meditate—it feels great!" I thought. It was only several weeks later, after I discovered that I was not able to reproduce the blissful episode during subsequent meditations, that I quietly asked an experienced meditator what I was doing wrong. Only then did I discover that these experiences did not occur regularly to others. I had no way to label my meditation experience, until a few years later, when I read some of Gopi Krishna's books on kundalini.

This is one of the reasons why labeling Spiritually Transformative Experiences can be so useful. Giving an unusual experience a non-pathological name—and learning that it has parallels in many cultural and spiritual traditions—helps us integrate it into our lives.

A Canadian Doctor's Story

Gopi Krishna's experience fits the description of kundalini awakening described in the yogic tradition so closely that you might think such a classic awakening could happen only to someone steeped in the Indian culture, but this is not the case. In my work I have found that Spiritual Energy/Kundalini Episodes cross all cultural and religious boundaries and occur to people who have never practiced yoga or heard of any type of transformative energy. One of the most interesting stories I have heard was that of a young doctor named Gwen who practices family medicine. She had a dramatic kundalini awakening during her third year of medical school. Prior to her experience she had never done yoga, meditated, or practiced any Eastern or Western spiritual discipline. She did, however, have a strong innate spirituality and spent hours and hours in extremely deep concentration—an activity that may mimic in some ways the highly focused concentration and meditation called, respectively, dharana and dhyana in the Eight Limbs of Yoga (described in detail in Chapter Thirteen). Here is Gwen's story as she told it to me.

> I had just had a relaxing supper with a close friend one Saturday evening. I had been studying and in a very intense state of concentration for most of the day. In fact, throughout my university education, and especially during medical school, I studied very intensely, and frequently went into almost trance-like states of absorption during my studies. I think all this intense absorption and concentration is what inadvertently stimulated my kundalini.
>
> That evening, after the supper, I discovered that I had

an intense pressure headache. My friend suggested that he try giving me a head massage to relieve the headache. I sat down in a comfortable position, and he began to massage my scalp.

Suddenly, my whole body started shaking uncontrollably. I felt rushes of energy coursing up my body to my head, and my whole body jerked with the pulses of energy. My back, arms, and legs all jerked repeatedly as the energy pulse raced upwards. I could not stop the shaking. My body was rocked and shaken by these energy pulses from about 9:30 p.m. until 3:30 a.m. I was fully conscious the whole time, and was acutely aware of what was happening in my body.

I was very frightened during the shaking episode. I had no idea what was going on. I could not control my body; I could not stop the jerking movements of my body and limbs. I shouted out to my friend, asking what was happening. He did not know, and he just sat with me to comfort me. I knew it could not be a seizure, because I was fully conscious throughout the whole episode. Later I found it interesting that my headache had disappeared as soon as the energy pulses began. When the energy rushes and body shaking finally stopped, I felt overwhelmingly fatigued, as if I had experienced a tremendous release of some sort. I crawled into bed and went to sleep immediately.

In the morning when I awoke, I felt as if I had been reborn. When I opened my eyes, the world seemed to have become a magical place. I felt as if I were in love with the world, and that the universe and I were making love to each other. It seemed as if the world was filled with light; all the colors and dimensions of objects seemed clearer and more beautiful. Every sensation was enhanced. It was as if I was breathing in the life energy of the universe with each breath. I felt as if my consciousness had expanded to immense proportions, and I felt totally at one with the entire universe.

I felt the oneness of all things, and I felt that all was well in the Divine plan of the universe.

As I basked in this blissful state, I started to spontaneously recite scriptures that I had not yet read from the Koran and from the Bible. I started to spontaneously go into yoga postures and do yoga mudras, or hand movements, even though at that point I had never studied yoga.

In the weeks that followed, I remained in an expanded, mystical state of consciousness. I felt a tremendous physical energy during this time. I could easily run at full speed for four miles, even though I had not previously jogged. I seemed to suddenly have great psychic energy also, and I had spontaneously developed new psychic abilities. I was clairsentient, and could perceive emotional and physical problems in others. Several people told me that they experienced a healing of their pain when I would lay my hands on a painful part of their body. And when people needed help with emotional problems or pain, I would seem to automatically know what to say. I was also able to see auras around people and to perceive the energy of other things—plants, trees, rocks, everything.

I felt as if I had undergone a complete rebirth. The experience created a child-like innocence in me. I developed an utter trust in the wisdom of the intelligent power behind the universe. I felt a real sense of grace, of surrendering to a higher power. I felt as if my physical body had become an open vehicle for the life force to express itself through.

I also seemed, spontaneously, to develop tremendous new understanding of the realities behind the universe, and answers to the paradoxes of life and the universe. I could see the wisdom within the folly around us.

The blissful expanded mystical state of consciousness lasted for six months, then my consciousness contracted until it seemed to reach a state that was only somewhat larger than my original state of consciousness. It remains in this state today.

This entire experience changed me totally. It actually seems to have left me more intelligent than I was previously. I can think more clearly and more perceptively. After the experience I developed the urge to meditate daily on the divine. I have retained some telepathic abilities and remain psychically open, although not to the extent that I was during the six months of expanded consciousness. Although I never experience violent body jerking the way I did that first evening, I still experience recurrent energy surges that rush up my body towards my brain. I perceive this as the life force surging through me.

Immediately after her experience, Gwen found the changes in her perception and the expansion of her consciousness so overwhelming that she decided to take a year off school. She spent the time traveling, learning about different spiritual traditions, and meeting people with similar interests around the world. After a while she managed to integrate the experience and what she learned from it into her daily life. She returned to medical school, completed her studies, and has become an excellent, dedicated physician.

Kundalini Awakening and Breathwork

In *The Stormy Search for Self* Christina Grof describes her kundalini awakening. It has several of the characteristics of the Spiritual Energy/Kundalini Episode. One of the things that makes Christina's story so interesting is that she may have inadvertently stimulated her kundalini through the combination of a longtime practice of Hatha Yoga and Lamaze childbirth-breathing techniques. These techniques are similar to some pranayama exercises—the breathing techniques used by yogis to stimulate kundalini. Christina's case is, of course, unusual. Most women do not need to worry that practicing either Lamaze or the gentle yoga stretches appropriate for pregnancy could have such dramatic results.

Christina's kundalini awakening occurred during the birth of her first child.

> *Lying on the delivery table, I glanced up at the immense surgical lamp and the kind, curious faces of the doctor, the assisting intern and nurses, and my husband. After only a few hours of labor, my son was suddenly and rapidly making his way into the world as I enthusiastically cooperated. As the people around me encouraged me to "push . . . push . . . nice and hard, remember to breathe," I felt an abrupt snap somewhere inside of me as powerful and unfamiliar energies were released unexpectedly and began streaming through my body. I started to shake uncontrollably. Enormous electrical tremors coursed from my toes up my legs and spine to the top of my head. Brilliant mosaics of white light exploded in my head, and instead of continuing the Lamaze panting, I felt strange, involuntary breathing rhythms taking over.*
>
> *It was as though I had just been hit by some miraculous but frightening force, and I was both excited and terrified; the shaking, the visions, and the spontaneous breathing were certainly not what I had expected from all of my months of preparation. As soon as my son was delivered, I was given two shots of morphine, which stopped the whole process. Soon, the wonder faded and I became embarrassed and fearful. I was a restrained, well-mannered woman who had a strong sense of authority over my life, and now I had completely lost control. Very quickly, I pulled myself together.*

During the birth of her second child, Christina had an even stronger kundalini experience. This time she was given tranquilizers which stopped the experience, just as the morphine had during the birth of her first child.

Even though she had studied yoga, Christina did not know exactly what had happened to her. The fact that heavy medication stopped both experiences added to her feeling that what she had undergone was a sign of illness.

Four years later, her spiritual journey began in earnest when she had another powerful experience while meditating with an Indian guru. After this her life changed radically. As with many people who experience continued "high-voltage" kundalini activity, she had periods of anxiety and depression as well as periods of spiritual awareness and bliss. Eventually she met her future husband, Dr. Stanislav Grof, who helped her see her experiences as part of a process of personal growth and transformation. The Grofs' work is discussed further in Chapter Thirteen.

Kundalini and Alcoholic Recovery

In my clinical experience, some people involved in the intensive psychological and spiritual healing work of recovering from addictions will experience a Spiritual Energy/Kundalini activation. Often, this happens once they "hit bottom," and from this mental and spiritual abyss, desperately cry out for help to the divine. In my opinion, this was true of Bill Wilson, the co-founder of Alcoholics Anonymous, whose "hot flash" or "white light experience" has all the clear signs of a Spiritual Energy/Kundalini Episode. Here is the description of Bill Wilson's experience as described in AA's *Pass It On*:

> ... he and Lois were waiting for the end. Now, there was nothing ahead but death or madness. This was the finish, the jumping-off place. "The terrifying darkness had become complete," Bill said. "In agony of spirit, I again thought of the cancer of alcoholism which had now consumed me in mind and spirit, and soon the body." The abyss gaped before him.
> In his helplessness and desperation, Bill cried out, "I'll do anything, anything at all!" He had reached a point of total, utter deflation—a state of complete surrender.

With neither faith nor hope, he cried, "If there be a God, let Him show Himself!"

What happened next was electric. "Suddenly, my room blazed with an indescribably white light. I was seized with an ecstasy beyond description. Every joy I had known was pale by comparison. The light, the ecstasy—I was conscious of nothing else for a time.

"Then, seen in the mind's eye, there was a mountain. I stood upon its summit, where a great wind blew. A wind, not of air, but of spirit. In great, clean strength, it blew right through me. Then came the blazing thought, 'You are a free man.' I know not at all how long I remained in this state, but finally the light and the ecstasy subsided. I again saw the wall of my room. As I became more quiet, a great peace stole over me, and this was accompanied by a sensation difficult to describe. I became acutely conscious of a Presence which seemed like a veritable sea of living spirit. I lay on the shores of a new world. 'This,' I thought, 'must be the great reality. The God of the preachers.'

"Savoring my new world, I remained in this state for a long time. I seemed to be possessed by the absolute, and the curious conviction deepened that no matter how wrong things seemed to be, there could be no question of the ultimate rightness of God's universe. For the first time, I felt that I really belonged. I knew that I was loved and could love in return. I thanked my God, who had given me a glimpse of His absolute self. Even though a pilgrim upon an uncertain highway, I needed to be concerned no more, for I had glimpsed the great beyond."

Bill Wilson had just had his 39th birthday, and he still had half his life ahead of him. He always said that after that experience, he never again doubted the existence of God. He never took another drink.

...he often referred to his enormous, intense, mystical, life-changing spiritual experience as a "hot flash." He *did this so often that other A.A.'s began using the same term, never realizing that Bill was deliberately "deflating" his own experience (and his own ego) by describing it thus.*

Bill Wilson's experience had clear and classic symptoms of a Spiritual Energy/Kundalini Episode: an energy movement that he described as the spiritual wind blowing through him, heat sensations, inner sounds of wind blowing, intense white light, and the associated mystical experience. This experience had a profound, spiritually transformative impact. He became less materialistic, more service-oriented, and developed deep, unshakable spiritual convictions. The experience also opened him to other STEs. He became convinced of the reality of past lives and had both psychic and inspired creative experiences. In my clinical work I have met several other recovering alcoholics who have had similar, if perhaps less dramatic kundalini awakenings when hitting bottom. These awakenings launched them to their journey of recovery and healing.

Downward-Flowing Spiritual Energy

Not everyone who experiences a Spiritual Energy/Kundalini Episode experiences sensations of the kundalini moving upwards through the body. In fact, some people report powerful Spiritual Energy/Kundalini Experiences where it feels like the energy is coming down from above and descending into the experiencer. These types of experiences are sometimes referred to in Christian traditions as "descent of grace" or "descent of the Holy Spirit." They are usually accompanied by the other signs of a Spiritual Energy/Kundalini Episode—perceptions of light, inner sounds, energy rushes (sometimes downwards), vibrating, jerking, or spiraling, plus the associated mystical or paranormal experience.

Jyoti, a friend and fellow kundalini researcher, describes such a downward-flowing kundalini episode in her autobiography,

An Angel Called My Name.

> *On the evening of April 30, 1983, I was taking a shower when a loud buzzing noise began. It became so loud I felt sure that everyone else could hear it . . . The loud buzzing seemed to reach a peak at which point a bright Light appeared above me. A beam shot down from it and poured into the top of my head, traveling throughout my entire body. My body seemed to be drawn forward. I felt totally nurtured and the process went on for quite some time. I fell deeper and deeper into an altered state of consciousness. After a while, I returned to a more functional state, but I still felt altered in some way . . . I decided to meditate . . . The energy was extremely strong, and again the loud buzzing returned. The Light returned, hovering over my head. As it descended, a sense of calmness and beauty seemed to fill the room in an all-encompassing, ever-present glow. I felt great empathy with it. Four figures in white-hooded robes appeared, one on each side and two at the end of the bed. Their form was wavy like heat coming off a road, but their appearance was distinct. They stood quietly and serenely, as if in a ceremony . . .*
> *Richard and I lay down on the bed . . . Again the energy returned. I visualized it as a white light that drew a circle around us encompassing our bodies. The energy seemed to flow across both of us. I found myself in a white swirling tunnel that had a bright red sphere at the other end. Its light radiated out and filled the tunnel with a red glow. People were standing in the tunnel. They disappeared leaving only one man, who began to walk toward me and then motioned with his arm to come . . . The scene changed, and I was looking into the corner of a living room with a couch, a chair, and a lamp. The scene changed again and I saw a city street scene. It appeared to be European with trees lining the area between the street and the sidewalk. It was a busy street*

with cars rushing to and fro. Each scene seemed so distinctly different that no connection could be made. Again the scene changed, displaying a beautiful, sunny landscape. The sun began to shine more brightly and filled the scene with such a brightness and intensity that only the silhouette of a tree in the center remained.

Following this scene, I found myself flying over a terrain of rolling hills. I enjoyed the sensation so much that I began to indulge in it, flying closer to the ground—up and down and over the hills. Suddenly, something pulled me up. I realized that I was in outer space looking down upon what appeared to be the planet earth. How in the world did I get out here? Outer space wasn't dark, but rather produced a sense of clarity. The earth was breathtaking in her hues of blue and green. . . . I had the distinct feeling that I would soon realize my true origin. At that moment I sensed my concentration being broken

I got up. . . My head was confused and my heart full. I sobbed for hours not knowing why. Upon returning to ordinary reality, I was filled with completeness, fullness and total commitment. . . . I am not sure I will ever be able to verbalize the intense meaning this evening held for me . . . I can only say that Spirit shook my world once again and impregnated me with an overwhelming sense of love and wholeness.

Jyoti has continued to have repeated Spiritual Energy/Kundalini Episodes over the years, and is in a process of long-term spiritual transformation of consciousness.

Kundalini by Any Other Name

Many—if not most—people who have Spiritual Energy/Kundalini Episodes are not aware that they have had what is called a kundalini awakening in the yogic tradition. Others simply choose to give the experience another name, such as "Holy Spirit" or

"White Light Experience." Dr. William Brugh Joy, a California doctor who specialized in internal medicine, has had many profoundly moving spiritual experiences in his life. He has become a well-known and highly respected speaker at conferences on spiritual subjects and has written a number of books. This story in *Joy's Way: A Map for the Transformational Journey* contains most of the elements of a Spiritual Energy/Kundalini Episode.

> *In a morning meditation in February 1976, I had the sensation of a motor turning on in my chest area, and then I saw a momentary flash of blinding white light. In each subsequent meditation, and each night just after I went to bed, I experienced the same blinding intense flash of light; it was far more intense than looking at the sun or at any other brilliantly lighted object I had ever seen. I began to try to hold the light in my awareness, but I could not do it. The light was just too bright. A second was more than I could stand.*
>
> *The experience, sometimes skipping a few days but always of the same quality, continued until November 1976. Then, one night, I was lying in bed, just about to fall asleep, when the motor came on; but this time it was not the usual motor. This time it was like a diesel truck. Its vibration shook not only me, but also the king-size bed. It was first centered in my chest area, then moved into the lower abdomen, then up toward my head. On came the superbrilliant light. It was not just a flash, and it did not stop. For a moment, I was terrified. Then I heard a voice say, "What do you think you have been preparing for?" I accepted it and relaxed into the experience. It lasted for about six hours: intense, intense, intense white light and the quaking of my whole body.*

Joy's experience is typical of many of the stories I have heard. Often people having a Spiritual Energy/Kundalini Episode have no prior knowledge of kundalini and have no idea what is happening to them. Some are terrified initially. Others think that they are dying or going crazy. Some even think an alien force or UFO is causing the intense energy experience. Still others think it is a normal, blissful, meditation-related or prayer-related experience. It is reassuring to know that most people who have Spiritual Energy/Kundalini Episodes tend to function quite normally between them and, although the physical symptoms sometimes continue, they generally do so at fairly low intensity between the peak episodes.

The many people I have met who have had Kundalini Episodes have eventually become tremendously uplifted and inspired by the experience. Once they had a name for their episode, a framework in which they could understand this very physical yet paranormal experience, they could relax and grow from the profound energetic opening. I think it is essential that awareness of kundalini awakening and its associated physical symptoms be spread throughout the Western world, so that persons experiencing it will have such a framework, and will also be given appropriate guidance and support throughout this dramatic spiritual awakening. Further, as I mentioned earlier, I think a Spiritual Energy/Kundalini Episode heralds the beginning of a journey of long-term psychological and spiritual transformation of consciousness. In the same way as mystical experiences, Spiritual Energy/Kundalini Episodes create an intense spiritual yearning in the experiencer, which draws them to strive to complete this journey, to reach transcendence, God-consciousness, the farther shores.

CHAPTER 5

Near-Death Experiences

The term "Near-Death Experience" was coined by Raymond Moody, M.D., an American psychiatrist, to describe a phenomenon he documented in his ground-breaking 1975 book, *Life After Life*. In his work, Dr. Moody observed that a surprising number of people seemed to have out-of-body and mystical experiences while very near death. After he documented more than one hundred cases in his book, Near-Death Experiences received a great deal of media attention. Doctors and psychologists from around the world began to tell of similar reports made by their patients, and scores of books have since been written on the subject.

One of the most significant of these is *Heading Toward Omega* by Dr. Kenneth Ring, an eminent American research psychologist and professor at the University of Connecticut. Another significant book is *Closer to the Light* by Dr. Melvin Morse, an M.D. who has become an authority on NDEs in children. Dr. Ring and Dr. Morse both went beyond merely documenting the existence of NDEs and focused on the positive changes in values, attitudes, and behavior occurring in people's lives after such experiences. Dr. Ring went even further, postulating kundalini awakening as a possible mechanism underlying NDEs. I support this hypothesis, and will expand on my own ideas about kundalini and NDEs in Chapter Eight.

Theologians have been as fascinated with the subject as are doctors and psychologists. In his recent book *Life After Death* Tom Harpur, a scholar, ordained Anglican priest, and respected Canadian author, analyzed NDEs as one of a number of subjects that are relevant to the question of life after death. Harpur examined the historical perspectives and surveyed much of the material that has been published on NDEs since Moody's book. Harpur concluded that expanding exploration and research in the field is "one of the most exciting developments of our time" and that he finds himself increasingly, if cautiously, "positive about the validity of the NDE as a witness to invisible realities beyond."

Even though there are still skeptics who believe that NDEs are caused by everything from overactive imagination to lack of oxygen in the brain, the number of people interested in the subject is rapidly growing. An organization called the International Association for Near Death Studies, of which I am a member, has recently been formed to facilitate dialogue and research on the subject. Both are clearly needed. More and more children and adults are reporting NDEs. One reason for this might be that improvements in technology—from emergency rescue equipment to medical resuscitation techniques—mean that far more people survive close brushes with death.

Still, not everyone who is near death and then resuscitated has an NDE. Statistics on the percentages of people who do vary greatly. According to Harpur, a December 1988 *Philadelphia Enquirer* reports that the consensus among most NDE researchers is that between 35 and 40 percent of persons who are questioned after returning from near death report an NDE. We do not yet know why some people report having them and others do not.

We do know, however, that NDEs are often spiritually transformative experiences. It is one point that writers like Ring and Harpur agree on. And it is something I have found to be true—both from my own personal experience and those of people I have counseled.

Characteristics of Near-Death Experiences

One of the most interesting things about NDEs is how similar different people's experiences are. People often interpret the experiences differently, based on their cultural perspective, but the actual experiences are virtually identical in all cultures. Dr. Moody identified fifteen features common to NDEs; these features have now become the standard identifying factors used by most researchers in the field. Although most NDEs do not contain all the features Moody lists, it is usual for them to have at least eight of the fifteen. The features usually occur in the general order listed below. My work with NDE experiencers seems to indicate that the number of features people experience tends to increase with the length of time they were unconscious or close to death. Although I have modified and expanded on a number of points using my own experience and terminology, the following features are similar to the ones listed by Moody.

1. *Ineffability.* NDEs have dimensions and aspects that are beyond words and cannot be adequately conveyed, expressed, or described to others.

2. *Auditory awareness.* Clear and accurate recall of what others were saying while the experiencer was unconscious or clinically dead.

3. *Strong feelings of peace.* A feeling of peace, comfort, and tranquility; fear either dissolves or is completely absent.

4. *Unusual inner sounds.* An internal sense of "hearing" buzzing, ringing, roaring, whistling, wind, distant wind chimes, or even "celestial" music.

5. *Floating out of the body.* The individual's "point of perception"—or the spirit body—rises, allowing the experiencer to observe his or her physical body and the surroundings; the spirit body may travel to other locations, often to observe loved ones.

6. *Dark tunnel.* A sensation of moving away from

the physical body through a long, dark passage or tunnel with a bright light at the far end.

7. *Meeting spirits.* Contact with loving spirits, often those of departed loved ones, relatives, or friends, who are often seen as youthful and/or shining white figures.

8. *White light.* Encountering or being immersed in indescribable white light that emanates a powerful aura of intense love and unconditional acceptance. This aura of love may be overwhelming and may inspire awe, devotion, and/or a willingness to surrender; it is sometimes perceived as a "being of light" such as God, Jesus, an angel, or another religious figure.

9. *Life review.* A review or rapid re-experiencing of emotional or significant life events, including ones that may have been forgotten or repressed.

10. *Life barrier.* The perception of a barrier or border that the spirit body cannot cross if it wants to return to the physical body.

11. *Abrupt return to the body.* A sensation of rapidly traveling back down through the tunnel and/or of being suddenly pulled down, sucked down, or being sucked back into the physical body, often through the top of the head; the sensation of suddenly re-entering the physical body, sometimes with a jolt.

12. *Conviction of the reality of the experience.* An absolute certainty that the experience was real and not a fantasy or a dream—even in the face of disbelief or ridicule.

13. *Transformational impact.* A life that is changed in one or more ways: (A) psychologically—the person may mature rapidly, appreciate life more, feel enriched, gain new insights about life or lifestyle, or rapidly or spontaneously resolve psychological issues; (B) spiritually—he or she may gain new insights into the nature of the universe, learn important lessons

about love, the basic unity of the world's religions, or other spiritual matters, or become stronger, more courageous, or more willing to speak the truth as they see it; (C) psychically—he or she may notice the development of intuition or psychic abilities or an increase in these faculties.

14. *New views of death.* The loss of fear of death and an increase in the certainty that the spirit lives on after death of the physical body.

15. *Independent corroboration.* Events observed on the physical plane during the out-of-body experience that are corroborated by other people or evidence.

The Story of a Young Judge

The following story was told to me by a young female lawyer whom I'll call Sylvia. She was extremely successful in her work and had held a position as a judge for two years before her experience.

I was driving home late one night after work along a dark, winding desert road. The evening seemed quite usual. As I drove, I was looking forward to getting home, greeting my husband, and spending some time playing with my two-year-old son. Suddenly, a huge transport truck raced around a bend, pulled into my lane, and faced my small car head-on.

My immediate reaction was to panic; I realized that I could not avoid crashing into the truck. I thought, "I'm going to die!" In a flash, I felt my consciousness leave my body and float above the car as I watched the accident happen below. I saw my body become cut and battered by the impact of the collision, but I felt no pain or fear, only a sense of peace and calm.

Then I suddenly found myself at the entrance to a long, dark tunnel, with a bright light glowing at the far end. Progressing along the tunnel, I began to experience an instantaneous replay of the events of my life. Once the "life review" was finished, I found myself in the dazzlingly brilliant white light at the end of the tunnel and perceived a number of loving beings who seemed to be made of light. Although I was not certain who they were, I sensed they might be deceased family or friends who loved me. They greeted me with warmth, acceptance, and love. I felt I was enveloped by the loving light of God, or the intelligence behind the universe. It was the most intensely beautiful and uplifting feeling I had ever had.

Quite suddenly, I felt myself being pulled away from the light. It seemed as if my "soul" was sinking down into a darker, smaller space. With a sudden jolt, I found myself waking up in my battered body. Groggy and aching all over, I discovered I was in a hospital emergency department where, I learned later, I had been brought by an ambulance and resuscitated.

Sylvia was profoundly moved by her experience, but she was also confused. She had never heard of Near-Death Experiences, and she did not know what to make of what she had undergone. Thinking that the doctors would not understand, she did not tell them of the experience. Her husband was the first person she told. But he thought she had imagined the whole thing, and he became angry whenever she wanted to talk about it.

Wanting desperately to understand what had happened to her, Sylvia remained preoccupied with the experience. Her husband became increasingly hostile about her fascination with it, and eventually they separated. They are now divorced.

In her search for understanding, Sylvia also tried to talk to the pastor of her local fundamentalist church. He told her that the experience must have been the work of the devil and that she should repent. Unwilling to agree with this interpretation, Sylvia went to her medical doctor, a physician who had never heard of Near-Death Experiences. He recommended that she see a psychiatrist, which Sylvia did.

The psychiatrist was also unfamiliar with NDEs. Observing

Sylvia's emotional intensity when she talked about the impact of the experience, the psychiatrist suggested that an unresolved emotional conflict had triggered the "delusion." He suggested that she uncover the conflict and resolve it through long-term psychotherapy and that, once this was done, the delusion would be eliminated. He then suggested she take some tranquilizers for the "anxiety" she was experiencing. Sylvia decided not to take the medication or try his psychotherapy.

Sylvia began to feel very confused and alone. Although she sensed she had undergone some type of mystical experience, no one around her seemed to think there was any validity to her story. Still, she was aware of many positive changes in her life. She had lost her fear of death and came to see God as the loving, intelligent divine force driving the universe rather than the vengeful judge she had once conceived of. She also came to believe that the founders of all the world's religions were trying to understand the same truth. Sylvia steadfastly refused to believe that such wonderful spiritual insights could have come from a delusion or a figment of her imagination.

Sylvia recovered physically from the accident, returned to her work as a judge, and adjusted to life as a single mother. She didn't become familiar with the concept of Near-Death Experiences until many years later when she came across Kenneth Ring's book *Heading Toward Omega*. What she read there confirmed the reality of her own experience and helped her understand why and how it had transformed her life.

Anyone Can Have an NDE

It is important to realize that people of all ages, of any educational background or level of intelligence, can have NDEs—Dr. Morse has documented more than a hundred cases of children who have had them. In my clinical experience, I have encountered people who ranged in age from their teens to their eighties when they had these experiences. NDEs can be triggered by any type of life-threatening illness or accident, even attempted suicide.

One of the most moving experiences that I have ever heard occurred to a forty-three-year-old mentally challenged woman I'll call June. Her NDE occurred after an attempted suicide. This is the story as she told it to me.

It was just after Christmas. I was very depressed. My family did not want to see me at Christmas and I was all alone. I knew that there was something wrong with my brain, and people called me retarded. I knew I could never have a normal happy life like you see on TV so I decided to kill myself. I took my whole bottle of anti-depressant pills and drank a whole bottle of vodka. Somebody had told me that would kill me.

When I passed out, I remember floating out of my body and looking down at my body passed out on the floor. I felt sorry for my body. It was all covered in vomit. I must have thrown up and then passed out on it. I felt very calm, though, and I looked up and saw a dark tunnel with a light at the end of it. I went through the tunnel, and I came out at the most wonderful place you could ever imagine. There was this really bright light, and I saw my grandparents and other relatives who had already died around me. I felt love coming from every-where, from everyone. I felt like I was being hugged by God. It was so beautiful. But my relatives told me that it was not my time to die. They told me in the nicest, lov-ing way, that I should not try to kill myself, that I should go back. Suddenly I was back in my body again, and I woke up, covered in vomit on the floor.

I don't think I will ever try to kill myself again. But I know that there's nothing to be scared of when you do die. It's nice. But somehow I know that in the big plan of things I am supposed to live in this body with a retarded brain. Maybe I will teach somebody something . . . maybe there is something good I am supposed to do, even in this messed up head and body.

June's experience was typical of many people who have an NDE while attempting suicide: They discover that they need to come back and deal with their lives to the best of their ability.

Frightening Near-Death Experiences

Unfortunately, not all NDEs are positive. Tom Harper cites Margot Grey's research that reports that up to one in eight of NDEs are perceived by the experiencer as negative. The reasons for this are not yet understood—and probably will not be until more research is done. Here is the story of a negative NDE told to me by Anna, a survivor of a Nazi concentration camp.

> *I was about twenty years old when the experience occurred. I had been captured and put into this concentration camp three years earlier. I had seen both of my parents die of starvation. They had insisted upon giving me some of their food because we were not being given enough to eat. They thought that out of the three of us, I had the best chance to survive. The winter after they died, some sort of infectious diarrhea struck the camp. Sanitation was poor, and therefore the infection spread quickly. Many people died from the effects of the diarrhea.*
>
> *I became so weak from the fever and the diarrhea that I was unable to leave my cot. As I became severely dehydrated, I became too weak to eat or drink. I remember feeling my consciousness fade, my vision grew black. Suddenly I felt myself slip up, out of my body. I was floating above my unconscious body, looking down on it. I felt terrified. "No! No!" I screamed inwardly. "I do not want to die too!" I felt overwhelmed with fear and panic. I wanted desperately to get back into my body and wake up. I do not know how long I stayed out of my body, but it was the most horrible, terrifying sensation I ever had. The next thing I remember is waking up in my cot the next morning. My fever had come down during the night.*

Anna's NDE was clearly not an inspiring or uplifting event, but as yet we do not know why. One fact Dr. Ring has discovered in his research, however, is that there does not seem to be any relationship between the precipitating event and whether the NDE is positive or negative. In other words, people who have very similar accidents or illnesses can have very different NDEs.

One factor contributing to a negative NDE that I have observed is whether or not the dying person surrendered to or turned to God. Several persons who recounted terrifying NDEs told me that they resisted going to the light, that they resisted or refused to turn to God. Anna certainly fought against the experience. Her thoughts did not turn to God, and she did not surrender to the experience.

Lucille, a thirty-eight-year-old housewife who had a terrifying NDE, describes her experience as follows:

> I was at home one Saturday afternoon when I suddenly developed an excruciating headache. I called out to my husband and my daughter as I collapsed onto the kitchen floor. I lost consciousness. My husband dialed 911, and an ambulance came and took me to the hospital. The doctors discovered that I had suffered a severe brain hemorrhage, and I had to undergo emergency surgery in order to save my life.
>
> At some point after I lost consciousness, I felt myself float out of my body. Suddenly I was up by the ceiling, and I could see my husband and daughter, worried, huddled over my unconscious body. "No! I am not going to die!" I screamed inside my soul. I saw a tunnel with a bright yellow-white light at the end. I felt myself being pulled down the tunnel, towards the light. "No!" I screamed. I fought against the pull towards the light. Somehow I knew that the light was God, and I thought going to the light would mean death on earth. I desperately struggled against the pull towards the light. I thought constantly of my daughter, and I vowed that I would let nothing take me away from her. The struggle

to resist the pull was horrible. I felt as if I was desper-
ately clawing my way, swimming against a very strong
current in a river. I struggled to stay away from the light.
I felt anger and fear. "No!" I kept saying to myself.

Finally, I regained consciousness in my body. I was
now in the recovery room of the hospital, following my
brain surgery. I was glad to still be alive, but I felt terri-
bly upset by the ordeal I had been through.

Clearly, Lucille resisted the urge to turn to the light in her experience, and in fact it seems that this resistance was what made
her NDE nightmarish. When I asked her if there was anything
unpleasant about the light, or the tunnel itself, she stated that
there was not. In fact, she said the light radiated a very intense
feeling of love. It was by this intense radiation of love that she
recognized the light to be God. In tears, she admits that she just
was not prepared to surrender to God, that she desperately
wanted to stay alive, to be with her daughter.

Sometimes experiencers describe an NDE as negative not
because it was negative in itself, but because they did not want
to return to their body! They would have preferred to stay in the
beauty, love, and peace of the light. Several people have told me
that they felt angry about the NDE experience for this reason.
They were living in physically abusive and psychologically
destructive home situations at the time of their NDE. They felt
angry at God afterwards for sending them away from the light
and back into their abusive situations.

One of the most dramatic negative NDE stories I have ever
heard is the one told to a fellow International Association for
Near Death Studies researcher, Dr. M. Taylor Bach, and recorded
on his video *A Message of Hope.* Pastor Howard Storm describes
his NDE, which began as negative but then shifted into a profoundly positive experience. He was a businessman and atheist at
the time of the NDE. I have paraphrased his description.

About five years ago, I almost died from a bleeding ulcer.
I recall lying in my hospital bed, awaiting emergency

surgery, when I felt myself go faint, slipping into dark-ness. I tried to call out or move, but I could not. Suddenly I found myself standing at the side of my bed, looking down at my unconscious body. I tried to call out to the nurses, but I was unable to make any noise. I felt I was in a dark, heavy space. I thought that I must have died. The thought crossed my mind that I should pray, but I did not. I had been a vehement atheist for the last forty years of my life, and I was not about to change now.

The darkness grew heavier. I felt myself go out of the room and down what seemed like a dark hallway, into a very dark and uncomfortable space. Slowly I became aware that there were dark presences in the shadows of the dark-ness. These presences started taunting me, poking my body and saying rude things using offensive language. I shouted at them to go away. Once again I had the thought that I should pray, but I did not. The taunting voices became louder, and their pokes started feeling as if their hands were claws and they were ripping my flesh. I was in agony and terrified. I begged them to stop hurting me, but they laughed and kept jeering at me and tearing at my flesh. Finally I felt completely destroyed. I was writhing in agony, crying out in physical pain and emotional devastation.

Once again, the thought crossed my mind to pray. This time, I thought, "What do I have to lose?" How-ever, I didn't know how to pray. Suddenly I recalled a phrase from a hymn I had sung in my childhood, "Jesus loves me, this I know." I began to sing "Jesus loves me," making up words in parts where I had forgotten them. The taunting voices shouted at me as I sang "Stop that! It's no use! There's nobody to hear you!" But as the voices ordered me to stop, I continued to sing, and then I started to pray, with heartfelt sincerity. "Please, Lord Jesus," I prayed, "If you really are out there, please help me!" As I continued to pray and sing, the dark entities seemed to move away. "Stop that, the light is hurting us," they said. I continued to pray earnestly.

Suddenly, I noticed a speck of light, far away, like a shooting star, moving towards me through the darkness. As the light moved closer and closer, the dark presences seemed to disappear, or dissolve in the light. As the ball of light drew near, I felt as if I was lifted out of the darkness and raised into the protection of this loving bubble of light. Although no words were spoken, I immediately sensed that this loving light was a spiritual being—Lord Jesus. The being of light carried me up through space, and into a phenomenally immense, even more brilliant light, which I recognized in my heart as God. As we moved into the light, I felt my soul embraced by God's infinite love.

I wept. I felt myself unworthy of such love, of such compassion. I felt ashamed of my many years of having maligned those with spiritual faith. I trembled, saying to the divine light that I was unworthy, that there must have been some mistake. Without words, the light—God—informed me that there are no mistakes, that all are deserving of divine love. I wept with joy and ecstatic bliss.

When my body was resuscitated in the hospital, I abruptly returned to the earthly plane. I was bursting with joy at this profound spiritual awakening, and I could not wait to share this story with all who would listen. I changed my life work, and am now a pastor, eager to tell everyone about God's love!

Howard Storm's story demonstrates that a negative NDE can be turned into a positive one through turning to God. This once again supports my hypothesis that a critical element in a negative NDE is the failure or refusal of the individual to turn to or surrender to God.

When I counsel people who have had a negative NDE, I first try to understand which aspect of the NDE seemed negative to them—the experience itself, the possibility of death, or the return to life. Then I try to help the person understand what psychological and spiritual lessons can be learned from this negative reaction to the NDE. Usually, I have found that persons who have had a negative NDE can transcend the negative impact by trusting in the divine wisdom of the loving light which they encountered, and by addressing whatever psychological and/or spiritual issues need to be addressed—here on the earthly plane.

The issue of negative NDEs is complex and deserves a great deal more research.

NDE-like Experiences and Facing-Death NDEs

Technically, when doctors and researchers refer to Near-Death Experiences they are talking about an experience in which the person is clinically dead—or extremely near death—and then resuscitated. However, in my work I have come across many people with a broad spectrum of experiences that are very similar to NDEs even though the experiencers have not been clinically dead, unconscious, or resuscitated. In my clinical practice I have found three main groups of NDE-like experiences. Facing-Death NDEs in people who thought they were about to die, Deathbed Visions in people who had the experience several hours or even a few days before they did actually die of a terminal illness, and Death-Watch Experiences in people who were emotionally close to a loved one who died. Occasionally, people will report an NDE-like experience occurring during meditation, when there is no risk of death.

In Facing-Death NDEs one common factor seems to be that the experiencers come face to face with their own mortality—whether or not they are, in reality, in danger of dying. In my experience people who report Facing-Death NDEs often describe only a few of the typical features of an NDE although they may report features of a full NDE. "Paul," a thirty-eight-year-old engineer, had a Facing-Death NDE in his mid-twenties when he came extremely close to losing consciousness and drowning.

I was canoeing with an inexperienced friend in Canada in early spring just after the ice melted on the lakes. The canoe accidentally overturned, and we fell into near-freezing water. We were both wearing heavy parkas and boots, and my partner could not swim. Panicking, my friend tried to climb on top of me and pushed me under the water.

After struggling for a few moments, I felt certain I was going to drown. Suddenly, I felt my consciousness float up, out of my body. I became very peaceful and calm. As I looked down from above, I saw a motor boat appear out of nowhere, race over toward us, and pull us out of the water a few moments later. When our rescuers pulled my head out, I gasped for air and was instantaneously aware of being back in my body.

Paul was never actually unconscious during this episode. It lasted only a brief time and, following the pattern I've noticed, he experienced four of the typical features of NDEs: an out-of-body experience, a deep feeling of peace, an abrupt return to his body, and, later, an unshakable conviction concerning the reality of the experience.

Since Paul's experience had only some of the classic features, most researchers wouldn't consider it to be a true NDE. However, I believe experiences like Paul's are genuine, and are important because they can open a person's mind or even, in some cases, begin a process of spiritual transformation.

People who simply think they are about to die sometimes report this type of experience. In these cases, the significant factor may be that they face death psychologically even if they don't actually come close to it physically. Several former soldiers have told me stories of Facing-Death NDEs, having out-of-body experiences on battlefields, seeing their lives flash before their eyes, or feeling the presence of protective, loving spirits when they were in situations so dangerous that they were convinced they were about to die. Automobile accidents that we think of as close calls are another common trigger for Facing-Death NDEs. A man I'll call Jonathan describes his own close call.

I was driving home from college, after a dormitory party rather late one evening. I was really tired, probably too tired to drive safely—but I often sped and drove recklessly. I was racing along the deserted highway in my fiberglass-bodied sports car, rushing to get home and into bed.

The rain was drizzling and the roads were slippery. Unexpectedly, I lost control of my car as I approached a cement underpass. I must have been going close to 100 miles per hour at the time. I knew instantly that I had absolutely no hope of surviving the impact. At the speed I was going, the fiberglass body could crumple completely.

As my car spun out of control, I saw my life flash before my eyes. I saw myself with my father, walking along the beach when I was about five years old. Then I saw myself playing with my brother up at the cottage. In the next scene I saw my mother sewing me a new jacket one Christmas. Another was my high-school graduation party. More and more scenes like this flashed before my eyes. As I watched these events, I felt as if I was out of my body, floating above my car. Abruptly, my car came to a stop at the far end of the underpass. By some miracle it had crashed into a metal railing and totally missed the cement abutment. Then, just as suddenly, I was back in my body again, totally in the present.

I knew that I had just narrowly missed dying. I felt humbled and sobered by the experience. I realized that my life was very precious, and that I should be treating myself with more care. From that day I quit speeding and driving recklessly. I had been badly shaken by the close call I'd had and by the realization that I had come so close to death.

Jonathan had five features of a typical NDE: an out-of-body experience, a life-review, an abrupt return to body, a conviction that the experience was real, and a transformation of his lifestyle. It seems clear that his experience—even though he was not unconscious or physically harmed in any way—falls within the spectrum of various types of experiences that are in some way related to classic NDEs.

Deathbed Visions

Experiences like those of Jonathan and Paul raise questions about what exactly triggers an NDE. The experiences of another—and very different—group makes the questions even more intriguing. These are people who know they are going to die and who have experiences that parallel classic NDEs, but who have their experiences several hours or even days before they reach the actual moment of death. Dr. Melvin Morse calls this phenomenon a deathbed vision.

In my work as a family physician, I often deal with elderly patients hospitalized with illnesses that will ultimately cause their death. On several occasions these people have told me about having a vision or dream that relates to their impending death. Many of my medical colleagues' patients have related similar accounts. We have all noticed that the people who have this type of vision often are extremely peaceful and serene at the moment of death.

Deathbed Visions often have a number of typical NDE features. They may include a sense of peace and calm, a loss of fear of death, a vision of the luminous spirits of deceased loved ones who come to reassure them or accompany them, a long, dark tunnel with a brilliant white light at the far end, and/or a vision of a prophet or important figure from the dying person's religion, such as Christ or Moses.

I have found that people who have these experiences often interpret them as a clear sign that they will be dying soon. They are often considerably changed by the experience; they accept their impending deaths much more calmly and become more deeply at peace. Frequently, they use their remaining time to tell their family members that they love them and to urge them not to grieve. They assure their friends and family that they are not afraid to die. Sometimes they even say that they welcome death.

The dying person's loved ones may also feel deeply reassured if they are told about the vision. One of the most striking examples of this I have ever heard was told to me by a woman who had lost two young sons at different times.

My son Billy got leukemia when he was seven. He had been taking chemotherapy, and he seemed to be doing well. The doctors were optimistic, and we didn't expect him to die. Then one morning he told me that he had had a dream the night before. He said that in it his brother Bruce had come to see him and that he knew now that he would be dying soon, but that he wanted me to know that everything would be all right. Then he turned to me and said, "Mom, why didn't you ever tell me I had a brother named Bruce who died?" I was so overcome, I didn't know what to say. When Billy was an infant his brother Bruce had died in a car wreck, and somehow we had never been able to tell him about it. The next day Billy died, too. And losing him was so hard, but I just held on to the idea that he and Bruce were together now, and somebody, somewhere was taking care of my babies.

Even though the loss of her sons had happened years before, the woman was in tears as she told me this story. Still, she said again and again how much Billy's dream had reassured her and helped bring her some sense of peace.

Death-Watch Experiences

A Death-Watch Experience is another NDE-like experience that happens to people who are not close to death themselves. Rather, this experience may happen to those who are physically and/or emotionally close to somebody else who dies. Usually, a Death-Watch Experience occurs around the time of death. Although I have found that they are more likely to happen when a person is physically at the bedside of the dying person, they can also happen when a person is at a distant location.

Often Death-Watch Experiences are brief visions of what appears to be the spirit of the dying loved-one, giving a final blessing of love, delivering a message, or saying goodbye. Sometimes Death-Watch Experiences very closely resemble a full NDE.

Such was the case of Louisa, who told me her story as follows:

> I was sitting at my husband, Jim's, bedside, holding his hand. His cancer had hit him very fast and very hard. It was just three months since he was diagnosed, and we both knew that he would not live much longer.
>
> We had talked very deeply and lovingly to each other over the last few days. We seemed to have healed any differences that we had had between us, and I felt very much in love, very close indeed to my husband. I basked in the glow of this feeling of mutual love as I watched him drift off to sleep.
>
> Suddenly, I felt myself rise above my body, and I felt myself and Jim moving upwards. We were rapidly moving together up through a dark tunnel towards a bright light. The light was radiating intense love. Part way up the tunnel I felt myself abruptly stop moving towards the light, as if I'd been stopped by an invisible force field. Jim kept on moving upwards. For an instant he stopped and turned his head to look at me. His face looked young and radiant. He smiled a smile that radiated a wave of love towards me, as if to say goodbye, then he turned his face away and continued to move up towards the light.
>
> I struggled to push myself up towards him. I wanted to go with Jim! The next instant I was aware that I was in my body, at Jim's bedside, holding his now lifeless hand. Jim had died.

Although Louisa felt a tremendous loss at the death of her beloved husband, she said that her Death-Watch Experience, her glimpse of Jim going to the loving light of God, has been a great comfort to her throughout her grief. Neither Jim nor Louisa had been particularly religious or spiritually minded people before the death. But this glimpse has made Louisa realize that truly there is nothing to fear in death—that a loving God awaits us all if we turn to the light.

A Continuum of Experiences

From a clinical standpoint, my own NDE is interesting because it contained elements of both a Facing-Death NDE and a classic NDE. My Facing-Death Experience began immediately after the second engine on the plane failed and we rapidly began to lose altitude. As soon as the words "Oh God, I'm going to die" came into my mind and I psychologically faced death, the spiritual part of my experience began. I was filled with peace and calm, and quotes from the scriptures poured into my consciousness, comforting and reassuring me. I became certain that God existed and that the divine plan was unfolding as it should. Later, as my body began to freeze and I physically faced death, I experienced more and more of the classic features of NDEs. I heard an inner sound, then I floated out of my body and experienced the sensation of being embraced by a universal, loving, omnipotent intelligence and of being surrounded by a loving light. By this point I was filled with the deepest sense of bliss I have ever known. After the experience, I was absolutely convinced that it had been real—in some ways more real than what we generally think of as "reality." What's more, it began a lifelong transformative process.

Based on my own experience and my work, I have come to suspect that individuals who have had Facing-Death Experiences might well have gone on to have classic NDEs if their experiences had lasted longer or if they had come physically closer to death. It seems logical to me that the different types of NDEs we have been discussing exist along a continuum.

NDEs and Transformation

Although some scientists still question the validity of Near-Death Experiences—and the role of kundalini awakening in NDEs is still subject to scientific verification—few people can deny the transformative impact NDEs often have on experiencers. In some ways NDEs are the most clear-cut type of Spiritually Transformative Experience. The moment of near-death is usually so clearly defined and dramatic that experiencers can see distinctly the differences in their lives before and after the event. Betty Eadie and Dannion Brinkley are two NDE experiencers who are now famous from their books that describe their NDEs and spiritual transformations.

In my own case, transformation occurred in several areas of my life. Although in 1979 I was only twenty-six years old and I had a great deal of personal growth and healing ahead of me, I noticed an immediate improvement in my relationships with members of my family, my capacity to love and forgive increased, my spiritual convictions were greater, and my commitment to standing up for the truth was stronger. I also had my first clear-cut psychic experience—or what is called, by some researchers, a "psychic opening." Over the years, the number of different types of psychic experiences I have had has increased gradually. Some are simply strong intuitive feelings about what I should or should not do; others are fairly dramatic instances of clairsentience and clairvoyance. I try not to make too much of them, since I realize that many, many people have similar experiences. Something has simply been added to the way I perceive reality: my sensitivity has increased, a change in my consciousness has occurred.

In retrospect, I now realize that my NDE was not my first STE. As mentioned in Chapter Four, almost three years earlier I had had what I now consider my initial kundalini awakening. I think that this spiritual energy awakening in 1976, and my regular prayer and meditation practice since then, probably made me very susceptible to the NDE in 1979.

Over the years, I have continued my regular prayer and meditation practice. I have also embraced my psychological-spiritual healing and learning—my psycho-spiritual housecleaning. I have been graced with other mystical experiences, not only when near-death, but usually related to times of intense heartfelt prayer and meditation. These mystical experiences have been a blessing in my life, for which I am grateful. They have uplifted and comforted me in times of intense emotional pain, as well as giving me clarity, peace, and guidance at time of major life changes. Spontaneous inspired creativity began in 1990, and it occurs periodically in the form of poetry, spiritual insights, and prose.

These changes in consciousness have been accompanied by a number of physiological sensations of kundalini activity. The first symptom I noticed was rushes of energy that move rapidly up my spine. These rushes occur with STEs and often during meditation or during quiet contemplation at the exact moment that I receive a sudden spiritual insight or intuitive flash. When the rushes and insights occur together, I often have the feeling that one somehow verifies the other. During highly creative periods, I feel waves of heat and burning in my spine. These energy rushes and heat sensations began after my awakening experience in 1976 and continue to this day.

I began to notice the next physiological sensation around 1983: a recurrent inner sound. Initially, the sound would occur only when I was meditating or deeply contemplating a spiritual topic, but its occurrence became more frequent, then constant. At first it sounded a little like the chirping of crickets, later like a gentle motor rumbling. Eventually it began to sound more like distant wind chimes or tinkling bells. During intense meditation or spiritual contemplation, this high-pitched tinkling sound becomes louder and is sometimes accompanied by a low-pitched, rumbling sound.

In the mid-1980s, I had recurrent expansions of consciousness. At times I felt as if the space occupied by my mind had grown and expanded outside my head. Sometimes this expansion seemed to stop a few feet from my head; occasionally it seemed to stretch out to very large dimensions. My dream life has become very rich, punctuated with strong life messages, glimpses of past lives, and recurrent mystical visions. My meditations bring stillness, peace, and clarity.

I also seem to have new, and increasing, light experiences. I sometimes have episodes of "luminosity," when the world suddenly seems to be illuminated by a brighter light. These episodes can occur in any setting, indoors or outdoors, day or night, when I am highly spiritually focused.

Following my NDE, changes also began to occur in the way I

wanted to live my life and in the way I viewed myself. Although I'd been interested in spiritual matters for much of my life, I developed an even greater urge towards prayer, meditation, yoga, and reading spiritual books. Over the years I've also noticed gradual changes in my personality. As my awareness of the inter-connectedness, the "oneness" of all, grows, it becomes increasingly important to me to be of service in whatever small way I can. As this process continues, I am also repeatedly forced to face my emotional and psychological issues. My "shadow" tendencies in life situations, whether it be anger, fear, guilt, shame, distorted thinking, selfishness, or insensitivity, are often thrown, quite spontaneously, by my subconscious mind into my conscious awareness. The psychological "housecleaning" that results is often challenging, or even painful, but very healing and enriching. I know I have to go on with this psychological inner work, and I have a strong inner desire to do so.

Most importantly, my meditation experiences and feelings of the connectedness of us all to the Higher Power have deepened immensely over the years. Meditation is now an entry into the "stillness between thoughts," what I believe is meant by "Be still, and know that I am God." I now perceive God's presence in the world at all times, as a loving force that is invisibly guiding all of us in our life journey of healing and learning.

The process of spiritual transformation is clearly one that propels us to more deeply experience our connection to the Higher Power, to see ourselves as we really are and to—slowly but surely—grow. As I will outline in detail in Chapters Fifteen, Sixteen, and Seventeen, this psycho-spiritual housecleaning is what I believe to be the progressive inner work of the spiritual journey.

CHAPTER 6

Psychic Awakening

A tremendous amount of research has been done on psychic abilities and psychic phenomena over the last few decades. And although not everyone believes they exist, and many people today share the perception that psychic phenomena are not real but rather are based on deception or trickery, many respected scientists, psychiatrists, doctors, and psychologists do think some psychic phenomena are genuine. Stanislav Grof, Kenneth Ring, and Carl Jung are among those who have written about paranormal phenomena and have been convinced of their reality.

Psychic Awakening—or psychic opening—has become a generally accepted term for describing the onset of psychic experiences in a person who has not previously had them or the development of new, different, or more powerful experiences in a person who has already had some type of psychic experiences.

In general, the term "psychic experience" can refer to almost any type of paranormal experience in which the experiencer perceives something that cannot normally be perceived by the five senses. In my clinical experience I have found that Psychic Awakenings and psychic experiences are extremely common in people who have had Mystical Experiences, Classical Kundalini

Episodes, and Near-Death Experiences, and I have become convinced that they are a natural part of the process of spiritual transformation of consciousness. In fact, almost every person I have ever counseled who has had an STE has noticed either the onset or the development of psychic abilities at some point after their STEs began. Extremely powerful Psychic Awakenings and psychic experiences can also be STEPs. As mentioned in Chapter Four, the opposite is not true. Not everyone having psychic experiences is undergoing spiritual transformation.

Psychic experiences, of course, take many different forms, and they are defined in a variety of ways. For these reasons, I have made a fairly extensive—but not exhaustive—list of common psychic experiences and provided definitions based on those developed and used by the Academy of Intuitive Studies in California.

Types of Psychic Experiences

1. *Abstract intuition.* Automatically knowing the answer to a problem without having to go through the logical steps of thinking and learning.

2. *Astral travel.* Episodes in which the spirit (sometimes called the astral body or spirit personality) seems to leave the physical body and travel to another place, time, or dimension.

3. *Automatic writing.* Writing or some other creative endeavor done without conscious thought by the experiencer; it is often assumed that a "spirit guide" connects in some way to the experiencer's hand or arm and uses it to write messages, paint, draw, or play a musical instrument.

4. *Clairaudience.* Mentally perceiving or actually hearing sounds or voices that are beyond the range of natural hearing.

5. *Clairsentience.* The ability to feel and know the true feelings of another, including the ability to locate pain in another by perceiving it in one's own body.

6. *Clairvoyance.* (1) The ability to see auras, subtle energy fields, or chakras; (2) the ability to see meaningful colors, patterns, or symbols which are not normally visible; (3) the ability to see objects or events that are concealed or beyond the natural range of sight (sometimes called "remote viewing").

7. *Psychic or spiritual healing.* The ability to heal others by touch (also called "the laying on of hands"); the related experience of being healed by the touch of another, or being healed through prayers or focused thoughts.

8. *Out-of-Body Experiences.* Episodes in which the spirit seems to leave the physical body, but remains within sight of or in the general location of the physical body.

9. *Past-life recall.* The ability to know, see, or clearly sense what seems to be previous-life incarnations.

10. *Precognition.* The ability to see, know, or emotionally sense the future; this includes having premonitions, prophetic dreams, and premonitory visions.

11. *Psychometry.* The ability to receive intuitive information about a person or object by touching either the person or the object with one's hands.

12. *Communication with spirit guides.* The ability to communicate with what seems to be a spirit helper, guardian angel, or guide by seeing, hearing, feeling, knowing, or smelling their presence.

13. *Telekinesis.* The ability to move objects by thought or mental influence.

14. *Telepyrokinesis.* The ability to start fires by thought or mental influence (also called pyrokinesis).

15. *Telepathy.* The ability to send and/or receive thoughts or mental images to or from another person.

16. *Trance channeling.* A phenomenon in which the experiencer's own personality or spirit seems to step aside, and another personality or spirit seems to use

the experiencer's physical body to communicate, write, or draw.

A Psychic Awakening

Sudden Psychic Awakenings are sometimes confusing or disrupt the experiencer's life. This is particularly true when the awakening is a powerful one. However, the onset of the mildest psychic abilities can be disruptive—or even frightening, especially if the experiencer is convinced psychic phenomena do really not exist or believes they are bizarre or somehow connected with "the devil" or "dark forces."

Even people who believe in psychic abilities and think they are positive can be unsettled by their own experience of them. Since so many scientists and doctors still scoff at the existence of psychic phenomena, some experiencers wonder for a while about their own sanity. Others think that these abilities belong only to a few rare and gifted individuals and may be afraid that their imaginations have run wild.

The following is the story of Dagmar, a child-care worker whose Psychic Awakening occurred about three years ago. The experience was Dagmar's first STEP. She was initially quite confused by it and by the psychic experiences that followed.

> All my life, I was a very intuitive person, but I had never had any clear psychic experiences. When I was thirty years old, my father died of pneumonia in our home. I was very saddened by the loss of my father because I had loved him very dearly.
>
> About one week after he died, I was thinking about him while I was at work, and suddenly I saw my father standing there, in the corner of the room! My first reaction was delight. "Dad! It's so good to see you!" I thought. In a second or two, I realized he wasn't physically there, that he had died—but I could still see him as clear as could be.

I sensed in my mind that my father was telling me that he was okay, that death was nothing to fear. The vision lasted for about half an hour, then slowly disappeared. I was very happy to have had a chance to see my father again. But I was very confused because I didn't know how or why it had happened. And even though I knew on one level it was real, I started to wonder if I might have been seeing things or if I was losing my mind. I didn't tell anybody about this for almost a year, because I was afraid that they would think I was crazy.

After that I started having many types of psychic experiences. They have included psychic visions, psychic dreams, and premonitions. One of my most dramatic psychic visions had to do with another death. About one year ago, my neighbor's son died. He was only three years old. The entire family was grieving deeply over their tragic loss. At the funeral, suddenly I could see the little boy standing there, behind his family, watching the funeral service. I could also see that he was not alone; he was accompanied by a number of beautiful beings that seemed to be made of light. He looked directly at me and smiled.

I thought about it carefully and decided to tell the boy's mother what I had seen. Right after the funeral I spoke with her and simply told her that I was absolutely sure her son was at peace and that others were caring for him. I was surprised at how much comfort she seemed to find in my words and, perhaps, by the conviction I felt. Later, when we were alone, I told her in detail about the psychic vision. Since then she has thanked me over and over for telling her.

Experiences like this continue to happen to me. I have no idea why I suddenly started having them. At first, I was worried and was afraid I might be going crazy. Now I think these experiences are a gift and a part of my spiritual unfoldment.

In adjusting to her psychic experiences, Dagmar went through what seems to be a fairly typical pattern. At first she found them unsettling and confusing. She was convinced, on the one hand, that they were real and, on the other, that her "seeing things" might indicate some type of mental problem. She was also very reluctant to tell others about them for fear they would say she was "crazy." Over the past few years Dagmar has become far more comfortable with her psychic abilities. She has come to accept them as part of her own particular spiritual journey. Whenever she has a psychic experience, she prays for help in understanding its significance and for guidance about what she should do with the information she has gained. Dagmar now understands that she can have these visions and still be a completely normal, mentally healthy individual. Although she has learned to respect her psychic impressions, she knows not everyone believes in the paranormal, so she tends to keep her experiences relatively private and share them only with those who will understand. She also keeps them in proper perspective and views them as a sidelight rather than the main focus of her spiritual journey.

An Experience of Clairsentience

Psychic experiences take so many different forms that even people who are aware of most types can be troubled or caught off guard when they have an experience that they are completely unfamiliar with. In my work, I have found that a surprising number of people are experiencing clairsentience even though they have never heard of it. Since this particular type of psychic experience often involves sensing or feeling another person's pain in one's own body or emotions, it can be particularly distressing until the experiencer discovers exactly what is happening to him or her. The following story provides a good example of this. It happened to Jeneane, the businesswoman whose mystical experience was described in Chapter Three. After her experience of perceiving the Bodhisattva, Jeneane began to have an increasing number of spiritual experiences. Still, when her first experience of clairsentience occurred, she wasn't sure what was happening to her.

About two years after I began my regular practices of Hatha Yoga and Jungian dream analysis, I had an extremely unusual experience one day during a meeting with a regular client. While we were speaking, I suddenly felt a strong pressure-like pain in the middle of my chest. A few moments after this occurred, my client broke into tears and confided to me that his wife had left him a few days earlier.

I sensed that the pain in my chest might be somehow related to my client's "heart pain," but I wasn't sure, and the pain in my own chest did not stop for one full hour, until after the client had left my office. Concerned, I went to my doctor for a checkup and tests on my heart later that week. The doctor told me that my heart was fine and that the transient chest pain could have been caused by gas or muscle tension.

Although it reassured me to know there was nothing wrong with my heart, I couldn't accept the doctor's explanation. I was especially puzzled since I had begun to notice that this intense pressure and pain returned to the middle of my chest whenever I was with a person who was experiencing emotional pain. Eventually, each time the chest pain returned I asked the person I was with if something was bothering him or her—and I almost always got an affirmative response.

Over the next few weeks, I began to notice another unusual physical sensation: a painful pressure in the center of my forehead. I soon discovered this sensation was occurring when I was around people who were angry or in mental turmoil. This pain would sometimes become agonizing for me when I was in a crowded public place like a subway train.

Even though Jeneane eventually developed a good sense of what was happening to her, she had no idea what to call it. After learning of my interest in the paranormal she approached me, described her experiences, and asked if I had ever heard of such a thing. She found it reassuring when I was able to provide her with a label for the experience and tell her that this and other types of Psychic Awakenings were common for those who were on the spiritual journey. She also found it helpful to learn that there were techniques (see Chapter Fifteen) which would help her block, ease, or eliminate the pain she was "picking up" from others.

Psychic from Childhood

Many people who have a marked psychic openness have had this ability since early childhood. Denise, a forty-year-old nurse, told me about her experience of growing up with psychic abilities. Denise's psychic experiences have always been an integral part of her life. Still, she has had one experience that was extraordinary enough to be a STEP. Of course, for someone who had never had any psychic experiences, the onset of even a milder version of Denise's abilities might be a profound transformative experience.

I have had frequent psychic visions for as long as I can remember. As a young child I remember seeing energy patterns and colors around people. For many years I thought everyone saw those colors. It was only when I was around six or seven that I realized that other people couldn't see them. Now I know that I was seeing people's auras; this ability is still with me.

As a child, I found it sort of confusing when I knew what people were feeling or was aware of something about their past that they didn't know I knew. Sometimes I would look at somebody, for instance an aunt, and I would see images in my mind of things that had happened to her. When I talked about these images my parents became very upset with me and would tell me to keep my mouth shut about my "wild ideas." Eventually, I learned that I should not talk about the information I received about other people's lives.

Once I grew up, I managed to cope fairly well with my psychic experiences. As I matured, I found I developed even more psychic abilities. I became very spiritually focused, and I started having mystical visions and episodes of bliss that were related to prayer and meditation. By this time I felt I'd managed to integrate my psychic abilities into my life.

However, when I was about thirty, I suddenly started recalling some of my past lives. The first time it occurred was when I was on holiday in Massachusetts. One day my husband and I went to visit the town of Salem. While there I suddenly had a clear recollection of living there with my brother—and I knew that my brother in that life was my husband in this one. As the memory unfolded, I saw myself being arrested unjustly and being put on trial as a witch. My brother had left on a long trip the week before I was arrested and he wasn't there to help me. I felt abandoned and was extremely angry with him. Still, I was very fortunate, for I was eventually released from prison, and I escaped the horrible fate that so many other women met there.

At first, having this past-life memory was overwhelming and confusing. But over time I learned to use the information I gained from the past-life experience to help me understand the complicated relationship I had with my husband in this life. I had a great deal of unresolved anger towards him, and I did not trust him. Seeing the connection I had had with him in a past life and realizing that some of the negative emotions I had might have come from there helped me understand my marriage and allowed me to work spiritually and psychologically on letting the emotions go. I have also come to believe absolutely that karma and reincarnation are very real.

Still, to this day, I keep my psychic abilities hidden from most people. I use my psychic perceptions to help me in nursing patients with emotional difficulties, and in counseling friends about personal problems. I have developed a reputation of being a gifted nurse. Very few people know what my secret method is!

Denise's first past-life memory represented a new level of Psychic Awakening and was a STEP for her. It had a spiritually transformative effect on her and helped her work out psychological issues that she had been unable to resolve before the STEP occurred.

She provides a good example of someone who has adjusted well to having psychic experiences, has a very successful life, and has learned to use her gifts constructively to help herself and others.

Encounters with Unidentified Flying Objects

A UFO encounter is generally defined as an experience in which an individual actually sees and communicates with—or has some other type of close contact with—beings that appear to come from another dimension or planet. The experiencer sometimes has the impression that he or she was taken to an alien spaceship or to other places or dimensions. In this case the experience is sometimes perceived as an abduction in which the experiencer is medically examined or taught spiritual lessons. Simple UFO sightings do not fit into this category of experience.

UFO encounters are the paranormal phenomenon that I am least familiar and least comfortable with. But in my work I have spoken with several people who believe they have had this type of experience. And, of course, the question of the existence of alien life forms opens up a whole range of spiritual and scientific issues that are beyond the scope of this book. Still, I think it is important to include UFO encounters because they frequently seem to have a profound transformational effect on the experiencer.

Dr. Kenneth Ring recently conducted a carefully controlled research project on this subject and reported on it in his third book, *The Omega Project*. During his research Dr. Ring discovered that individuals who reported having close UFO encounters or abductions also scored very high on a scale he devised to rate kundalini activity. He also found that a UFO encounter often had the same type of transformational impact that a Near-Death Experience had.

Further evidence that the UFO encounter can precipitate spiritual transformation is given in an essay by Keith Thompson, "The UFO Encounter Experience as a Crisis of Transformation," that appeared in the Grofs' book *Spiritual Emergency*. Thompson discusses in depth how the perceptions of those who report UFO encounters are changed and says that, perhaps, the UFO encounter—like NDEs, mystical visions, and other paranormal phenomena—acts like a prod that pushes us on to the next level of consciousness.

A Classic UFO Encounter

One of the most classic and best-documented cases of a UFO encounter is the story of Betty Andreasson, which was published in the book *The Andreasson Affair*. Andreasson was taken to another "place" by UFO beings, subjected to what seemed to be a medical examination, taught a number of spiritual lessons, and then returned. She did not recall her experience immediately after it happened, but only after she was hypnotized during therapy some time later.

This gradual recall is common among UFO encounter experiencers and seems to follow a fairly consistent pattern: at first, the experiencers do not recall anything about the experience. They are, however, aware of a period of time that they can't account for or for which they have no memory. Then, over time, memories of the encounter begin to surface, sometimes more and more rapidly, until finally the experiencers are able to reconstruct much, if not all, of the encounter. Often this process of remembering occurs in dreams, during hypnotic regression, or in what the experiencers describe as flashbacks. The following is a classic example of one type of UFO encounter that fits this pattern. It was told to me by a medical doctor whom I'll call Shawn. She was in her mid-thirties when it occurred and had meditated regularly and been involved in the process of spiritual transformation for several years. Even though she had had a number of psychic and paranormal experiences, she was extremely skeptical about UFO experiences.

> One summer weekend I was driving to a medical con-ference that was being held at a retreat center in the country. As I was driving along a fairly remote road, I was contemplating some spiritual concepts I had recently been discussing with friends. I wasn't in any particular hurry, because I was only about a half-hour from the site and the conference wasn't due to begin for more than an hour. Suddenly, I felt as if I had just "dropped" into my body. I had had this sensation sometimes when I first woke up in the morning, and it seemed as if my spirit had left my body while I was sleeping and then suddenly dropped back into it when I awakened. But I certainly had never had it when I was already awake or driving. After feeling this marked sensation, I looked at the sur-rounding countryside—which I had driven through many times before—and felt totally disoriented. I had a feeling of jamais vu, as if I had never seen the area before. I didn't recognize anything, and I didn't know where I was. Glancing at the clock on the dashboard, I saw that it was almost time for the conference to begin. I assumed that I must have been so absorbed in my thoughts that I'd been driving on "automatic pilot" and that I must be very close to the conference. Just then I rounded a corner and came through a small town that I recognized. Amazed, I realized that I was still a good twenty minutes from the conference. More than half an hour had elapsed, and I had no memory of what had happened during that time.
> At first I pushed this out of my mind and concentrated

on the conference. But the next day there was an occurrence that, in retrospect, made me think something unusual might have happened to me. One of the presenters at the conference, a psychologist, mentioned the subject of UFO abductions. The moment he did, I found waves of intense fear washing over me. This was a very unusual reaction for me to have in any circumstances, let alone the one I was in.

About a week later, I was going about my busy daily life when I began to have flashbacks. At first they were flashes of images of what seemed to be alien beings and of being examined by them. The flashes were so disconcerting that I began to meditate and pray each day, asking for divine guidance to help me understand exactly what these flashes were. I was beginning to sense— although I wanted to deny it—that they might be a memory that was trying to resurface, and I needed to know if this was the case or if they were simply flights of my imagination. As I continued to pray and meditate on this over the next few days, the images became clearer, additional details began to fall into place, and then the memory of what had occurred coalesced into a whole.

I have a clear visual image of being asked telepathically to lie down on a table. I was in some sort of strange room with illuminated control panels on some of the walls and with subdued lighting that was a shade of royal blue. The beings communicating with me had faces shaped like upside-down pears and huge dark eyes. I noticed that the irises of their eyes were pigmented; some had brown eyes, others had blue or hazel green. They also had eyelids and they blinked. My medically trained mind seemed to make a particular note of this. Several years earlier, I had seen the movie Communion, which had similar-looking beings whose eyes were portrayed as eyelidless, black pools.

An overpowering, invisible force seemed to push my body onto the examining table, and I felt frightened. As I began to silently pray to God to protect me, one of the *aliens looked down at me, smiled as I prayed, and said telepathically, "Do not be afraid. We do not want to hurt you. We just want to see how you are doing." This alien exuded an aura of gentleness and love. The eyes gazing down at me were dark blue and looked compassionate.*

I was subjected to some sort of physical examination that I have only vague memories of—there may have been some sort of rectal probe and some sort of thin wire-like probe that was inserted through my umbilicus or my lower abdomen. When the examination was over, I was released from the table, taken to what looked like a television or computer screen, and made to look at some information on the screen. Although I do not recall the content of the material, I do know that it was written in a language that I do not currently understand. It had symbols that looked like three-dimensional drawings and a little like broad hieroglyphics.

The appearance of the aliens was slightly different from the impression I had gained from reading and hearing about the subject. The skin that I could see on their reverse-pear-shaped heads had a texture that was slightly heavier than human skin, rather porous and leathery looking. It was paler than human skin and had a slight milky-gray undertone. Their noses had little prominence; they were small and fine and had narrow nostrils. Their mouths were small with very thin lips. They spoke to me and each other telepathically and did not move their lips to speak.

I clearly recall one of the alien's hands: he or she had very long fingers with spatulate ends and fleshy, ruddy-colored fingernails. There seemed to be one long thumb and only two, or perhaps three, fingers.

The aliens were about four and a half feet tall. They wore loose-fitting clothing and had some sort of boots or shoes on their feet. They walked about but also seemed to be able to levitate.

Through a doorway at the far right end of the room, I could see another room. In it was another being who seemed to be looking at an illuminated screen and who looked different from the others. Although I don't recall communicating with him, he seemed to be taller and looked more like a human/alien mixture.

Just before I was sent back, the being who examined me sent me a telepathic message: "Keep up the good work!"

The impact of remembering this incident was shattering. I was a respected medical doctor who had always considered these types of experiences questionable. I wondered if I was becoming mentally ill. I was afraid to tell anyone about it in case they might think I was losing my mind. I was also afraid for my children and began to pray daily to protect them from an alien abduction.

Shawn's experience has some features typical of psychic experiences: for example, she reported feeling as if she had returned to her body after an out-of-body experience and being communicated with telepathically. After the episode, Shawn had a marked increase in other types of psychic experiences. As you read on you will discover some possible reasons for this.

Another Type of Close Encounter

The stories of UFO encounters I have heard have convinced me that these experiences are often STEPs and overlap in many ways with other types of Spiritually Transformative Experiences. Here is the story of a patient of mine called Lisa.

My experiences started early, I think around the age of three. I remember lying in bed one night, waiting to fall asleep. Suddenly I saw two little men wearing hooded cloaks standing at the foot of my bed. They didn't scare me. They didn't do anything, they just looked at me. I

looked back at them. These little men—the "little monks,"
I called them—appeared in my bedroom many evenings.

I told my mother about them, but she didn't believe me.
Eventually, I stopped trying to tell her. But I continued to
see these "little monks" in my bedroom on and off for
years. It made me think I might be partially crazy or some-
thing, so I never talked about it and just tried to live my
life normally.

From a very early age I also remember having sponta-
neous spiritual insights. I can remember reading the
Bible as a child and thinking that my church (Roman
Catholic) had gotten things all mixed up and missed the
point of what Christ was trying to say. Also, when I was
about seven years old I spontaneously came up with the
concept of reincarnation. I didn't know what to call it,
but I thought that it explained the immortality of the
spirit. I also believed that reincarnation was what Christ
was really talking about when he discussed eternal life.
About fifteen years later, I was reading some Eastern
philosophy for the first time and was surprised to dis-
cover that others had the same idea and that they called
it reincarnation.

When I was around twenty, I got interested in medi-
tation and began to meditate regularly. A few years later,
my most intense contact with the "little monks"—I now
think of them as aliens—occurred. As I was meditating
one day, I suddenly got the feeling that the little men
were in my room, so I opened my eyes. Sure enough,
there they were. This time they seemed to be staring at
me with incredible intensity, and the room seemed to be
filled with a very bright white light. I felt as if they were
trying to take me somewhere with them, and I started
floating out of my body. The aliens just seemed to glide
through the air. But I knew I did not want to go with
them and I fought against it. At the same time, I felt as
if my head was going to explode and I was aware of a
terrible burning pain in my back, as if my whole spine

*was on fire. All the while I fought to stay in my body,
and I kept telling the little men to go away.*

*Finally they just disappeared, and I felt totally back in
my body, in my room. I had an intense splitting headache
for three days afterwards, together with this weird burning back pain. Eventually, both these pains went away. I
never told a doctor or anyone else about this because I
thought they'd think I was crazy.*

*It never occurred to me that the little monks could be
aliens or that they could have anything to do with UFOs,
until I read an article in* Scientific American *three years
ago that described the experiences of people who were
abducted by UFOs or saw aliens. One of the descriptions
of a type of alien that was commonly seen was identical
to the little monks that I had been seeing since childhood.
After reading the article, I began to wonder if I had ever
been abducted by a UFO, but just couldn't remember it.
Then I thought that maybe they were trying to abduct me
that day I had such a powerful experience, but that they
couldn't take me because I fought back.*

A Tentative Hypothesis

It is interesting to note how many of Lisa's symptoms were sug-
gestive of a kundalini experience: the burning pain in her back,
the pressure and pain in her head, the sensation of floating out
of her body, and the perception of the white light. This is especially interesting given the fact that Dr. Kenneth Ring has found
such a high correlation between UFO encounters and signs of
kundalini awakening.

Although this relationship may seem strange at first, there may
be a number of logical explanations for it. In some cases, people
who are unknowingly having the sensations and paranormal
experiences associated with kundalini activity may have no idea
how to interpret their experience. And, in their struggle to make
sense of their experience and to find a way to describe it, they fit

it into the framework of the UFO encounter. For example, a person who is sitting in a forest one night and suddenly sees a blinding white light may later tell people that he has seen a UFO because he has no other way to identify or label the experience.

Considering the vastness of the universe, it is conceivable that sentient life forms living on other planets and galaxies may exist. It is also possible that some of these beings may have a technology more advanced than ours and may have physically observed or visited our planet. I think that some UFO sightings may be due to these visitors. These UFO sightings do not have a spiritually transformative impact on the viewer.

It is my clinical conclusion that many UFO encounters, however, may be a type of transdimensional psychic experience. Many physicists today believe that we live in a multi-dimensional universe even though we can normally only perceive three of these dimensions with the physical eye (height, width, and depth). For hundreds of years, trance channels and mediums have claimed that they could communicate with beings or entities living in other dimensions. When the activity of kundalini begins to bring about the changes in consciousness that result in an increased ability to perceive other levels of reality, the mind may begin to glimpse these other dimensions and the life forms that fill them. It is possible that UFO experiencers may perceive contact with "aliens" in another dimension—or place—clairvoyantly, or that they might be astral traveling there. In other cases, it may be that the beings associated with UFOs are moving into our dimension to make contact.

Although my clinical experience of people having UFO experiences is limited, my observations have led me to develop two further hypotheses: First, persons experiencing other types of STEs may be more receptive to transdimensional experiences. Second, it may be that the transdimensional contact with extraterrestrial beings in itself stimulates the kundalini mechanism and/or opens psychic capacities in the brain. This idea is not as far-fetched as it first might seem. It has long been held in the yogic tradition that a person with an awakened kundalini can awaken it in another. This phenomenon is called shakti pata or shakti put. Although the term refers literally to the transfer of shakti (kundalini) from one person to another, it seems to me that this may be accomplished, in actual fact, through a kind of resonance in which the level of activity of kundalini in one person stimulates a similar level of activity in another. In the same way, contact with the intense psychic energies of extraterrestrial beings may stimulate the energies of the person having the experience, making him or her temporarily more psychically open and, thus, able to perceive the other beings and/or dimensions. This stimulation may also leave the experiencer permanently more psychically open. Many UFO encounter experiencers describe a dramatic psychic opening after the encounter.

The story of Shawn provides an excellent example of this. She had been undergoing spiritual transformation for years and had had many psychic and paranormal experiences. Thus, she was already psychically open or, in a sense, susceptible to a transdimensional psychic experience. The experience itself also seemed to further stimulate her psychic capacities, resulting in a marked increase in her psychic experiences after her UFO encounter. It is interesting that during the two years before her experience she had been having a number of signs of kundalini activity, including sensations of heat and energy in her spine and visions of inner light.

Adjusting to Psychic Abilities

In my clinical practice I have observed that people who have a psychic awakening and continue to have psychic experiences adjust in stages to their new abilities. First, they are often puzzled, confused, or frightened. They question the nature of what they have experienced; they wonder where the experiences have come from and why. At this stage, experiencers are usually very reluctant to tell others their experiences, because they believe people will think they are crazy. However, as the psychic experiences keep occurring, most experiencers try to talk to friends or family about them. In some instances, they are rebuffed or ridiculed and find it extremely difficult to speak about their experiences again. In other cases they discover people who are eager to talk about psychic phenomena. Although this can be helpful, psychic experiencers often pick up a good deal of misinformation in this way. One of the most common problems is that they begin to get an inflated idea of themselves or the uniqueness of their abilities. In general, I have found four common problems that people have in adjusting to new psychic gifts.

1. They may become self-inflated, thinking that they have a rare gift and that they are special, or they inflate the importance of the abilities themselves.

2. They may incorrectly believe that their psychic information is infallible.

3. They may lack restraint and immediately blurt out psychically received information when they receive it.

4. They may lack judgment and indiscriminately share psychic information with anyone, or at inappropriate times or places.

One of the clearest cases of a lack of judgment was a man I worked with, whom I'll call Daniel.

A highly educated and extremely successful businessman, Daniel had started his own company and become wealthy at an early age. When he was in his early thirties he began to receive channeled material. In a one-year period, he received the material for three books that dealt with the spiritual nature of humanity, the need for humanity to reconnect with nature, and the importance of taking immediate action to save the environment. However, Daniel also began to believe he had a mission to save all the endangered species, and he developed a strong desire to communicate telepathically with whales.

These latter experiences were unusual, and when

Daniel came to me as a patient it became apparent that he was exhibiting some signs of delusion. Still, a good deal of the information he was receiving psychically was, in fact, correct. Further, Daniel functioned quite normally most of the time. During these periods of normal functioning, however, Daniel exhibited some of the typical problems listed above, all of which involve a lack of judgment.

After receiving channeled material for a while, Daniel came to believe that he had been in some way "chosen" as the person who would ultimately save all the whales. After receiving some information that was shown to be accurate, he began to think he was special and was having experiences that were far beyond anyone else's.

He also lacked the ability to discern when it was appropriate to talk about his experiences. Once, during a meeting of a non-profit—but not environmental—group, Daniel insisted that "save the whales" be added to the list of organizational goals that were being discussed.

Believing that the material he was receiving was infallible, he would bring the information that related to his channeling up at business meetings and try to get his fellow board members to make investments and commitments based on it.

Ultimately, he began to discuss his psychic experiences indiscriminately. He talked about them with his accountant, his secretary, his housekeeper, and people he met in restaurants or bars.

A Balanced Perspective on Psychic Gifts

Daniel exhibited a number of the problems that many mentally healthy individuals exhibit after they begin to develop paranormal abilities. In counseling people who have started to have psychic experiences, I have found that these difficulties are, in fact, quite common.

In order to help people put their experiences in perspective, I encourage them to look at psychic gifts as an extension of intuition and point out that some people have much stronger intuition than others but that this does not make these people special. It is also important for them to realize that both intuition and psychic experiences can be colored a great deal by a person's emotional make-up, thoughts, and feelings: Wishful thinking is often misinterpreted as psychic or intuitive information.

Since psychically received information is not always correct, I point out that well-adjusted, highly intuitive people have learned to balance intuition and intellect; they use their intellectual skills critically to examine and judge the information they receive through intuition or psychic experiences. They have learned that this is only a tool—one of several sources of information that need to be considered in making well-informed, rational decisions.

When I had my own first psychic experience, I can remember being so startled that I paused and prayed for guidance. This guidance helped me handle the information I received correctly. When I clairvoyantly saw the image of my friend Susan's brain covered in pus and realized that the picture somehow symbolized meningitis, I tried to balance this "psychic information" with the reality of the situation. Using my logic, I gathered information from Susan about her medical condition. When I found she had a few of the symptoms of meningitis, I didn't jump to the conclusion that my psychic information—or my interpretation of it—must have been 100 percent correct. I simply outlined the symptoms for her and advised her to get tested for meningitis if any more of them developed. As it happened, this approach had a very positive effect: Susan got early treatment for her disease and was cured. If, however, I had become fanatical about what I had seen in my vision and insisted on her going to the emergency department immediately, the result might not have been so favorable. Had she done so, the doctors almost certainly would not have tested her for meningitis: her symptoms were simply not clear enough. She would have probably been sent home, and then been very reluctant to return when her symptoms worsened—and this could have led to tragedy.

How Yogis Saw Psychic Abilities

Since ancient times, yogis have considered psychic gifts or sid-dhis to be a natural by-product of progress along the spiritual path of yoga. However, these gifts have also been held to be potential distractions from the true goal of yoga—the realization of oneness with God or Brahman. It has long been believed that these psychic gifts should never be sought in themselves. If they do occur, they are to be acknowledged, learned from, but not dwelt upon excessively. It is held that the yogi who focuses excessively on psychic gifts may lose sight of the true spiritual objective and thereby become nothing more than a "magician," never obtaining ultimate realization.

There is also a long tradition among respected psychics that one should not try to use these gifts to gain personal power or wealth. Although this is an ethical consideration, it also has its practical side. Following the initial experience, psychic episodes often recur only irregularly and unpredictably, and even highly psychically open experiencers find they can't always make the abilities appear consistently.

Almost all the individuals who have become known and respected as actual "psychics" say that they do not, ultimately, control their abilities. Even though they can often put themselves in a frame of mind that makes a certain psychic experience more likely to occur, they cannot force it to happen. This is perhaps how some stage psychics get into trouble: They become over-confident of their psychic abilities, then when they are required to produce abilities on demand, and they can't, they resort to trickery.

There are also people who try to use their psychic powers to harm or manipulate, or play "psychic games" of some kind. Although some researchers believe it is simply not possible to use psychic abilities for harmful purposes, others disagree. I will dis-cuss the topic of psychic assault in Chapter Twelve.

Clearly we need to gain a far greater understanding of psychic phenomena. In the meantime, I hope that anyone who is devel-oping psychic abilities as part of the process of spiritual transformation will be cautious, use discernment, and will pray for guidance as to how to use their insights for the highest good. It helps to keep psychic abilities in proper perspective by realizing that they are a common sidelight on a journey whose actual purpose is the process of spiritual transformation.

CHAPTER 7

Inspired Creativity and Genius

In my work with people who are undergoing spiritual transformation, I have found that many of them notice an increase in their creativity. They begin to feel an urge to keep journals or write poetry or stories, to draw or paint, to express themselves through music. I have found that this increase in the creative urge is common regardless of the types of STEs the person is experiencing. Although these people do not generally produce works that are outstanding or particularly remarkable, their new-found—or increased—creative expression seems to be very much a part of their spiritual unfolding.

In a few cases, however, the creative experience is so powerful or so deeply intertwined with a mystical or paranormal element that it becomes a STEP in its own right. For some people, these creative inspired experiences are the most prominent type of STE. In the yogic tradition it is said that a partial flow of the kundalini to the brain yields inspiration, rather than liberation. The yogis also warned that such inspiration may hold great truths, but be mixed with half-truths due to the impurities in the consciousness of the partially realized individual. Discernment is needed when contemplating the truths in inspired works, just as with intellectual works.

"Inspired creativity" is a particularly apt name for this type of experience since, in its theological sense, the word "inspiration" refers to the influence of the divine on the human mind or soul. Some people who experience profound inspired creativity produce writings, musical compositions, or artwork that is outstanding or remarkable in some way. Others may spontaneously develop creative gifts or abilities in areas in which they previously had no talent whatsoever. The STE category of Inspired Creativity and Genius is not limited to artistic inspiration. This phenomenon can also manifest itself as profound intellectual insights or discoveries, or the development or advancement of theories in the sciences, humanities, or philosophies.

The relationship between creativity and spiritual experiences may not at first be clear. However, one only has to look back in time to discover many examples of an overlap between creativity or genius and profound spiritual experiences. Many saints and mystics have created wonderful works of art, poetry, or music or made significant contributions to science. And many creative geniuses from both the arts and the sciences have had mystical experiences and have said that their great works were divinely inspired. One of the classic examples of a mystic who had a tremendous capacity for creativity was the Catholic saint Hildegaard of Bingen, born in 1098.

Hildegaard, even in childhood, had a spiritual nature. When she was eight years old her parents sent her to be educated in a Benedictine convent. When old enough, she took her final vows and became a cloistered nun. Although she had visions and psychic experiences from an early age, her life in the cloister proceeded fairly normally, and she eventually became head of the convent.

Five years later, she had a mystical experience more profound than anything she had ever experienced. She wrote later that the "heavens were opened" for her, and she received a prophetic calling.

She soon began to write extensively, to paint, and to compose music. In much of her writing she tried to describe her visions and capture their symbolic beauty and meaning. But she also wrote poetry, several books on natural history and medicine, and a morality play. She began to paint her visions and to compose music. Her paintings have been likened to those of William Blake, and her music is still sung and played today. Some of her herbal remedies are still in use.

Hildegaard once wrote that she constantly experienced a vision of what she called "a reflection of the living light" that was "far, far brighter than a cloud that carries the sun." On rarer occasions, she even experienced directly what she called the "living light" itself. The scope of Hildegaard's creative output went far beyond her education, and she made it clear that the material for it came from inspiration: "as the sun, the moon, and the stars appear in water, so writings, sermons, virtues, and certain human actions take form for me and gleam within."

Many individuals who have been known primarily for their creative genius rather than their mystical natures speak about inspiration in similar terms.

The great composer Johannes Brahms called upon his Maker when he felt the urge to compose and would sometimes receive his music from divine inspiration:

> *I immediately feel vibrations that thrill my whole being. . . . These are the Spirit illuminating the soul-power within, and in this exalted state, I see clearly what is obscure in my ordinary moods; then I feel capable of drawing inspiration from above, as Beethoven did. Above all, I realize at such moments the tremendous significance of Jesus's supreme revelation, "I and my father are one." Those vibrations assume the forms of distinct mental images, after I have formulated my desire and resolve in regard to what I want—namely, to be inspired so that I can compose something that will uplift and benefit humanity—something of permanent value.*
>
> *Straightaway the ideas flow in upon me, directly from*

God, and not only do I see distinct themes in my mind's eye, but they are clothed in the right forms, harmonies, and orchestration. Measure by measure, the finished product is revealed to me when I am in those rare inspired moods.

Clearly, for Brahms the creative experience was also a deeply spiritual one. Similar examples can also be found in the world of scientific genius. Nikola Tesla, who is considered by many to be the greatest inventor of the twentieth century, received detailed plans for many of his inventions in blinding flashes of light. He developed a deep spiritual awareness of reality, and recognized that his abilities and ideas came to him from a reality beyond the physical.

Albert Einstein, too, saw the relationship between the spiritual experience, inspiration, and genius. Although he did not speak publicly about any spiritual experiences he may have had himself, he often wrote about what he called the "cosmic religious experience." Further, he wrote about it in a way that makes it almost certain that he was speaking from some type of personal experience. In *Living Philosophies*, he noted: "It is enough for me to contemplate the mystery of conscious life perpetuating itself through all the universe which we can dimly perceive, and to try humbly to comprehend even an infinitesimal part of the intelligence manifested in nature. . . . The most beautiful thing we can experience is the mysterious. It is the source of all true art and science."

In *The World As I See It*, he wrote, "I maintain that the cosmic religious experience is the strongest and noblest insightment to scientific research." He added that the most important function of both art and science was "to awaken this feeling and keep it alive in those who are capable of it."

STEs and the Creative Experience

Historical cases of creative genius such as St. Hildegaard, Einstein, and Brahms show a definite relationship between profound spiritual experience and creative inspiration. Of course, not everyone who has STEs of Inspired Creativity becomes a creative genius or creates works of the caliber of a St. Hildegaard or an Einstein.

As is the case with other types of STEs, experiences of Inspired Creativity occur along a continuum, varying in intensity and in the quality of the creative material produced. Some individuals who have this type of STE create works of great quality or even genius, but this is rare. For the rest, the experience centers not so much on the creation of works of genius as on the sudden, spontaneous development of a particular creative ability where none was present before.

Creativity and Altered States

The following is the story of a woman whom I'll call Ellen whose experience of Inspired Creativity was a STEP that changed her life completely.

Until she was nearing middle age, Ellen worked as an engineer. She was extremely well educated, had obtained a Master of Science degree in engineering, and had risen to the top of a field in which it is extremely difficult for women to succeed. She was married to another equally successful engineer. The two of them had worked on important projects around the world and had earned a lot. Although Ellen's most dramatic STEP occurred when she was about forty, her process of spiritual transformation began a few years earlier. Here is the story she told me about her experiences and their tremendous transformative impact.

> *When I was in my late thirties, I began to feel discontented and to sense that something essential was missing from my life, even though I had no idea what it might be. By most socially accepted standards, I should have been happy with my life: I had a good marriage, a great deal of money, and a highly successful career. Confused and troubled by my discontentment, I began Jungian analysis.*

During this process I kept a journal, recorded my dreams in detail, and spent far more time in introspection.

One morning, shortly after arising, I was overcome with fatigue and felt I had to lie back down on my bed. I had begun to drift off when, without warning, sensations of energy began to stream up my body and into my head. Suddenly, I seemed to be immersed in a beautiful intensely brilliant, white light. For a moment, I felt myself merge with what I can only describe as the intelligence behind the universe, the cosmic power, or the cosmic white light. When the experience ended I felt overwhelmed and profoundly moved.

Shortly after what I have come to call my "white light experience," my dreams become more vivid. They also seemed to be providing me with clear images of paintings and directions on exactly how these paintings could be done. At the time, this seemed extremely strange to me. I had never had any artistic talent or any interest at all in drawing or painting. Still, I recorded the dreams carefully, as I was in the habit of doing.

Eventually I began to draw or paint these dreams. Over a period of time, the urge to spend my time painting grew. Ultimately it became so strong that I quit my job in engineering and enrolled in art school. Once in art school, I mastered techniques with amazing speed. After only a year in the program, my professor took me aside and told me that I had learned all I possibly could from the school and that it was time for me to leave and get on with my artwork.

While I was studying art, I had continued to record my dreams and had been attempting to paint the images. Although I didn't fully realize it at first, I came to understand that my dreams were providing me not just with images but with information on innovative techniques and unusual materials that would be needed to reproduce the images.

Since leaving art school six years ago, I have worked

*full-time as an artist and have continued to paint my
dream images. I have created a tremendous volume of
high-quality work and, in fact, have produced enough
material to have six separate, individual showings of
new work put on in five years—an accomplishment that
is remarkable among even the most talented and prolific
artists.*

*In spite of the success of my work, I feel a great deal
of humility about my art. Rather than thinking of myself
as the creator, I like to consider myself simply a
"receiver" or an instrument who brings the dream
images into physical reality. I strongly believe that I
receive my ability and my inspiration from a source
beyond myself.*

Except for Ellen's "white light experience," Inspired Creativity
has been the main feature of her transformative process—and
the process has clearly been a spiritual one. Many of the paintings are symbolic depictions of transformation and growth. A
number of them represent such clearly spiritual subjects as
kundalini awakenings. Many others give the viewer a powerful
sense of the oneness of all things, and some seem to resonate
with a life force of their own.

As soon as the creative process began, Ellen's life also began to
develop an increasingly spiritual focus. She continued to delve
deeply into the works of Jung, but also began to seek out others
who wrote on spiritual subjects. She became extremely interested in
works such as Bucke's *Cosmic Consciousness* and began to read
avidly the works of Gopi Krishna. She now feels that this has helped
her to integrate her experiences into her life and to understand that
kundalini drives the tremendous transformation she is undergoing.

Like many people's spiritual journeys, however, Ellen's has
been in some ways a difficult one. Even though she has adjusted
to the tremendous creative urge that now takes up so much of
her life, her family has not. Ellen's husband and the other members of her family initially ridiculed her decision to give up her
financially successful career and the lifestyle that went with it.

The differences between Ellen and her husband grew until they finally divorced. Fortunately, Ellen's family has been able to accept the change and support her new direction in life.

In spite of the difficulties that Ellen has had to work out, she is confident that she made the right decision. Her painting brings her tremendous satisfaction, and she knows she is doing what she was meant to do. She has finally discovered the dimension that was missing from her life.

When Ellen is painting her dream images she often finds herself in a trance-like state that she feels allows her to become a conduit for inspiration. Many of the great artists, composers, writers, philosophers, and scientists have described this type of experience. Truly inspired creative episodes often seem to be experienced in an intensely absorbed, paranormal state of consciousness that has mystical overtones. Composer Richard Wagner once wrote that inspiration came from "universal currents of Divine Thought vibrating the ether everywhere" and that "[when I am] in that trance-like condition, which is the prerequisite of all true creative effort, I feel that I am one with this vibrating Force, that it is omniscient, and that I can draw upon it to an extent that is limited only by my capacity to do so."

Many of the people I have known whose STEs included Inspired Creativity have spoken of similar experiences. One is a woman I'll call Gail who has a doctorate in neuroendocrinology. Gail was involved in research at a respected private university. Widely published, she had received a number of awards and grants and seemed to be on the fast track to academic success. Her colleagues were certain it was only a matter of time before Harvard or another top university invited her to continue work there. However, when she was in her mid-forties her direction in life radically changed.

> *I developed a flu-like illness which left me profoundly exhausted. After almost two years of visiting specialists, the illness was diagnosed as severe Chronic Fatigue Syndrome. In my case the illness left me not only terribly exhausted, but also unable to concentrate. Even*

though I tried to battle the disease physically and mentally, I was eventually forced to quit my work at the university.

At some time during the first year of the illness I began to have dramatic sensations of light and of energy coursing through my body. Although the sensations were very powerful and unfamiliar, I was not worried about them: I thought they might be the result of my body's efforts to fight the illness. I even wondered if the illness might not have somehow stimulated some type of latent healing power in my body.

At about the time the experiences of light and energy began, I developed a tremendous urge to draw. I found this strange because I had never had any artistic tendencies. After a time, however, I decided to enroll in a part-time art course as I was still unable to work. On the second evening of the course, the instructor took me aside and told me that I shouldn't be taking the course, I should be teaching it. I was astounded; I had no idea how I had developed the artistic ability I suddenly seemed to be exhibiting. The instructor, also a woman, was fascinated by what I told her and suggested that we try working together.

When we did get together, we decided to experiment by working on the same canvas. As soon as we stood in front of the canvas and began to paint, a strange thing happened: Both of us spontaneously entered an altered state of consciousness, and we began to paint in a manner so synchronized that we almost seemed to be two arms of one painter.

For the past three years, my instructor and I have continued to paint jointly in this altered state of consciousness. Before we begin a new painting, we look at sketches we have made of our dreams and other subjects and at photographs we have taken. Eventually an idea for a painting will seem to grab both of us. With nothing more than this vague idea in our minds we begin to paint—usually on an extremely large canvas. Immediately

> *it seems as if we are somehow taken over and we become*
> *completely absorbed in our work. We become like two*
> *halves expressing one energy. We often work in this state*
> *for days with very little rest or sleep. Often, when a*
> *painting is completed, we collapse in exhaustion.*

Gail and her former instructor sometimes paint as many as two to three huge canvases a month in spite of her continued chronic fatigue. Many of these paintings have deeply spiritual themes. Vibrant with color and vitality, they are considered by many to be exceptionally good. No one looking at them can tell they were done by two people, one a trained, professional artist and the other a scientist who had no training or artistic ability until she was forty-five years old.

For Gail, her periods of Inspired Creativity have gone hand in hand with her spiritual growth. She spontaneously developed a strong desire to meditate and has joined a network of people interested in similar subjects. She is determined to continue her spiritual journey and work as an artist. Like Ellen, Gail has found that these decisions have met with a great deal of resistance from her family. Her husband became so incensed with her intense focus on painting that he slashed several of her canvases with a butcher knife. They have since separated. Some other members of Gail's family believe that she is mentally unbalanced. Still, Gail has a number of new and old supportive friends who care for her and believe in her. She feels confident that she is living her life as she should. In fact, one of the most fascinating aspects of Gail's story is that her long illness seems to have impaired her ability to concentrate on scientific material or focus her intellect for any length of time—and yet her creative ability has developed and flourished.

Creativity and Intense Absorption

Often people like Ellen and Gail who experience Inspired Creativity talk about entering what they describe as an altered state of consciousness. In many STEs involving Inspired Creativity, a strong feature is the intensity of experiencers' absorption in this altered state. A man I'll call Edward provided one of the best examples of this I have ever seen. Although Edward held a doctorate in social work, he had been painting for years and his artwork was an extremely important part of his life. Here is his story.

> *My desire to paint began spontaneously when I was an adolescent. When I paint, I feel myself going into an altered state of consciousness that is almost a trance. I become virtually oblivious to external stimuli and lose track of night and day and times for meals and sleep.*
>
> *I have also found that I cannot make these creative periods begin. My friends often try to commission work from me, but I am unable to begin a painting at will. It seems that the creative urge has to surface out of my innermost self and then propel me into the altered mental state that is necessary before I can express my creativity.*
>
> *Once one of these states begins, I go into a compulsive, highly energetic mode that I call my painting frenzy. I become extremely irritated if something interrupts me, and I resent it when someone tries to remind me of worldly schedules or commitments.*
>
> *I am able to paint only when I am in one of these trance-like states. I am also aware that my creative periods have a mystical quality. Although my paintings are all scenes from nature, I have been told they have a transcendental quality. I try to capture an otherworldly luminosity that I see in scenes of nature when I am in one of my altered states.*

It is interesting to note that Edward, like so many other people who experience Inspired Creativity, has felt rushes of energy up his spine for years.

Gifted Children and Creativity

A number of the people who are undergoing the process of spiritual transformation report powerful inspired creative experiences as children. Two of them could be considered child prodigies. Although the term "child prodigy" is sometimes associated with child geniuses such as Mozart, it is often used in the scientific literature to refer to any child who has produced original, high-quality music, writing, scientific insights, or artwork before the age of fourteen. One of the people who fits this category is a man I'll call Martin. He is now thirty and is working on his Ph.D. in physics. As a child, Martin showed an inspired ability to create and compose music that was closely related to mystical experiences. Here is his story.

> *From a very young age I felt that I did not fit in—that I was different. I went to the Roman Catholic church with my parents, and I heard talk there about mystical states, and how only Jesus, the apostles, the saints, and the Virgin Mary ever experienced them. I remember at the age of seven thinking that the church was wrong, because I went into these incredible states of bliss and awe whenever I surrendered to the inner music I felt pouring through my soul.*
>
> *At a very young age I learned to play guitar and piano, and I used to sit and play the music I heard resounding inside my head. I discovered that if I opened up to the divine I would experience feelings of bliss and ecstasy and I would hear extremely beautiful music pouring through my soul. The music I heard and played in this way was original. I had no sheet music for it, and I had never heard it before. It was simply flowing through me.*
>
> *I tried to talk to my parents about what I was experiencing, but they told me not to talk about such nonsense. They agreed I seemed to like music, but they thought that my talking about mystical experiences and bliss was*

> *the work of the devil or something evil. Slowly, I*
> *to believe that there must be something wrong o*
> *thing bad about the blissful state I went into when*
> *played. And, finally, when I was around ten I became*
> *convinced that what my parents were saying was true.*
> *One of the reasons for this was that the experiences felt*
> *too good—and I had learned by then that life wasn't sup-*
> *posed to feel that good. I started to actively suppress the*
> *music and not allow myself to go into the mystical states.*
>
> *I managed to keep them suppressed until about three*
> *years ago when I was working on my Ph.D. Suddenly I*
> *felt as if something inside of me cracked or exploded and*
> *I couldn't keep this incredible creative urge down any*
> *more. It terrified me, because I didn't know what it was.*

Martin's story is similar to those of many people I have worked
with who were exceptionally creative as children. Often parents
and even teachers don't recognize exceptional creative talents of
this type because they don't fit within the boundaries dictated by
the rigid, linear thinking so common in our schools and society.
At the urging of his parents, Martin succeeded in suppressing his
mystical/creative urge for many years. But this creative force
could not be held down forever. The same was true in the case
of a woman I'll call Sheila, who had an amazing gift for writing
when she was a child. She told me her story when she came to
me for counseling.

> *When I was about ten years old I began to write complete*
> *novels. While I was writing I would fall into an almost*
> *mystical state which was characterized by intense absorp-*
> *tion and wonderful bliss. Unfortunately, my ability was*
> *never recognized by my parents, who refused to read any-*
> *thing I ever wrote. I felt a deep inner urge to become a*
> *writer when I grew up, but my family scoffed at the idea,*
> *saying I would never earn a reasonable income.*
>
> *I excelled in school, and my parents urged me to*
> *become a lawyer. Many of my teachers agreed, and I*

eventually became convinced that going to law school would be the best thing I could do with my intellectual abilities. Still, although I kept it hidden from my parents, I continued to write.

Once I entered law school, however, I found I no longer had time to write. This situation continued until I had worked as a lawyer for three years. By this time I found that I was profoundly depressed. I felt my life was empty, even though I had worldly success. As a result of counseling, I decided to cut down on my workload and give myself time to write. Once I began to give vent to the powerful creative urge I felt and to write again, my depression lifted, and I began to find meaning in my life.

Child prodigies are rare, and my work with them has been limited. However, the stories of Martin and Sheila are typical of my experience: Both felt their creative experiences had a strong mystical component, and neither of them was able to completely suppress the creative force that flowed within them. Further, both Martin and Sheila grew into adults who have a very strong spiritual focus. Of course, further research would be needed to determine whether this is typical of all child prodigies and to discover exactly what the relationship might be between this type of mystical/creative experience and the process of spiritual transformation.

Milder Inspired Creativity and Poetry

Many cases of Inspired Creativity are much milder than those experienced by Ellen and Gail. Few people suddenly develop the outstanding degree of talent that they did or are able to begin new careers with so little training. However, the spontaneous development of milder forms of Inspired Creativity is very common in people involved in a process of spiritual transformation. Most of the people I have seen who have STEs—if not STEPs—involving Inspired Creativity have either been involved in spiritual pursuits for a long time or have become highly spiritually focused soon after the experiences begin. Further, in many cases, the creative material produced—whether it was scientific insights, philosophy, art, poetry, prose, or music—had a spiritual or transcendental quality.

A very common form of milder Inspired Creativity in STE experiencers is inspired poetry. I suddenly began to write inspired poetry around 1995, and many kundalini experiencers have told me of suddenly beginning to write inspired poetry, sometimes multi-page epics! One case of this type is that of a woman I'll call Cassandra, who was a housewife and mother.

> *Since my twenties, I have been actively involved in my own spiritual journey. It began when I took a course in meditation in which I had a mystical vision. That abruptly changed my life. I began to practice meditation, prayer, and self-reflection regularly. Soon the pursuit of spiritual understanding became the main focus of my life. Eventually I began to do yoga and martial arts.*
>
> *I steadfastly continued my meditation and spiritual practices for years, without feeling that I had any further spiritual experiences. When I was in my late thirties, however, I developed strong kundalini symptoms: heat, piercing back pain, energy rushes, and sometimes I went into spontaneous yoga postures. I suddenly developed an overwhelming urge to write poetry. I found that rhyming couplets relating to spiritual themes would float into my consciousness. As I wrote them down, more and more would flow into my mind. Eventually a poem—pages in length—would take shape. Sometimes the process of producing a poem occurred rapidly; at other times parts of the poem would come to me over several weeks. Gradually the poem took the form of a lengthy epic.*
>
> *I was amazed by this development. I had never thought of myself as a person who had any ability as a poet.*

Cassandra has found that she has little or no control over writing this poetry. She says it simply "comes to her" and seems to flow with little intellectual effort on her part. Although these inspired poetry experiences are not as dramatic as the artistic transformation of someone like Ellen, it seems clear to me that they represent a common feature of transformation of consciousness on the spiritual journey.

One of the most fascinating things about the people I've met who experience STEs with Inspired Creativity is that they all talk about going into some type of altered state when they have their experiences, and they all agree that there is a mystical component to the experience itself. I have also found that almost everyone who is having any type of STE tends to experience a noticeable—and sometimes extreme—increase in the urge to be creative. Surely this indicates that the relationship between Inspired Creativity, genius, mystical experience, and kundalini will be a fertile and fascinating area for future research.

Section 2

The Kundalini Model

CHAPTER 8

The Modern Kundalini Model

It should be clear from the case histories related in the first section of this book that many people are undergoing the types of extraordinary spiritual and paranormal experiences I call STEs. However, very little Western scientific research has been done to learn more about them in general and to discover whether the striking similarities and parallels found in these experiences might not be explained by some common denominator.

In the East, yogic mystics have studied and documented STEs and spiritual transformation of consciousness for thousands of years. Their scientific research method was inner and outer observation of the self, and comparison with the observations of other yogis. The kundalini model is the model of spiritual transformation of consciousness that has emerged from this ancient yogic research. Although agreeing on major points, diverse yogic traditions have developed slightly different understandings of the kundalini model, just as diverse world religions have developed slightly different understandings of the spiritual energy active in mystics! My first introduction to the kundalini model came from my meetings with

Gopi Krishna from 1977 to 1983 and from my intense study of his writings and theories. His model makes sense to me, and has helped me understand STEs and assist others with STEs. Therefore, I will describe Gopi Krishna's kundalini model in detail.

Pandit Gopi Krishna proposed a hypothesis or starting point for Western scientific research on kundalini and its relationship to Spiritually Transformative Experiences in 1967. A synopsis of this hypothesis is as follows: Kundalini, when awakened, is the biological-psychological-spiritual mechanism responsible for Mystical Experiences, Classical Kundalini Episodes, Psychic Awakenings, Near-Death Experiences, Inspired Creativity and Genius, and, when unhealthy, some types of mental illness with mystical features.

My clinical experience suggests that this hypothesis provides an excellent starting point for research. It would help explain the commonalities found in various STEs and provide a platform for future research that might come closer to determining the exact nature of the spiritual energy mystics have described for thousands of years. Current Western scientific theories about the nature of the universe and human consciousness cannot explain STEs. The modern kundalini model provides a missing link: a plausible theory to explain the spiritual transformation of consciousness.

A modern interpretation of the ancient kundalini model was first put forward by Gopi Krishna in 1967 in his still-popular book *Kundalini: The Evolutionary Energy in Man* and was described in increasing detail in his other eighteen books. Gopi Krishna theorized that kundalini was the biological-spiritual mechanism driving human evolution, transforming humanity's consciousness, and making it possible for us to attain the tremendously expanded states of awareness that he called "higher consciousness." He developed his ideas by researching the ancient yogic texts, by interpreting them in light of modern knowledge about the human body, by observing the workings of kundalini in his own body, and through inspired creative insights and revelations which he received as part of his spiritual transformation. The last forty years of his life were spent working to promote awareness of kundalini and to convince the

Western scientific community to investigate kundalini seriously.

Gopi Krishna proposed that the kundalini hypothesis could be tested in a number of ways: (1) Literary research which would involve researching the lives and writings of great mystics and geniuses of the past to see if evidence of kundalini awakening could be found, and collecting information from the vast literature on kundalini from the oral and written yogic traditions and other esoteric mystical traditions; (2) developing a questionnaire that would examine the experiences of people living today who are undergoing the profound paranormal experiences characterized as STEs in this book; (3) carrying out detailed medical and biochemical analysis of hormones and body fluids in individuals experiencing profound kundalini awakening and in people experiencing mental illness with mystical features; (4) developing a project in which selected people would begin a disciplined attempt to arouse kundalini while being scientifically and medically monitored.

Although no full-scale scientific investigation was ever launched during his lifetime, Gopi Krishna's hypothesis did attract the attention of some leading scientists and scholars. One was Dr. Carl Friedrich von Weizsacker, physicist and former director of the Max-Planck-Institute for the Life Sciences. In his foreword to Gopi Krishna's *The Biological Basis of Religion and Genius*, Professor von Weizsacker reveals his deep respect for Krishna's ideas and calls him "an eyewitness to the truth he represents."

Another avid supporter of Krishna was Dr. Karen Singh, a medical doctor who was the Minister of Health and Welfare for Indira Gandhi's government in India. Dr. Singh even gained approval and funding for a massive scientific project to test the kundalini hypothesis, but the Gandhi government fell just before the project was to begin.

A number of Kundalini Research Institutes and Associations have formed around the world, and some of the literary research Krishna proposed has begun. In 1990 a major step was taken when an international group of scientists, doctors, and researchers—myself included—met at the home of Dr. Bonnie Greenwell, a clinical psychologist and former director of the

Counselling Center at the Institute of Transpersonal Psychology, near San Jose, California, to discuss the possibility of collaborating on scientific research into kundalini. Those present came from a variety of backgrounds, represented diverse spiritual traditions, and held widely different ideas about kundalini, but all agreed on the importance of scientific research into the possible relationship between kundalini, mystical states of consciousness, and other paranormal experiences.

At the meeting the Kundalini Research Network was formed as a coalition of individuals and organizations whose top priority would be to increase the awareness of kundalini and its associated phenomena in the Western scientific, medical, and academic communities as soon as possible. For this reason, the KRN Questionnaire Research Project was begun. I was a member of the original project committee. In 1991, I became chairperson for the project, a position I held until 1998. In the same year, under my supervision, the questionnaire was developed and a pilot study completed. Shortly thereafter, the principal study was launched. A number of intriguing findings have been made. However, before we go on to consider them, we need to look at the concepts from the ancient yogic tradition that form the basis for the modern kundalini model. We also must examine how the awakening of kundalini might function as the biological-psychological-spiritual basis for Spiritually Transformative Experiences.

The Underlying Principles

The basic premise underlying the modern kundalini model is that the next goal of evolution is for humans to manifest an expanded range and higher states of consciousness, which will include mystical and paranormal perceptions. This expansion of consciousness will occur as a result of the activation of one or more presently dormant brain centers or functions. When, with the Grace of the Divine, the spiritual energy/kundalini is awakened in an individual, this transformation of consciousness is accelerated. According to Gopi Krishna, a healthy kundalini awakening causes two distinct, simultaneous changes in the body. One is that the body is stimulated to supply potent fuels to the transforming brain. Two psychic fuels, prana and ojas, are transported up the spinal cord to the brain. This is perceived as a movement and flow of energy up the spine. The other is the stimulation of a normally dormant region of the brain known as the brahma randhra in Yoga. As this area is stimulated into activity, it makes possible the expanded perceptions that are presently thought of as mystical and paranormal states of consciousness.

Circulation of Potent Prana—The Life Energy

According to the Yogic tradition, universal "prana" is an extremely subtle, super-intelligent cosmic creative force or energy—as yet unidentified by Western science—which fills all of creation. Each living body contains individual "prana," known in China as chi (qi), in Japan as ki, and in the West as universal life force, bioenergy, or life energy. According to Gopi Krishna, individual prana is a very subtle, biochemical sheath permeating and surrounding our bodies, sometimes referred to as the etheric body or subtle body. The individual prana, which acts to vivify each being, acts on all the cells and tissues of the body, and is continuously affected by universal prana. It circulates through the body in channels called the nadis—a complex system believed by some to include the nervous system. Individual prana is also identified with the psyche or the individual personality.

Although this process has been written about in detail in the Tantras, Gopi Krishna's writings help us understand to some degree how individual prana might function in terms of what we now know about the body and nervous system. It is thought that individual prana is produced by certain cells of the body as a part of their normal functioning. Prana is also absorbed from the air we breathe and from the food we eat. Once the prana is produced internally, or absorbed from outside the body, it is transported by the nadis or nerves and stored either in the central nervous system or in the sexual organs, or carried on to the brain, where it is used as "psychic fuel" for the functions that are carried out by our consciousness.

With the activation of the kundalini mechanism, however, cells are stimulated to produce a more refined, more potent form of prana and in greater quantities. The nervous system is stimulated into a higher degree of activity than normal in order to extract these greater quantities of prana from the cells, and from the nerves and the sexual organs. The flow of this highly potent form of the life-energy is sometimes perceived as an energy flowing up the limbs or back, or an inner luminosity as it pours into the brain.

Ojas—Sublimated Sexual Energy

In the yogic tradition, the sexual organs are also believed to be the main source of "ojas," another potent fuel for the transforming brain. It is believed that when the sexual secretions are sent downward or outward in the act of procreation, ojas, in its grosser form, is the vital principle that vivifies the egg and sperm. With the healthy awakening of kundalini, however, ojas is believed to be sublimated and transmuted into a finer form, and to travel up through the spinal cord into the brain. Ojas functions as a potent, nutritive source with rejuvenating properties for the transforming brain as the previously dormant brahma randhra activates and new brain functions develop. Sometimes the upward flow of ojas creates an exquisite sensation as it rises to the brain and is the "soma," "nectar," or "ambrosia" that is so often referred to in treatises on kundalini.

Ojas can also travel up the spine and out through the major nerve plexuses, or chakras, and irrigate the body organs. When ojas enters the body organs, it helps prepare and tone the organs for the increased prana production that is now required because of the tremendously increased activity of the brain.

In yoga, this transmutation and upward flow of ojas from the sexual organs is called urdhava-retas—literally, the upward flow of the semen. This process may be the equivalent of what is called "sublimation of the sexual energy" in modern psychology. The important role of ojas is thought to be one reason so many traditions recommend abstinence or, at least, sexual moderation for spiritual aspirants. It should be added that, although retas literally means semen, it is not semen, but sexual energy that is transmuted. Gopi Krishna, for one, made it clear that there is a parallel process in the female body and that women are as likely as men to achieve the successful awakening of kundalini. In my clinical experience, I have found that this is indeed the case.

Stimulation of the Brain's Dormant Region— "Brahma Randhra"

According to the kundalini model, as the increased quantities of more potent prana and nutritive ojas are streaming to the brain, stimulation and activation of a normally dormant region of the brain, known in the yogic tradition as the brahma randhra, is also occurring. (In Hinduism, Brahma is God, the creator; randhra means aperture.) The brahma randhra is sometimes called the "cavity of Brahma," a name that reflects the yogic concept that the awakening of kundalini is considered essential for the mystical path to God realization. Although the exact location of the brahma randhra is not known, some yogic traditions say it is near the center of the brain, directly above the palate—but it probably does not correspond directly to either the pituitary or the pineal glands, as is sometimes supposed.

With Divine Grace and with healthy lifestyle of the body, mind, and spirit, the kundalini may remain active, the brahma randhra continue to be stimulated, one or more new brain functions or centers may activate, and new channels of perception begin to develop. In other words, the transformation that occurs with kundalini activity slowly makes it possible for the brain to perceive mystical and/or paranormal realities, the levels of reality that are glimpsed in STEs. As we have seen earlier in this book, these changes in perception can occur in a variety of ways. With a healthy, slow, gradual transformation in which the brain continues to be supplied adequately with potent prana and ojas, the brahma randhra usually first functions in only a limited way. The new perceptual abilities may occur in brief flashes or in somewhat longer, but still transient, episodes.

With time, as the transforming brain center(s) activate more fully, and as an individual heals their emotional, mental and spiritual impurities, blocks to the clear flow of kundalini (see Chapter 15), the brain may become able to perceive with greater frequency or intensity the subtle spiritual realities that are normally beyond our perception. At first, these mystical states generally occur only during periods of meditation, prayer, deep absorption, or concentration. Eventually, they may begin to occur at any time and, finally, become more and more a part of the experiencer's normal daily functioning.

The profound change in conscious perception that allows one to see spiritual-paranormal dimensions of reality has been given names in various mystical and esoteric traditions. In yoga and Hinduism, it has been called "the opening of the tenth door" and "the shedding of the veils of Maya."

As explained in some detail in Chapter Four, kundalini activity occurs on a continuum. I believe that the degree and intensity of STEs correspond with the level of kundalini activity the person is experiencing. Once kundalini is active, these episodic, variable experiences of expanded states of consciousness may continue for the rest of the person's life.

It is important to always remember that the kundalini model describes a physiologic mechanism associated with a deeply *spiritual* transformation of consciousness. Individuals cannot control this process. The Higher Power, God, or The Absolute drives this spiritual transformation through its loving, creative aspect—spiritual energy. Spirit inwardly guides and teaches the individual how to surrender to and work with this transformation process.

Pranic Energy Flow and the Chakras

Before going on to consider these expanded states in more detail, we need to take at least a brief look at the concept of chakras, for they are mentioned repeatedly in the literature on prana and kundalini. As previously mentioned, the word "chakra" literally means "wheel," and, in yoga, the chakras are said to be energy centers or vortices along the spine and in the brain. Although the chakras are described in great detail in some yogic and Tantric texts, different esoteric traditions have widely varying views about them. A few believe them to be merely symbolic aids to meditation. Others believe they exist, but only in the etheric body—a subtle, "energy" body that is held, in a number of traditions, to exist in addition to the physical body. (It is often called the "subtle body" in yoga.) Some people believe the chakras exist only in the physical body and are simply the major nerve plexuses. Another view suggests that the chakras represent points of communication between these major nerve plexuses and the etheric body.

The exact number and location of the chakras is also debated in various traditions. Some Buddhist schools, for instance, hold that there are ten major chakras; others say five. In most yogic traditions, however, there are thought to be seven. The lowest chakra is located at the base of the spine; the second lies near the genitals; the third is close to the navel near the solar plexus; the fourth is in the region of the heart; the fifth is at the base of the throat; the sixth is located on the brow between the eyebrows at a point sometimes called the third eye, and the seventh is located at—perhaps even above—the crown of the head. Some traditions hold that an additional three chakras exist above the crown and there are smaller, minor chakras on the hands and feet.

Despite the debate about exactly what the chakras and the etheric body are, one thing is clear: Many long-time meditators, serious students of yoga, and people who are undergoing STEs begin to experience sensations in the areas in which the chakras are generally thought to be located. Some also begin to perceive, perhaps clairvoyantly, such things as colors, patterns, or energy flows in these areas. It often seems as if the chakras become increasingly active energetically, and more prominent with time, following a kundalini awakening.

Many people having STEs report that they are able to see a white, shining energy body or aura which seems to exist around their own or others' physical bodies. Others also report seeing colored auras. Further, many report that they feel as if their bodies are tingling with energy or that sensations of energy are flowing along their arms and legs or up their spinal column. These sensations and perceptions may be related to the tremendously increased production of prana in the cells and the increased activity that occurs in the nervous system—and/or nadis—as it transports the larger amounts of more potent prana and ojas to the brain when the kundalini mechanism is active. Some say they see the circulating prana as a beautiful, glistening, silver luminescence that circulates through the organs and travels upwards along the nervous system. Some say that ojas is perceived in the spine and brain as a beautiful, luminescent gold.

According to the yogic tradition, when the kundalini is activated, it must open and flow through a pranic nadi or channel up the center of the spine, called "Shushumna." The chakras each connect to the shushumna, as well as to many other nadis. The upward flow of kundalini through shushumna, from the root chakra at the base of the spine to the crown chakra at the top of the brain, may be blocked or distorted at lower chakras by mental, physical, or spiritual impurities.

NDEs and Kundalini Awakening

An example of how the modern kundalini model can explain STEs can be found by examining the relationship between NDEs and kundalini awakening. It seems to me that one way of understanding the order of progression of the typical symptoms in a Near-Death Experience as identified by Raymond Moody is to compare them to the order of progression of chakra activation which occurs during a kundalini awakening. For instance, in some branches of yoga it is believed that at the time of death the kundalini energy awakens at the root chakra, rises to the crown chakra, and thereby enables the spirit to leave the body via the crown of the head. Some esoteric writers even speculate that the silver cord which is said to attach the spirit to the body is really a manifestation of kundalini. There are a number of parallels between Moody's progression of symptoms and the progressive activation of the chakras. Let us compare the two.

Typically, one of the first sensations during an NDE is the loss of fear, a feeling of great peace and calm, a certainty that there is nothing to fear, that all is right with the universe. These feelings are typical of those experienced when the kundalini rises out of the root chakra, the seat of fear. As the NDE continues, the kundalini rises further up the body. When the kundalini reaches the third chakra, a psychic awakening occurs, with clairaudience (hearing what is being said around your unconscious or dead body) and then sometimes an out-of-body experience. In an NDE, this experience of floating above the unconscious or clinically dead physical body and accurately viewing what is happening below almost invariably occurs after the feeling of peace begins. According to the yogic tradition, a third chakra out-of-body experience is psychic, not mystical in nature. There is no sense of light or of a loving Higher Power.

If the NDE continues, the kundalini can continue to rise even higher, to the throat, third eye, or even the crown chakra. The classical symptoms of the kundalini reaching an upper chakra are light, expansion of consciousness, and a mystical experience with or without a mystical vision. This corresponds to such typical elements of NDEs as the dark tunnel with light at the end, feeling merged into the light, having mystical visions of saints, gurus, deities, visions of departed loved ones, and receiving spiritual life messages. Kundalini awakening is also associated with hearing an inner sound, another symptom frequently described by near-death experiencers.

According to the kundalini model, once the kundalini mechanism is initially activated or awakened, it rarely turns off completely. The kundalini returns to the root chakra after the NDE, but the shushumna remains partly open, up to the chakra kundalini reached, and the mechanism continues to be active, though only slightly. This supports Dr. Melvin Morse's research observations in *Transformed by the Light*, where he documented that only those NDE experiencers who saw the light were spiritually transformed afterwards, with a loss of the fear of death and an increase in spiritual focus.

I support Dr. Morse's views. There is a great difference between the transformative effect of a third chakra or psychic NDE, where there was no glimpse of the loving Higher Power, and an upper chakra NDE. The psychic NDE experiencers often find themselves open to more out-of-body experiences and other psychic phenomena, but they do not become spiritually transformed or convinced of the reality of a loving Higher Power. Further, I believe that once the kundalini's pathway to the brain has been opened it never shuts down completely, and is much easier to reopen. In the years following an NDE, those who have seen the light and opened the kundalini pathway to an upper chakra may have ongoing kundalini activity continuing to some degree, which gradually transforms the brahma randhra brain center. This kundalini activity may range in intensity from dramatic to virtually imperceptible.

For those persons experiencing ongoing kundalini activity after an NDE, the level of activity and the intensity of the symptoms tend to increase over time. These kundalini symptoms may eventually become perceptible to the NDE experiencer as ongoing or recurrent inner sounds, intermittent light perceptions, or intermittent rushes of energy up the body and/or spine. This activity gradually stimulates the brahma randhra brain center, resulting in more frequent psychic experiences, recurrent mystical experiences, or the development of Inspired Creativity. Those NDE experiencers who further stimulate their kundalini through practices of meditation, intense prayer, intense concentration, yoga, or other spiritual disciplines are likely to notice a more rapid increase in these kundalini symptoms over time.

The Sahaja State—Perennial Cosmic Consciousness

According to the kundalini model, with Divine Grace, healthy mental, physical, and spiritual practices, and after many years of stimulation by the kundalini mechanism, the brahma randhra region of the brain may reach a level of stabilized functioning that allows a person to concentrate on external realities and, at the same time, exist in a perennial state of mystical union. Such a person would live in a state of higher consciousness, constantly living in direct connection with the Absolute, the divine intelligence behind the universe, or what is sometimes called the "Brahmic splendor," and yet still be able to participate in daily, worldly activities. Such a person lives and walks in two worlds, the mystical and the physical. This state is known in yoga as "sahaja-samadhi," the "sahaja state," or the "turiya state." In Christian mysticism this is called ongoing mystical union.

It is an extremely rare condition. For centuries, the hundreds of thousands of seekers who embarked upon the path of yoga were told that only a handful would reach final liberation. In the *Bhagavad-Gita*, the Hindu deity Krishna says, "Among thousands of men, scarce one striveth for perfection, and of the successful strivers, scarce one knoweth me in essence."

The term "sahaja," meaning "co-emergent," describes the co-existence of two states of consciousness, mystical union and normal worldly mental functioning. It is also known as "Buddha consciousness" or "Christ consciousness," because it is held that both Buddha and Christ were able to function in the world while at the same time existing in a state of mystical union with the Absolute. Dr. Richard Maurice Bucke, a Canadian psychiatrist, described a state similar to this as being "permanently endowed with the Cosmic Sense" or with cosmic consciousness. Dr. Kenneth Ring calls it "Omega," using Teilhard de Chardin's term for what Teilhard believed was the goal for the evolution of consciousness. Bucke, Ring, and Gopi Krishna all hypothesize that perennial cosmic consciousness would represent the next major evolutionary step for the entire human race.

If thinkers like Bucke, Ring, and Gopi Krishna are correct in their belief in the evolution of consciousness, it means that an ever-increasing number of people will begin to experience kundalini and mystical states of consciousness, until the final goal of evolution is reached. Although reaching this goal might take millennia, Gopi Krishna predicted almost two decades ago that as a reflection of the rapid pace of evolution of consciousness occurring on our planet at the present time, we would begin to see evidence of increased kundalini activity—and the accompanying paranormal phenomena—in a large number of people before the end of this century. This is borne out by what I have seen in my medical and psychotherapy practice and what my colleagues around the world have seen in theirs. One of the reasons Gopi Krishna worked so hard to encourage scientific investigation into the kundalini model was concern that lack of understanding of the biological-psychological-spiritual basis for the experiences I call STEs would mean that the people experiencing them would not be able to get help in learning how to integrate them into their daily lives. Beyond this, he believed that the medical and psychiatric communities must be prepared to deal with the types of extreme difficulties he experienced with his own awakening; they could not do this, he knew, if they did not know about, nor believe in the reality of, kundalini and spiritual transformation of consciousness.

Gopi Krishna's Kundalini Awakening

Since Gopi Krishna's own experience is widely considered the most dramatic and well-reported case of classical kundalini awakening recorded in our times, it would be helpful, at this point, to look at it in more detail in terms of both the difficulties he experienced and the state of higher consciousness that he eventually reached. His own account of his initial kundalini awakening was included in Chapter Four. He describes his life in detail in his autobiographies *Living with Kundalini* and *Kundalini: The Evolutionary Energy in Man*.

After his explosive kundalini awakening at age thirty-four, Gopi Krishna began to notice dramatic changes in both his physical body and his consciousness. For several months these changes were extremely distressing. He had digestive problems and lost all interest in food. He felt an intense burning up his spine, and sensations of heat and flame replaced, for the most part, the incredibly beautiful silver "liquid light" he had experienced during the awakening. He was also plagued with insomnia and spent night after night completely unable to sleep. He suddenly found himself subject to labile emotions and fluctuating moods. He would find himself experiencing inexplicable and unprovoked episodes of anxiety, fear, anger, and depression which would well up spontaneously from his inner depths and would disappear as suddenly and inexplicably as they had begun. His deep and abiding love for his family even began to disappear, and it seemed to him as if he had actually lost the capacity to love. He also began to lose his ability to concentrate and his interest in meditation, work, and conversation.

Although he had been a practitioner of yogic meditation for years, he knew very little about kundalini. He began to read about it with what little concentration he could muster, and eventually became convinced that his first experience tallied very closely with the descriptions in the ancient texts of kundalini awakening. He could not, however, find any information on the persistent distressing, negative sensations that had followed it.

In his search he came across two pieces of information which he credits with saving his life. One was a line from a translation of one of the yogic texts that he found in Arthur Avalon's book *The Serpent Power*. It said that the yoga student who managed to awaken kundalini should never let his stomach become completely empty, but should eat a small meal every two to three hours. The other piece of information came from his brother-in-law, a student of yoga, whose guru had once told him that problems could arise if kundalini was awakened through any other nadi than the sushumna—the channel located in the center of the spine. The guru had said, further, that if kundalini was aroused through the pingala—the channel to the right of the sushumna—mental imbalances and sensations of unbearable heat could occur. (In yogic terminology, the pingala corresponds to the sun and heat.) The guru had painted such a bleak picture that Gopi Krishna immediately sought other advice on the subject, but unfortunately, he found none.

Over the next several weeks, his condition worsened. He had become almost completely unable to eat, and the sensations of heat, fire, and flame were almost unbearable. His eyes were sunken and glazed from lack of sleep, and he had lost a lot of weight.

Just when he thought he could not go on any longer, he remembered what his brother-in-law had told him. In a flash of what seemed to be divine guidance, it occurred to him that he should try to meditate on the ida—the channel on the left of the spine which is associated with the moon and cold—and see if he could neutralize the burning sensations. He lay on his bed and began to visualize a cooling force flowing up the center of his spine. Suddenly, a miracle seemed to happen. In his autobiography he writes,

> *There was a sound like a nerve thread snapping and instantaneously a silvery streak passed zigzag through the spinal cord, exactly like the sinuous movement of a white serpent in rapid flight, pouring an effulgent, cascading shower of brilliant vital energy into my brain, filling my head with a blissful lustre in place of the flame that had been tormenting me. . . . I immediately fell asleep bathed in light and for the first time after weeks of anguish felt the sweet embrace of restful sleep.*

On awakening, he found that his head was still filled with a glowing radiance and that he was in an expanded state of consciousness. He remembered what the yogic text had said about eating and knew he must follow this advice. His wife cared for him and fed him small meals of easily digestible food every two to three hours. Slowly, over the next few months, he regained his strength and mental tranquility. As time went on he learned the importance of following without fail the inner, divine guidance he received.

Although his condition had improved greatly, Gopi Krishna went through twelve difficult years of ongoing transformation.

During this period he continued to study the yogic texts and have discussions with holy men. This eventually helped him to understand why his difficulties had occurred. Not only had he originally awakened kundalini through the wrong channel, he had also awakened it abruptly with his intensive practice of meditation and had activated the brahma randhra before his body was able to provide it with the necessary psychic fuel, prana, and nutritive tonic, ojas.

Over the next twelve years he experienced a gradually increasing expansion of consciousness and became aware of an increasingly brilliant silver luminosity that bathed his inner and outer vision: a silvery flame in his brain and radiant currents of light that darted through his body and head. In addition, external objects seemed to be dusted with a whitish coating. Over time the luminescent circle in his head grew larger. He also noticed an inner sound, a buzzing in his ears that became louder with prolonged concentration.

During this time he often felt like a helpless observer; he watched his body and brain being remodeled, but he had no idea what the purpose or the end result of the transformation might be.

Throughout this period Gopi Krishna found that his system was more sensitive than before, especially to concentration and stress. He tired more easily, needed regular breaks from concentration at work, and had to sleep at least ten hours a night. He continued to eat several small meals at well-regulated intervals throughout the day. In addition, all of his five senses seemed to become keener and more refined. His intellect become more penetrating, his imagination more vivid. His lost love for his family returned and increased. He also felt an increased love for his friends and for the world. Although his moods and emotions were far more stable than they had been during his period of extreme crisis, they remained more labile than they had been before his experiences began. Almost daily, he felt ups and downs in his moods, and sometimes he had to exercise great effort in order to remain unruffled and calm in spite of the waves of anxiety or elation that would wash over him.

During this twelve-year period of gradual transformation, Gopi Krishna did undergo one other serious crisis. He had begun to meditate again, gradually increasing his time to three hours a day. Then, hoping to speed up the process of transformation that seemed to be occurring within him, he increased it more and more until he was getting up after only a few hours' sleep and beginning to meditate at midnight. At first, this intensive meditation propelled him to new heights, but after a few weeks the searing, burning sensations returned; the pleasant, buzzing inner sound became a harsh, tormenting noise, and his insomnia and loss of appetite returned. His suffering lasted for several weeks, but, over the next few months, by decreasing his time in meditation and forcing himself to eat small amounts of food frequently and regularly throughout the day, he was gradually able to rebuild his strength and regain his equilibrium.

Towards the end of this twelve-year period, he received his first indication that this transformative experience was leading to the development of new mental capacities and higher states of consciousness. One evening in 1949, he was strolling over a bridge with a friend. In the middle of their conversation, a deep absorption settled on him and he lost touch with his surroundings and was no longer aware of the voice of his companion. He writes,

> *Near me, in a blaze of brilliant light, I suddenly felt what seemed to be a mighty conscious presence sprung from nowhere encompassing me and overshadowing all the objects around, from which two lines of a beautiful verse in Kashmiri poured out to float before my vision, like luminous writing in the air, disappearing as suddenly as they had come.*

When he repeated the lines, his friend was struck by their incredible beauty. Both of them were amazed, since Gopi Krishna had never evinced the slightest ability to write or compose poetry.

This spontaneous, inspired creativity grew and developed over the years. In addition to the many books he wrote in prose, he composed several books entirely in beautiful and powerfully moving verse. One, *The Shape of Events to Come*, was written in less than three weeks. Over the years, he was also the recipient of prophecy and revelation. He eventually came to live in a state of perennial expanded consciousness while being able to function in the everyday world. In his autobiography, he described points of even deeper absorption:

> *Language fails me when I attempt to describe the experience . . . my lustrous conscious self is floating, with but an extremely dim idea of the corporeal frame in a vividly bright conscious plane, every fragment of which represents a boundless world of knowledge, embracing the present, past, and future, commanding all the sciences, philosophies, and arts ever known or that will be known in the ages to come, all concentrated and contained in a point existing here and everywhere, now and always, a formless, measureless ocean of wisdom from which, drop by drop, knowledge has filtered and will continue to filter into the human brain. On every visit to the supersensible realm I am so overwhelmed by the mystery and the wonder of it that everything conceived in this world . . . above all even my own existence, life and death, appear to be trite and trivial before the indescribable glory, the unfathomable mystery, and the unimaginable extent of the marvelous ocean of life, of which I am at times permitted to approach the shore.*

Eventually, Gopi Krishna came to think that, during the twelve years of adjustment, his body and nervous system was being remodeled. This biologically based process had been necessary in order to gradually transform his system so that it was able to produce and handle the increased flow of energies that were necessary for the brahma randhra to develop, mature, and stabilize. He thought that the basis for understanding this process lay in the yogic texts pertaining to kundalini and that the ancient masters of yoga had fully understood how important it was for the body, mind, and spirit of the student of yoga to be completely prepared for the awakening of kundalini. He came to believe that the eight-fold path of yoga contained the disciplines that would sequentially prepare the student physically, psychologically, and spiritually for a healthy awakening of kundalini. (See Chapter Thirteen for a detailed discussion of the Eight Limbs of Yoga.)

One of the modern kundalini model's greatest strengths is its view of kundalini—and the accompanying transformation of consciousness—as a multi-faceted process, a process that is biological as well as psychological and spiritual. Because of this biological basis, Gopi Krishna was confident that the reality of spiritual transformation of consciousness would eventually be documented and verified through scientific investigation.

We are Truly Spiritual Beings

If scientific research shows the modern kundalini model to be true, there are a number of significant implications. First, the widely held belief that life is merely transient and totally physical is fundamentally wrong. The insights gained throughout history from profound mystical and paranormal experiences indicate that we are fundamentally spiritual beings, existing in a multi-dimensional universe. Further, the purpose of our physical existence on earth is to provide an opportunity for our souls to learn spiritual lessons and grow.

The verification of the kundalini model would also suggest that the world's great spiritual leaders have all been highly spiritually evolved individuals who had awakened kundalini and whose brahma randhra region of the brain was fully functioning. In this expanded state of cosmic consciousness, they were able to be clear vessels for the divine, to bring divine inspiration to their respective cultures. The spiritual guidelines they taught represented inspired insights into the morality, behavior, and style of life that would increase the rate of spiritual growth and spiritual evolution. The great spiritual masters are like people who have been gifted with color vision in a completely color-blind society.

Although their messages were influenced by their culture, their time, and what was then known about the universe, there were also many similarities. All the masters taught that we are essentially spiritual beings and that certain ways of thinking and acting are necessary to realize a state of union with the divine—whether it be called God, Allah, Brahman, Yahweh, or any other name. None of these great spiritual prophets was more divine than the others. And none had all the answers to the riddles of the universe. They did not, for instance, reveal the laws of physics or discover the vaccines that would prevent devastating diseases. They did, however, have a more highly developed faculty for perceiving spiritual realities and being open to mystical insights and revelation. Of course, total and absolute knowledge is beyond the capacity of the human brain—it is a feature of the divine intelligence behind the universe, alone.

If spiritual transformation of consciousness and mystical experiences are universal human phenomena, then all human beings, from all cultures and from all religious backgrounds, have the potential to manifest mystical states of consciousness. This concept could unify all the world's races and great religions in pursuit of the same goal—unitive consciousness.

If the kundalini model is validated scientifically, it will mean that there is a biological basis for Spiritually Transformative Experiences. Once this is established, further research might help us understand how to promote the healthy stimulation of the brain and the transformation, ultimately, to perennial cosmic consciousness. This would have tremendous implications for medicine. As a doctor, I can imagine a time when promoting the lifestyle factors needed for healthy spiritual growth and transformation could be as important as promoting preventative medicine is today. I can even envision the dawn of spiritual health promotion as a field in the medical science of the future.

Finally, if kundalini—regardless of what it is called—is shown to be a reality and to be an integral component of mystical experience and Inspired Creativity, further research might help us understand how we could best nurture and develop the creative geniuses and mystics of the future. With the inspired help of mystics and creative geniuses we might improve our chances of dealing with the troubles that face our planet today—from environmental disaster, famine, and poverty to wars and the abuse of human rights—which, we have also seen, cannot readily be solved by the current human intellect. If the kundalini model is true, it offers hope that with God's help the world might emerge intact in the next millenium.

A number of doctors and scientists are convinced that more research must be done. Many people are having Spiritually Transformative Experiences, and the medical and scientific communities lack understanding of what STEs are or what they imply about the nature of consciousness. Investigating the modern kundalini model offers a good opportunity for eliminating this lack and for eventually providing us with a workable model for understanding the transformation of consciousness.

CHAPTER 9

The Kundalini Research Network's Pilot Project

When Dr. Bonnie Greenwell organized the meeting at her home that resulted in the formation of the Kundalini Research Network, she had pressing reasons for doing so. Dr. Greenwell had done her doctoral dissertation in transpersonal psychology on kundalini awakening. Her research and her work as a psychotherapist had convinced her that kundalini awakening was becoming far more common than was generally realized. She also knew that the phenomenon and the accompanying paranormal experiences were very poorly recognized in the medical and psychological communities. Further, she knew that health-care professionals and therapists who were not familiar with the ramifications of kundalini activity would have difficulty helping people integrate the experience into their daily lives.

The doctors, therapists, and researchers—including myself—who met with her shared her concern. We agreed that a questionnaire project would be the Kundalini Research Network's number one priority. Since becoming chairperson for the project,

I have co-ordinated the questionnaire's development, reliability testing, pilot testing, and, finally, world-wide distribution.

The questionnaire consists of a series of standardized inventories that can be used by KRN-affiliated researchers to collect detailed case histories and information about the experiences of people undergoing kundalini awakenings and the other types of spiritual and paranormal consciousness experiences. The eight inventories explore the different types of experiences that I call STEs, even though the terms STEs and STEPs aren't used on the questionnaire: (1) Consciousness Experiences Inventory; (2) Medical History Inventory; (3) Lifestyles Inventory; (4) Social History Inventory; (5) Family History Inventory; (6) Spiritual Practices History Inventory; (7) Detailed Consciousness Experiences Inventory, and (8) Kundalini Experiences Inventory.

One purpose of the questionnaire is to collect detailed descriptions of both the physical and consciousness experiences of persons having any type of STE and, especially, STEP. Inventories 7 and 8 cover Mystical Experiences, Near-Death Experiences, Psychic Awakenings, Inspired Creativity and Genius, and Classical Kundalini Episodes as well as ongoing kundalini symptoms. These two inventories give research participants an opportunity to provide detailed information on their STEs and STEPs. Most experiencers report STEs in more than one category—and all are asked to fill out the section dealing with kundalini symptoms. Participants also rate their initial, and most dramatic STEs, and the frequency of recurring STEs or STEPs.

A second purpose of the questionnaire is to discover whether there is any statistically valid evidence that all experiencers—regardless of their initial or most dramatic type of experience—might be undergoing kundalini activity. Among other purposes, the questionnaire was also designed to explore whether there are any statistically identifiable factors related to family history, medical history, lifestyle, social history, or spiritual practices that might predispose individuals to STEs.

The KRN Questionnaire committee has collected over 600 completed questionnaires from people around the world, including the United States, Canada, Switzerland, India, Australia, New

Zealand, and Russia, who are undergoing dramatic STEs. The questionnaire was also given to a group of control subjects who were not experiencing major STE activity. As of 1999, the data is being analyzed.

Before the current version of the questionnaire was completed, a pilot project was carried out to iron out logistical problems and to check the reliability of the questions. Although the pilot study looked at a relatively small sample, the preliminary results are so fascinating—and have such important implications for people undergoing STEs—that I want to share them with you in this chapter. They also seem to be fairly indicative of data that are coming in from the main study. These preliminary results were first presented and published in the conference proceedings of the 1991 Annual Meeting of the Academy of Religion and Psychical Research as "Spiritual Emergence Syndrome and Kundalini Awakening: How Are They Related?" The principal investigators were me, Michael Bradford, B.Sc., Paul Pond, Ph.D., and Bonnie Greenwell, Ph.D. Later research also involved Russel Park, P.h.D., Bruce Greyson, M.D., and Megan Nolan, P.h.D.

In the pilot study 30 questionnaires were completed. Of these, 23 were completed by high-level STEP experiencers and 7 by controls (low-level experiencers). Potential control subjects were found by canvassing people who were interested in the types of experiences I call STEs but who were not known to have had any dramatic STEs or STEPs, though the questionnaire revealed that they had all had some type of minor STE or related symptoms. For the purposes of the study, however, they were identified and labeled as controls by their scores on the Consciousness Experiences Inventory rather than by their own perception of whether they were a control subject or an experiencer.

The age range of the STE experiencers was from twenty-one to fifty-three years, with the average age being forty-three. The control group's age range was similar, from thirty-four to fifty-four with an average age of forty-one. Of the experiencers, 21 were women and 2 were men. In the control group, 2 were women and 5 were men. The experiencers tended to be highly

158 of Farther Shores

educated, with 17 of the 23 holding university degrees; 8 of these 17 had completed doctoral degrees.

The Results of the Pilot Study

The overall results of the Consciousness Experiences Inventory are summarized in Table 1. Two of the most interesting findings from the study have to do with mystical experiences and psychic episodes. The findings show that 100 percent of all experiencers—regardless of their initial or most dramatic episodes—reported having mystical experiences. In most cases, these mystical experiences occurred repeatedly and in almost all cases at least one of the mystical experiences was described as extremely dramatic. Three of the 7 controls had also had mystical experiences, but each was reported as a single isolated episode that was not dramatic in intensity.

Ninety-one percent of the experiencers also reported having ongoing or recurrent psychic episodes. In contrast, only two controls reported having a single psychic episode, and one control reported having two isolated psychic episodes.

Although definite conclusions cannot be drawn until the major study is completed, the preliminary findings in these two categories suggest that all types of STE experiencers have mystical experiences and that an extremely high percentage have a propensity for psychic experiences.

Another statistically significant finding was that 70 percent of the STE group experienced some type of inspired creativity. One had had outstanding creative abilities since childhood and was, in fact, considered a child prodigy. The other 15 reported the spontaneous development of some degree of creative gifts in adulthood. None of the control group reported any inspired creativity at any point in their lives.

Other interesting findings were that 13 percent of the experiencers reported having a Near-Death Experience and that 30 percent reported having had a sense of communication or contact with beings whom they perceived as being from another planet or dimension. None of the controls reported having either an NDE or a perceived UFO experience. Finally, essentially the same percentage (13 percent vs. 14 percent) of both groups reported having had a psychotic episode.

These statistics certainly show that people having STEs tend to undergo more than one type of experience. More important, however, in relationship to the hypothesis we are examining, is that a full 100 percent of the experiencers reported having signs of ongoing kundalini activity with several symptoms ongoing or recurrent for many years.

Table 1
CONSCIOUSNESS EXPERIENCES INVENTORY RESULTS

	STE Experiencers (n=23)	Controls (n=7)
Mystical Experiences	100%	43%
repeated	87%	0
once only	13%	43%
Psychic Experiences	91%	43%
repeated	91%	0
once or twice	0	43%
Inspired Creativity	70%	0
Kundalini Experiences	100%	86%
repeated	100%	43%
once only	0	43%
Near-Death Experience	13%	0
UFO (communication with a being from another dimension)	30%	0
Psychotic Episodes	13%	14%

Note: The tables are all based on the KRN Questionnaire Project Pilot Study 1991.

Three of the 7 controls also reported having kundalini-related symptoms on more than one occasion, and 3 other controls had one isolated transient experience; however, for all of these controls, kundalini symptoms were described as being much less intense and occurring far less frequently than those reported by the experiencers. None of the controls had ongoing kundalini symptoms. Thus it seems that a fairly high percentage of controls may have had at least a minor, transient taste of kundalini activity. If these findings are repeated in the major study, I would suspect that the reason might lie in the criteria for selection of participants. All potential participants are drawn from a body of people who are interested to some extent in spiritual and paranormal phenomena. It is my belief that there may be a direct correlation between having mild paranormal experiences and being interested in them. Since I also believe that kundalini is responsible for these experiences, it makes sense to me that people who are highly interested would also have had at least some minor experiences of the energy.

Future research might need to look at this issue more carefully. It might also be interesting to examine whether individuals who have absolutely no interest in or belief in the phenomena in question have ever had any brief tastes of kundalini activity.

Table 2 provides a more detailed breakdown of five specific signs of kundalini activity. Recurrent sensations of energy, light, or heat rising up the spine or through the body were reported by 100 percent of the experiencers and none of the controls. One control person reported an isolated episode of energy rising up the spine. The other kundalini-related symptoms listed were all reported far more frequently by STE experiencers than by controls. These symptoms included bliss episodes, described as sensations of profound bliss, all-encompassing love, or overwhelming joy; expansive episodes, described as a feeling of expansion of any or all of their consciousness, head, or body; perceptions of unusual light or sparks, pervasive luminosity, or enhancement of visual perceptions; and perceptions of inner sounds, described as similar to the buzzing of bees, the dull roar of distant waterfalls, the music of the spheres, etc.

Table 2
FREQUENCY OF KUNDALINI SYMPTOMS

Kundalini Symptoms	STE Experiencers (n=23)	Controls (n=7)
Sensations of energy rising up the spine or the body	100%	14%
Bliss episodes, overwhelming love	87%	43%
Expansive episodes	83%	43%
Perception of unusual lights	74%	0
Perception of inner sounds	61%	14%

Table 3 indicates the type of STE that the experiencers listed as their first and as their most dramatic. Mystical experiences are by far the most common first STE and most dramatic STE. Classical Kundalini Episodes and Psychic Awakenings were equally split as the next most common type of initial experience. None of the experiencers listed inspired creativity, an NDE, UFO communication, or a psychotic episode as being the initial experience.

Close to 75 percent of the experiencers questioned listed either a Mystical Experience or a Classical Kundalini Episode as their most dramatic type of STE, these two types of STEs with almost the same frequency as being the most dramatic. Psychic experiences, NDEs, and UFO experiences were listed by a few people as their most dramatic STE. Once again, no experiencer listed either inspired creativity or psychotic episodes as their most dramatic STE. Table 3 also shows that the average age at the time of the first STE was 17.7 years; at the time of the most dramatic, it was 37 years. No information for controls is given on this chart since no controls had what could be classified as a dramatic STE or STEP.

Table 3
FREQUENCY OF SPIRITUALLY
TRANSFORMATIVE EXPERIENCE TYPES

	First STE	Most Dramatic STE
Mystical Experiences	65%	39%
Kundalini Experiences	17%	35%
Psychic Experiences	17%	13%
Near-Death Experiences	0	9%
UFO Experiences	0	4%
Psychotic Episodes	0	0
Average age at the time	17.7 years	37.0 years
Age range at the time	3–42 years	20–48 years

Although the main purpose of the KRN Questionnaire Research Project is to prove or disprove the kundalini model, many other important pieces of information are being gathered from it that will further our understanding of STEs and help people adjust to them. One relates to the types of activities or situations that appear to trigger dramatic STEs, or in some cases STEPs. The findings from the pilot project, shown in Table 4, are similar to what I am finding in my work. Meditation was listed as the most common trigger, followed closely by intense prayer. Triggers reported more than once were NDEs, breathwork, sex, and music. Triggers reported by one person only included yoga, a vision quest, contact with a guru, attending a church service, a UFO experience, concentration, nature, reading a spiritual letter, death of a beloved relative, and love.

Table 4
TRIGGERS FOR SPRITUALLY TRANSFORMATIVE EXPERIENCES

	First STE	Most Dramatic STE
Meditation	3	6
Prayer	3	4
NDE	0	3
Sleep	3	0
Breathwork	2	2
Sex	2	1
Music	2	0
Yoga	0	1
Vision quest	0	1
Contact with guru	0	1
Love	0	1
Church service	1	0
UFO	1	0
Concentration	1	0
Nature	1	0
Reading spiritual letter	1	0
Death of a relative	1	0
Don't know	2	3
TOTAL	**23**	**23**

What Helps—and Doesn't Help—Adjustment

Although much of the rest of the book deals in detail with ways of integrating STEs into daily life, it is interesting to look at what the pilot study indicated in this regard.

When the experiencers were asked to rate the things they found most helpful to adjustment and integration after an STE or

STEP, they listed meditation, reading books about spiritual topics, talking with supportive friends, prayer, talking to others with similar experiences, nature walks, and a decrease in workload.

The items rated as least helpful were talking with family members, advice from medical doctors, advice from traditional religions, and the use of prescription medications. If this list is borne out by the major study—and based on my clinical experience I believe it will be—it has some serious implications. It indicates that traditional medicine and traditional religion—the two most likely places for people to turn when faced with psychological or spiritual experiences they do not understand—are currently not very helpful to people undergoing these experiences. And family members, the people we most naturally look to for support, are providing as little, or even less, help.

Fortunately, the situation seems to be improving slowly. The American Psychiatric Association has recently approved a new diagnostic code for inclusion in the *DSM-IV*, the 1994 edition of a handbook used by psychiatrists, doctors, and psychologists in diagnosing mental illness and defining psychotherapeutic foci. This diagnostic code, called "V62.89 Religious or Spiritual Problem," was proposed by a California psychologist, David Lukoff, and two California psychiatrists, Frances Lu and Robert Turner. The inclusion of this category in the *DSM-IV* means that the academic core of the American psychiatric community has officially recognized the occurrence of spiritual experiences. It is my hope that this breakthrough, along with the transpersonal psychology movement's increasing vocalness on spiritual issues, indicates that Western health-care professionals are becoming more aware of, sensitive to, and supportive of Spiritually Transformative Experiences.

The results of the KRN Questionnaire Project pilot study clearly support the contention that there is a relationship between kundalini activity and the other types of STEs. Although very few experiencers had a classical kundalini awakening as their first experience, all of them reported the development, over time, of the signs of either recurrent or ongoing kundalini activity. And all of the experiencers reported feeling repeated rushes of energy up the spine—one of the classic signs of kundalini.

In addition, all of the experiencers—regardless of their initial or most dramatic type of STE—had had mystical experiences. Although for the purposes of this study, mystical experiences and kundalini awakening have been put in separate categories, it is important to remember that, in the yogic tradition, the purpose of the awakening of kundalini was the attainment of mystical states of consciousness. Thus, the fact that all the experiencers had both mystical experiences and some signs of kundalini activity lends even more credence to the idea that the kundalini model might eventually be proven to be correct and that science might some day come to recognize kundalini as the biological-psychological-spiritual mechanism responsible for Spiritually Transformative Experiences.

Section 3

Long-term Spiritual Transformation— The Mystical Path

CHAPTER 10

Physical Symptoms
of STEs

A long-term spiritual transformation process often begins in individuals after mystical, kundalini, and near-death STEs. This life-long process is sometimes called "kundalini process" or the "mystical path." It has definite physical, psychological, and spiritual symptoms. This long-term transformation and its symptoms have been alluded to in the yogic tradition, as mentioned in Chapter Eight, in the Buddhist tradition, as mentioned in Chapter Two, and in Christian mystical traditions. Evelyn Underhill wrote of the physical, psychological, and spiritual transformation process of Christian mystics as follows: "Living union with the One . . . is arrived at by an arduous psychological and spiritual process—the so-called Mystic Way—entailing the complete remaking of the character . . . It is an organic process . . . ."

When I speak of "symptoms," I am not using the word in the medical sense, but rather in the more general sense of a sign or indication that something else exists or is happening in the body—in this case, long-term spiritual transformation. In my work I have found that all STE experiencers undergoing long-term transformation tend to have a number of symptoms from three broad categories: the physical, the psychological, and the paranormal. This is true regardless of which type of STE the person had initially or most dramatically or continues to have most frequently or most dramatically. This overlapping of associated symptoms provides even more support for the idea that a common biological-psychological-spiritual basis underlies all STEs. What's more, the information we have about kundalini—gained from the modern kundalini model and from ancient yoga theory—explains why a great many of these unusual symptoms occur in the body, mind, and spirit.

The symptoms tend to be ongoing or to reappear from time to time. They generally begin at about the same time as the first STE or STEP or shortly afterwards and tend to continue with varying intensity over time. They also tend to be more marked around times of intense STE activity, and especially around the same time as STEPs. In fact, they may follow any one of the seven patterns of development that STEs follow over time.

STE Patterns over Time

1. *A slow gradual increase occurring over many years.* This pattern is frequently experienced by long-time meditators and practitioners of spiritual disciplines and by intensely religious individuals. In this pattern the intensity and frequency of STEs and the associated symptoms increase slowly and gradually over time, with some fluctuating, short periods in which experiences and symptoms are somewhat more marked.

Frequently, people experiencing this type of pattern tend for many years to ignore, minimize, or simply not recognize their spiritual transformation–related experiences and symptoms as anything out of the ordinary. Eventually, however, the individual finally has to admit that something unusual is happening. After that, they recognize that what is happening is part of a spiritual process. Sandy, a thirty-eight-year-old public school teacher, is an example.

When Sandy volunteered to complete a KRN pilot project questionnaire, she offered to be part of the "interested control group." She did not think she had had any mystical, spiritual, paranormal, or kundalini experiences. However, on the questionnaire Sandy reported having had numerous psychic experiences for at least ten years. She also reported having moderately intense, repeated symptoms associated with kundalini awakening such as rushes of energy up the spine. These sensations had been going on for more than eight years. She also reported having mystical experiences and bliss episodes from time to time over the years while she was meditating.

When I informed Sandy that her score on the part of the questionnaire that identified people as either "controls" or "experiencers" had moved her into the experiencer category, she objected, saying that everybody had the types of experiences she was having. Suggesting that this wasn't necessarily so, I described the pattern of slow, gradual increase in experiences over a number of years and explained how this could be stimulated by regular, long-term meditation such as hers.

Sandy said she'd think about what I'd said. The next time I saw her, she admitted that, after much reflection, and after talking openly with some of her closest friends, she had finally concluded that she probably was having STEs and that they seemed to be following the pattern of slow, gradual increase over a period of years. For Sandy this was an amazing realization. She had previously believed that meditation-related spiritual and paranormal experiences were "normal" and that the types of experiences I call STEs included only earth-shattering experiences.

In terms of the modern kundalini model as I interpret it, this type of pattern comes about when there is a slow, gradual increase in kundalini activity over the years. The resulting changes in the physical and subtle bodies and in consciousness may be almost imperceptible and are often not even noticed until the activation of the brain center progresses to the point where repeated paranormal consciousness experiences begin to manifest.

Gopi Krishna contended that this type of slow, gradual transformation of consciousness was currently occurring to many highly intelligent or highly spiritually focused individuals without their being aware of it. This pattern of transformation often seems to be the least fraught with difficulties, because it gives the physical, psychological, and spiritual aspects of the individual time to adapt slowly to the changes that are occurring.

> 2. *Episodes of profound STEs separated by periods with few or no experiences.* People with this pattern have episodes of STEPs or marked STEs that vary in intensity. These profound or very marked experiences are then separated for varying lengths of time by periods of either low or no STE activity. These in-between periods are often characterized by normal levels of conscious functioning. However, some experiencers fall into periods of lassitude or depression.

The stormy lives of many creative geniuses such as Nikola Tesla, Edgar Allan Poe, and Dylan Thomas have been characterized by periods of amazing inspiration, insight, and productivity alternating with periods of deep depression. Mystics have exhibited similar patterns, notably St. John of the Cross, who described the bleak periods that sometimes followed his mystical experiences as "the dark night of the soul."

According to the kundalini model, alternating peak and normal periods may simply be the result of periods of higher and lower levels of kundalini activity. During periods of positive, peak experiences the brahma randhra is functioning to some degree and the body is able to supply the necessary amounts of more potent prana and ojas. During the periods of normal conscious functioning, it seems likely that the activity level of the brahma randhra has slowed down and, with it, the demands for prana and ojas. During periods of deep depression the brahma randhra may stop functioning or continue to function at some level, but the body may be unable to supply consistently adequate amounts of pure or potent enough prana and ojas and this results in depression. Highly creative individuals who experience periods of depression and some people who have cyclothymic disorders may, in fact, be experiencing this type of pattern.

In cases where the discrepancy between the level of activity in the brahma randhra and the need for psychic fuel and nutritive tonic is less extreme, a person may simply experience periods of mental dullness, writer's block, or a temporary inability to draw on the source of creativity within.

A regular, balanced lifestyle (discussed in detail in Chapter Fifteen) is essential to the process of spiritual transformation, as it can help minimize the degree of fluctuation.

> *3. Episodes of STEPs separated by periods with gradually increasing levels of STE activity.* In this pattern STEPs or episodes of intense STE activity recur but are separated by varying lengths of time. In the early stages of this pattern the periods between experiences may be characterized by no or extremely little STE activity and/or no or few symptoms. As time goes on, the amount of STE activity and the number of symptoms in the periods between the STEPs and high STE activity gradually increase, and may continue to increase until low-level or recurrent mystical, psychic, or inspired creative experiences and symptoms of kundalini activity become ongoing in the experiencer's daily life. STEPs also continue to occur at intervals.

According to the kundalini model, this pattern is explained by gradually increasing but fluctuating kundalini activity. The first STEP indicates the beginning of kundalini activity and a first opening of the brahma randhra. The activity of kundalini and the brahma randhra slows down between STEPs but does not stop completely as it does in Pattern 2. Often stimulated by spiritual practices, this level of activity gradually rises over the years and raises the normal level of consciousness closer to the level experienced during STEs. However, as in the previous pattern, when the needs of the transforming brain center are not met, lassitude, dullness, and even depression can ensue. Also, intense emotional upheavals may occur as the Spiritual Energy/Kundalini strives to cleanse the subtle body and the unconscious mind.

This is a common pattern for people who had an initial mystical experience, Spiritual Energy/Kundalini Episode, or mystical NDE, after which they further stimulated the kundalini and their spiritual transformation process with prayer, meditation, depth psychotherapy, and/or intense psychological recovery work. This is the pattern my own kundalini process has followed since 1990. A prayer-related mystical experience in 1990 seemed to accelerate my spiritual transformation process, shifting me from Pattern 4 to Pattern 3.

> 4. *One STEP followed by a slow, gradual increase in experiences.* Although this pattern can be experienced by anyone, it is particularly common among people who have had a Near-Death Experience. In this pattern, a single intense STEP occurs that is sometimes followed by a return to normal conscious functioning. Then STE activity and the associated symptoms begin to increase gradually over a number of years. The level of activity and number of symptoms may fluctuate. As in the first pattern, these changes may be so gradual that they are virtually imperceptible until a certain threshold is reached.

This is the pattern that my own experiences followed from 1976 to 1989. Five years after my NDE I finally had to admit to myself that something extraordinary had been happening to me. It was several more years before I became convinced that some kind of ongoing spiritual change was occurring in my body and consciousness.

According to the yogic tradition, kundalini can awaken and rise rapidly to the brahma randhra for a short time in a number of different situations. This may be through divine grace, sincere spiritual practices, intense heartfelt prayer, meditation, selfless service or Near-Death Experiences. For example, when a person is on the verge of death by suffocation, it is believed that the kundalini mechanism can activate and send a potent stream of prana and ojas to the brain, nourishing it and protecting it from the deadly effects of oxygen deprivation. The activated kundalini stimulates the brahma randhra, and the experiencer enters a paranormal or mystical state of consciousness.

That this belief has long been held in the yoga tradition is evinced by an arcane, dangerous yoga technique called khecharimudra. In it the yogi, over a number of years, bit by bit, cut the frenulum—the flap of skin that attaches the tongue to the bottom of the mouth—to enable him to bend his tongue further and further back. The yogi's goal was, eventually, to deliberately block off his air passage with his tongue, and, with this asphyxiation, trigger a kundalini awakening. His years of yoga would then—he hoped—provide him with enough discipline to manage to remove his tongue while he was in the midst of a profound mystical experience. This is a dangerous practice and one that I would never recommend; many yogis are said to have died while attempting it.

In NDEs, it seems probable that once the body is resuscitated kundalini activity slows down, almost to a stop, and the person's consciousness returns to normal after a period of time. Since the brahma randhra may have been activated once and the shushumna channel opened to some degree, a small amount of residual kundalini activity may continue. Over time this activity may gradually increase and, in turn, further stimulate the brahma randhra and cause increasing STE activity. Further, the once-awakened kundalini may be more sensitive and more easily stimulated by spiritual practices, so that people who begin or continue such practices after a dramatic awakening may begin to have noticeable STEs sooner than those who do not and may switch to Pattern 3 as I eventually did.

As more and more people are resuscitated from near-death

situations, I suspect that there will be more reports of profound NDEs and, later, reports of ongoing spiritual transformation and the development of different types of STEs.

> 5. *A profound, explosive STEP followed by continuing high STE activity.* This rare pattern is the most dramatic and, usually, the most disruptive to an individual's life, particularly when it occurs to someone who has not been properly and systematically trained in preparation for a profound spiritual transformation of consciousness.

According to kundalini theory, this pattern occurs when the kundalini mechanism leaps suddenly into activity and maintains a constantly high level of activity—often due to stimulation caused by extremely intense concentration or spiritual practices. The kundalini mechanism continues to function at high levels, causing a rapid, dramatic transformation of the brahma randhra and constant activity in this region.

This type of spiritual awakening is the one most prone to difficulties. The stress that this transformation may put on the brain itself is phenomenal and the strain on the physical body, as it is suddenly forced to attempt to consistently supply vastly increased amounts of purer, more potent prana and nutritive ojas, must be tremendous.

This type of awakening can result in sudden, intense, and long-lasting mystical or inspired creative states of consciousness. It also tends to produce pronounced physical discomfort and pain and distressing, fluctuating mental states as the spiritual energy purifies the unconscious mind. The difficulties associated with this pattern can only disappear when the body is able to consistently provide the transforming brahma randhra with enough psychic fuel and nutritive tonic, and when the psychospiritual purification has progressed deeply. Unfortunately, this process of stabilization may take many years, as it did in Gopi Krishna's case—and only rarely does it result in the stabilized, tremendously expanded consciousness that he eventually reached.

A man I know stimulated this type of pattern with the extreme concentration required in completing two doctoral degrees in succession. From the onset of his kundalini awakening, he experienced nine years of mental turmoil, during which he was often completely dysfunctional. After nine years, the pattern suddenly altered and the kundalini activity slowed dramatically. Only then was he able to resume a normal life. This illustrates once again just how unwise it can be to follow extremely intensive spiritual practices, attempt to forcefully awaken kundalini, or spend too much time in intense concentration.

> 6. *Ongoing high activity from birth.* In the yogic tradition it is believed possible, in extremely rare cases, for an individual to have an awakened kundalini from birth. Depending on the degree of kundalini activity, these rare individuals are child prodigies or, in the case of a fully activated brahma randhra, a spiritual master who would have mystical experiences and profound spiritual insights from a very early age.

Guru Nanak, who is believed to have written profound spiritual poetry and dispensed spiritual wisdom long before school age, provides a classic example of this type of pattern. The same is probably true for other great religious prophets. Even though traditional sources tell us little about Christ's early childhood, I believe he was born with a fully awakened kundalini and, therefore, manifested a state of God consciousness.

Sometimes, an individual may have a partially active kundalini from birth, which spontaneously awakens to high activity later in life. These people are "born spiritual," and are drawn from early childhood to God and spiritual concepts. The yogis believe this happens to souls who were mystics or highly spiritual in their past lives.

> 7. *Prepared shaktipat awakening.* According to the yogic traditions, the spiritual transformation process least fraught with difficulties follows a kundalini

awakening stimulated by "shaktipat." Under a guru's supervision, the spiritual aspirant practices the eight limbs of yoga to prepare and purify their body, mind, and spirit before the kundalini awakens. When the guru perceives that the aspirant has adequately prepared himself or herself, the guru awakens (activates) the kundalini in the spiritual aspirant by "shaktipat." "Shaktipat" is the yogic word describing the sacred act of transmission of spiritual energy from an enlightened being or great saint to another individual. In many yogic ashrams today, aspirants seek such a prepared shaktipat awakening.

In some individuals the pattern of STE activity may change. For example, my experiences have changed from Pattern 4 to Pattern 3. Kundalini activity may also virtually stop, as it did in the case of the man I mentioned in Pattern 5. However, my practice has led me to believe that, in almost all cases, once the process of spiritual transformation has begun it continues throughout the person's lifetime, unless it is blocked by something such as drugs or alcohol.

Regardless of the ongoing, long-term STE pattern, all experiencers share many of the same types of physical, psychological, and paranormal symptoms. Learning to recognize these symptoms and coming to understand that they are a normal part of the process of spiritual transformation can allay a great many fears and help make the process much smoother.

Common Physical Symptoms

It is important to remind STE experiencers, their friends, and their families that all unusual or marked physical symptoms need to be investigated by a qualified medical doctor, even when the experiencer feels certain that the symptom is nothing more than the expression of the transformative energy in the body. One can be experiencing kundalini activity and also have physical problems that need medical attention. People on the spiritual path are not immune to illness and disease. It could be a serious, even life-threatening, mistake to assume, without medical guidance, that any of the symptoms listed on the following pages do not have a medical cause. Also, having a physical problem diagnosed and treated can sometimes help facilitate a healthier flow of spiritual energies.

The physical symptoms often associated with STEs can be divided into seven broad categories: (1) Kriyas and sensations of pranic activity; (2) undiagnosable body pains and chakra sensations; (3) metabolic changes; (4) changes in sleep patterns; (5) changes in sexual energy; (6) energy fluctuations; and (7) Yogic phenomena. The following section looks at each of these in detail, examines how they may be related to the awakening of kundalini, and considers a number of ways in which they can be minimized when people find them uncomfortable or distracting.

Kriyas and Sensations of Pranic Activity

"Kriya" is a yogic term for an involuntary jerking movement of muscles that sometimes accompanies the awakening of kundalini. Gwen, the young Canadian doctor discussed in Chapter Four, described a classic experience of kriyas when she said "my whole body started shaking uncontrollably. I felt rushes of energy coursing up my body to my head, and my whole body jerked with pulses of energy. My back, arms, and legs all jerked repeatedly. . . . My body was rocked and shaken by these energy pulses."

Although Gwen was beginning a STEP when this occurred, many people who have ongoing STEs also experience kriyas from time to time. They are often much milder than Gwen's, are generally not painful, and often last only a short period of time. Although the spontaneous or repeated jerking seen in some types of kriyas may resemble a seizure, there is no loss of consciousness as there would be in a true seizure. Kriyas generally seem to occur most often and more intensely at times when STE activity is high. Here are some of the forms the episodes commonly take:

- Involuntary jerking of one or both arms or legs, sometimes associated with rapid rushes of energy.
- Abdominal contractions or spasms, or spontaneous pumping of the diaphragm, sometimes associated with energy rushes up the spine.
- An arching or jerking of the back, usually associated with energy rushes up the spine.
- An arching back of the head and neck, often accompanied by a rolling upwards of the eyes and a fluttering of the eyelids, may be associated with energy rushing up the spine and sometimes into the brain.
- A vibration or fine tremor in the arms or throughout the entire body, or a fluttering of the diaphragm.
- Sensations of energy rushing, trickling, jumping, spiraling, or flowing through the body or up the spine.
- Sensations like currents of energy flowing through parts of the body, for instance up the arms or legs or through the organs.

Along with a number of other doctors and therapists, I believe that kriyas are probably the result of the increased flow of prana through the body that occurs after a kundalini awakening. This seems logical, since experiencers, like Gwen, often report that sensations of rushes of energy accompany the involuntary jerking and movements of the body. Some experiencers say they feel as if energy is flooding or "supercharging" their entire body.

In her book *The Energies of Transformation*, Bonnie Greenwell quotes a number of yogis, such as Swami Sivananda, who explain kriyas as the result of increased pranic activity. In addition to the types of kriyas I have seen in my practice, she adds such things as involuntary dancing, hopping, or spinning, and a sudden rigidity or freezing of muscles that may result in falling down. She also postulates that, in some cases, kriyas might be the result of the intensified energy affecting specific areas of the brain and stimulating involuntary muscle contractions.

Kriyas usually last for only a short period of time, often ranging from a few seconds to a few minutes. They are normally not painful and can often be tolerated until they stop of their own accord. For many experiencers, simply knowing that kriyas are a normal feature of STEs reduces the anxiety sometimes felt when they occur and makes them much easier to tolerate. They can also be minimized by performing the grounding activities described in Chapter Fifteen which help stabilize kundalini activity and the flow of prana. Physical exercise, such as walking, swimming, bicycling, or running, sometimes temporarily stops the kriyas. Eating more frequently and decreasing the amount of time spent in concentration and meditation can also help decrease them.

Undiagnosable Body Pains and Chakra Sensations

These pains differ from those associated with physical illnesses. They often migrate to different locations and come and go without any obvious physical reason. Even when they are thoroughly investigated with extensive medical testing, no physical cause or abnormality can be found. Severe low back pain, for example, may appear and disappear at very irregular intervals, change location, and not be related to any type of disease, spinal injury, physical exertion, or muscular back strain. Although these medically undiagnosable pains may occur in—and move to—any part of the body, they are often associated with the spine and the areas where chakras are believed to be located. These pains seem to be felt to some degree by almost all people who have STEs, and they are often more pronounced or persistent in people who have forcefully or unexpectedly awakened kundalini or who have never done any type of preparatory psychological housecleaning, bodywork, or a discipline such as yoga or Tai Chi.

Common undiagnosable pains or sensations are:

- Pressure or "pulling" sensations in the pelvic area. May be associated with the root chakra.
- Low, central back pains or burning sensations. May be associated with the first two chakras.

- Low back pain or burning sensations on one or both sides of the lower spine; may be associated with kundalini rising up the pingala, which is located on the right, or the ida which is located on the left, rather than through the sushumna or central nadi. Might also be associated with kundalini meeting a block in either nadi.
- Sharp, piercing, sword-like pains pushing up the spine. May be associated with kundalini rising up the sushumna.
- Central abdominal pressure or pain, with or without nausea. May be associated with the third, or solar plexus, chakra.
- Central chest pains or pressure, sometimes mistakenly confused with a stomach disorder or even a heart attack. May be associated with the fourth, or heart, chakra.
- Mid-back pain or pressures. May be associated with the heart chakra.
- Tightening of the throat or esophagus, sometimes described as feeling as if there was a constricting band around the throat. May be associated with the fifth, or throat, chakra.
- Pressure or pain between the eyebrows or on the forehead. May be associated with the "third eye" or the sixth chakra.
- Pressure or pain at the crown of the head, sometimes described as feeling as if the skull is too small or as if something were pushing forcefully up through the crown of the skull. May be associated with the seventh, or crown, chakra.
- Unusual headaches and sensations of pressure in the head, jaw, ears, or tempero-mandibular joint. May be associated with general kundalini activity.
- Marked, unusual sensations of energy or pressure in the center of the brain. May be associated with activity of the brahma randhra.

According to yogic theory of the subtle body, these types of sensations and pains may be caused by or related to "blocks" or "knots" that exist in the complex system of nadis or, more often, in the chakras. These blocks—associated by some with "samskaras," unresolved unconscious psycho-spiritual issues—are thought to hinder or interrupt the increased flow and circulation of prana associated with the awakening of kundalini and result in sensations of discomfort or pain in the areas where the prana is unable to push through the block or knot. Some blocks may be caused by physical factors such as impurities in the body, muscular tension or spasms, or misalignments of the spine. Some blocks may be caused by unresolved psychological issues from either this or other lifetimes. It is believed by some that ridding the body of impurities, freeing the blocked areas through such activities as bodywork, and resolving psychological issues by doing personal recovery work or depth psychotherapy can remove the blocks, free up the flow of prana, and eliminate some of the physical sensations and pains.

The following story was told to me by a thirty-five-year-old police officer who developed undiagnosable body pains after beginning intensive spiritual and martial arts practices.

> *I have been very active in the martial arts since I was six-*
> *teen. Over the years I have practiced karate, kung-fu,*
> *and kick-boxing. About two years ago I was introduced*
> *to meditation and yoga. I started meditating daily, and I*
> *have been meditating for two hours per day for the last*
> *six months. I also started practicing Hatha yoga for*
> *about one hour each morning.*
>
> *One year ago I joined a Tai Chi club, and then learned*
> *the practice of Chi-Kung. I have now added Chi-Kung to*
> *my daily practice. About six months ago I started notic-*
> *ing sensations of energy circulating throughout my body*
> *during the Chi-Kung. This was not painful or unpleas-*
> *ant. However, recently I have noticed that I get severe*
> *abdominal pain just to the left of my solar plexus start-*
> *ing within a few minutes after I begin my Chi-Kung*
> *practice. When I stop the Chi-Kung, the pain slowly goes*
> *away. I went to my medical doctor for a complete*
> *checkup. My doctor says I am in excellent health, and he*
> *could find no physical cause for the pains.*

This man was suffering from the typical undiagnosable body pains which can occur after a kundalini awakening. When I questioned him closely, he recalled that around the time he started noticing energy currents moving through his body during Chi-Kung, he also started noticing energy rushes going up his body during meditation. Probably he was undergoing a gentle kundalini awakening, stimulated by the intensive meditation and yoga practices. Further, his system was probably "ripe" for a kundalini awakening due to the many years of practicing the various martial arts, which also clear nadis and may stimulate kundalini. The pain in his abdomen was possibly due to a block to pranic energy flow that was now being pressed upon. I advised him to cut back on his meditation and yoga practices for a while, to slow down the stimulation to the kundalini. I also suggested he consider psychotherapy, to help resolve any psychological issues which might be acting as an emotional block to his process. When he did these things, the undiagnosable body pain during his Chi-Kung practice stopped.

Pains or sensations at the chakra points may in some cases be the result of clairsentience, which is discussed in more detail in Chapter Twelve.

I have seen a number of cases in which the resolution of psychological issues through either therapeutic or spiritual work has indeed eased the pain and unusual sensations associated with blocks. Sometimes prayer, light meditation, or positive visualization on the block itself can help a repressed memory to surface so that it can be dealt with. Yoga, Tai Chi, chiropractic, Shiatsu, deep body massage, and other forms of bodywork can also help release blocks. It should, of course, be remembered that dealing with repressed memories is sometimes traumatic and is often best done in a therapeutic, or at least extremely supportive, environment. A number of helpful strategies and techniques are given in Chapter Fifteen. Grounding techniques can also help bring relief.

Of all the uncomfortable physical sensations associated with STEs, back pain is one of the most common. In my practice, I have found that doing yoga or Tai Chi with a skilled instructor sometimes helps provide relief. Avoiding slouching or poor posture and taking care to sit or stand with the spine erect and aligned can also help minimize the pains. Pains located to the right or left of the spine—and possibly related to energies flowing up the ida or pingala instead of the sushumna—can sometimes be relieved by sitting erect, meditating lightly, and visualizing the energy shifting slowly towards the central channel.

Metabolic Changes

Many people experiencing STEs notice some episodic changes in the bodily processes that are related to metabolism. During periods of frequent or more intense STEs, people often remark that they feel as if their bodily functions have sped up. The digestive and the cardiovascular systems seem to be most affected.

Common symptoms associated with metabolic changes are:

- Increase in appetite, from slight to very marked.
- Craving for specific foods, especially for high-protein foods, dairy products, fresh fruits, or vegetables.
- Aversion to specific foods, often to concentrated sugars, alcohol, red meat, caffeine, or fried foods.
- Perception of a need to eat more frequently or more regularly, for example every two to three hours.
- Desire to eat smaller meals at each sitting.
- Loss of appetite and/or development of nausea, a nervous stomach, or overacidity of the stomach.
- Fluctuations in appetite.
- Increased frequency of bowel movements, for example increasing from an average of once a day to several per day during times of high STE activity.
- Increased bowel gas related to the increased bowel activity.
- Episodic racing of the pulse and pounding of the heart.
- Intolerance to heat or sensations of intense body heat, often described as "burning up"; hot flushes or night sweats.
- Cold or chills.

In terms of kundalini awakening, these metabolic changes would seem to be related to the way in which the body's various systems are stimulated into greater activity in order to provide the increased amounts of more potent prana and of ojas that are needed. Prana is believed to be extracted from the food we eat and the air we breathe in addition to being produced by some of the body cells. If this is indeed the case, it logically follows that changes in metabolic processes would occur with the activation of kundalini. (See Chapter Fifteen for more information on diet.)

I have noticed several of the above metabolic changes related to my own spiritual transformation process. I usually eat three meals a day: breakfast at 7:30 a.m., lunch at 12:00 noon, and dinner at between 6:00 and 7:00 p.m. During times of high kundalini activity I often seem to require a small mid-morning snack, a mid-afternoon snack, and perhaps also an evening snack. During these high-energy times I also find that I intuitively feel the urge to eat smaller, lighter meals at each sitting. I develop an urge to eat protein-rich foods, fruits, and vegetables, and develop an aversion to heavy starches and especially to sugar-laden sweets.

Many people undergoing STEs have found that the best technique for coping with these changes is to learn to listen to what their bodies are trying to tell them and to follow their intuitive urges. A craving for meat during high STE activity, for example, may well be a signal that the body needs more protein in order to produce greater amounts of more potent prana. I have sometimes seen people resist an urge to eat more protein after awakening kundalini because they mistakenly believe that all yogis and mystics are vegans or strict vegetarians or that it is better or more spiritual to be a vegetarian. This is not so. Further, while it is essential to learn to respect your body's inner guidance, one needs to use common sense in interpreting these intuitive urges. In cases of extreme loss of appetite, for instance, common sense tells us that the body needs fuel and that every effort should be made to eat at least small amounts of highly nutritious food at frequent intervals. In fact, many people find one of the keys to dealing with kundalini activity is to eat small nutritious, well-balanced meals or snacks every two to three hours. People who are unsure about the appropriateness of their dietary urges should discuss them with a doctor or nutritionist.

Doctors should, of course, be consulted regarding changes that cause any concern, particularly where a history of medical illness is involved. For example, a racing pulse is a normal, temporary symptom that can be easily tolerated by most people. However, a person who has a weak heart should definitely consult with a doctor so that medication to slow down the heart can be prescribed if needed.

Several techniques can be used to moderate sensations of heat and cold. Often a simple change of clothing is all that is needed. Dressing in layers so that clothing can be taken off or added as needed is often helpful for people who are away from home throughout the day. Extreme or persistent sensations of heat are sometimes relieved by remaining in a cool environment or taking frequent cool baths or showers. Yogis sometimes recommend rubbing a sandalwood paste on the third-eye center, taking cold baths, eating cooling foods such as yogurt, and avoiding hot or extremely spicy foods.

Some yogic breathing techniques are also believed to have a cooling effect. One involves protruding the tongue slightly and forming it into "U," inhaling through the mouth, and swallowing the somewhat cooled saliva at the end of the inhalation. The yoga technique of alternate-nostril breathing is thought to help relieve symptoms of heat and cold. The hand is held in front of the nose, and the thumb and fourth finger are used in alternation to block one nostril at a time. Each inhalation and exhalation is done gradually to the slow count of four. For a cooling effect, block the right nostril first and breath in through the left nostril. Then block the left nostril and breath out through the right nostril. Leaving your left nostril blocked, breathe in through the right nostril. Block the right nostril and breathe out through the left nostril. Repeat the cycle of alternate-nostril breathing a few times and end the last cycle with an exhalation through the left nostril. For a warming effect, begin by inhaling through the right nostril and end by exhaling through it.

Changes in Sleep Patterns

Many STE experiencers notice changes in their sleeping patterns, particularly during periods of high STE activity. Although the reasons for changes in sleep patterns or biorhythms are unknown, I speculate that the increased need for more—and more regular—sleep and rest are probably related to the body's need to replenish itself frequently during periods of intense pranic activity.

Common changes in sleep patterns include:

- Frequent middle-of-the-night wakening, often between 2:00 and 4:00 a.m.
- Need for more sleep per night than previously.
- Increased desire for naps in the middle of the day.
- Insomnia or inability to fall asleep during periods of very high STE activity.
- Decreased requirement for sleep during periods of high energy activity.
- Profound fatigue, especially just after periods of very high STE activity, or sometimes just before such periods.
- Interruption of sleep by night sweats and heat sensations.
- A feeling of being "hung over" or excessively groggy when sleep requirements are not met or the regular sleep schedule is disrupted.

Some yogic traditions contend that less sleep is needed after a kundalini awakening. My own clinical experience is the opposite. I find most STE experiencers find they need regular or increased amounts of sleep. The desire for more sleep and rest probably reflects the body's changing needs. However, the best way to meet the body's need for sleep is to establish regular times for sleeping and waking and to stick with them even on weekends and holidays. Current sleep research shows that a set wake-up time is the most important factor in helping the body restore healthy sleep cycles. If tired, go to bed earlier at night, rather than sleeping in. Adequate amounts of sleep are also needed; this is often as much as eight to ten hours a night for people undergoing STEs. If brief naps are needed, they should be taken, as long as set waking times are still maintained.

Cutting out stimulants such as coffee, black or green tea, chocolate, and caffeine-containing carbonated beverages can help return sleep patterns to normal in cases where excessive energy or sensations of pranic activity cause sleeplessness.

Current studies on insomnia say that light reading or other quiet activities are more likely to assist in falling asleep than exercise or watching exciting TV shows. People who have difficulty falling asleep should also increase their grounding activities. In general, increasing physical activity during the day, eating heavier, more protein-rich foods, and taking supplements of B vitamins, especially B-12, may all help. When insomnia persists, herbal sleeping preparations may solve the problem. If necessary, a doctor should be consulted about getting a prescription for a mild sleeping pill. Taken for a few nights, a mild sedative can break the cycle of sleeplessness and will do much less harm than many sleepless nights.

Over the years, I have experienced many of these changes in sleep patterns. The most noticeable change in my sleep pattern is the frequent middle-of-the-night waking. In fact, a great deal of the first draft of this book was written between 2:00 and 4:00 a.m.! My body was often awake during this time period, and the house was quiet because my young son was asleep, so I used the time to work on the manuscript. Now I generally remain in bed during that time, pray, meditate, or read some spiritual material. When I talk to various groups about STEs and kundalini, I often ask the audience how many of them suffer from middle-of-the-night waking. In a room full of people experiencing STEs, it's usually around 90 percent.

Changes in Sexual Energy

Sexual sensations and changes in sex drive are the physical symptoms that frequently cause the most distress in people undergoing long-term spiritual transformation. Fortunately, the unusual sexual sensations seem to occur only periodically and the changes in sex drive are usually only temporary. In fact, the vast majority of STE experiencers who have consulted me regarding changes and fluctuations in their sex drive have found that the problems resolved themselves after a period of time. For many, simply learning that these sensations and changes are a normal part of the process of spiritual transformation provides tremendous relief.

Common sexual energy changes are:

- Periods of mildly to markedly decreased sex drive.
- Periods of markedly increased sex drive, often to the point of distraction or discomfort.
- Periods of marked sexual tension similar to being pre-orgasmic but unrelated to sexual activity.
- Unusual fluctuations in the level of sex drive.
- Temporary confusion about appropriateness of one's regular sexual partner.
- Temporary confusion about sexual orientation.
- Fluctuations in the size of the erect penis; it often becomes larger during times of increased sex drive and smaller during times of decreased sex drive.
- Episodes of swelling or engorgement of the labia in women, generally during times of increased sex drive.
- Unusual increases or decreases in the amount of ejaculate produced by men or vaginal secretions in women.
- Unusual sensations in the sexual organs, often described as an internal, upward sucking sensation.
- Unusual pelvic pumping sensations—sensations of activity in the sexual organs.
- Menstrual irregularities in women.
- Spontaneous orgasms related to meditation, prayer, or spiritual contemplation.
- Sexual orgasms centered in the spine or head (orgasms of this type may vary in intensity and are similar in sensation to genital orgasms; the orgasmic sensation is simply located in another part of the body).

- Sexual orgasms associated with an out-of-body experience, psychic experience, or mystical experience.

These sensations and changes in sexual functioning are logical when they are considered in terms of the activation of kundalini. The relationship between the sexual energy and kundalini is well recognized in yoga, particularly in the Tantric tradition. The sexual organs have long been held to be the body's greatest reservoir of prana and ojas. If this is true, the sensations of "activity" in the genital area so often described by people undergoing STEs may well be simply that: a heightened activity that has been brought about by the transforming brain's increased need for psychic fuel and nutritive tonic. The genital "sucking" sensations may be the result of prana and ojas being drawn out and pulled upward towards the brain. These sensations are sometimes reported as being extremely strong and may be associated with spontaneous orgasms.

Further, when the genital supplies of prana and ojas are being used and depleted in this way, the process could result in a decrease in the normal, downward pressure of the sexual energy that fuels the drive for procreation. In other words, the normal sexual drive temporarily decreases and, in some cases, disappears completely for a period of time. Once the body is able to provide and maintain an adequate supply of prana and ojas, the sex drive returns to normal. In some cases, the production of prana and ojas may be stimulated more than necessary for the brain's needs and the excessive amounts of these substances stored in the sexual organs. This could lead to a buildup of energy that causes increased downward pressure on the sexual organs and a subsequent increase in sex drive. These startling changes in the activity of the sexual organs may also explain the marked changes in the amount of ejaculate and vaginal secretions.

When understood as a normal part of spiritual transformation, the fluctuations in sex drive and other unusual sexual symptoms are often coped with more easily. It also helps experiencers to know that these changes are a common sign of ongoing kundalini activity.

However, since kundalini awakening and sexual energy are so closely related, this is an area that STE experiencers need to pay careful attention to. Common sense—as well as many spiritual traditions that point to moderation and abstinence—would seem to indicate that unusual periods of decreased sex drive are the body's way of indicating that the sexual energy is needed elsewhere and that the frequency of sexual release needs to be decreased. The energy may be being sublimated into creative endeavors or may, as discussed in detail in Chapter Four, be needed to nurture the process of transformation that is occurring in the brain.

When one is involved in an ongoing sexual relationship with another person this can, of course, cause difficulties that will need to be worked out with as much open, honest communication as is possible given the nature of the relationship. Regardless, it is important that experiencers understand the reasons for their diminished sex drive and that they avoid blaming their partner, blaming themselves, or feeling guilty about the situation. People undergoing STEs cannot simply force their sex drives to return to normal and, according to kundalini theory, they shouldn't try. In my practice I have heard many reports of negative consequences from people who engaged in sexual activity and had orgasms during periods of little or no sex drive. These included sensations described as "complete mental blackness," feelings of being "completely disgusted," and an experience like "falling down an unending, black well." Other experiencers have described feeling physically and/or emotionally drained, and some have even entered into states of despair. All of these experiences make sense when one considers the possibility that the highly activated brahma randhra center might be being deprived of much-needed prana and nutritive ojas when these substances are expended at the wrong time through sexual activity.

Although my advice is to follow the urges of the body when the sex drive is low, I am afraid my experience leads me to say almost the opposite when it comes to periods of intense sex drive. During these periods it is probably best to exercise self-control and maintain a moderate sex life, even when one gets strong urges for excessive indulgence, so that the much-needed supplies of prana and ojas are not completely depleted. Spiritual teachers from many traditions recommend decreased sexual activity and even abstinence at certain times during the spiritual journey. Based on his own experience, Gopi Krishna recommended, for example, that people following the moderate spiritual path limit the frequency of sexual release to somewhere between twice a week and once every two weeks. He also said that, during periods of high kundalini activity, sexual release could be extremely detrimental to the process.

Some people involved in spiritual transformation believe these difficulties can be circumvented by refraining from having orgasms but remaining sexually active. The advisability of having non-orgasmic sex—instead of being abstinent or moderate when needed—is, however, controversial. I do not recommend it. Other people, however, promote the idea that the sexual energy stimulated in this way can then be sent back up the spine and into the brain. Some of these ideas may even be based on ancient Tantric practices. These practices—controversial in themselves—were developed in a culture and setting completely different from our own and were considered advanced esoteric practices. Further, I think that finding a spiritual teacher today who is knowledgeable enough to guide one safely through these practices would be difficult. Beyond this, some experts on kundalini, such as Gopi Krishna, say that during sexual arousal the energy is transformed into a grosser form and that this grosser form cannot be transformed back into the more subtle form that is needed to nourish the brain.

In general, I think it is much safer to practice moderation and abstinence when they are required than to indulge in non-orgasmic sex. It will undoubtedly be a long time before we understand this process completely, and it is far better to err on the side of safety.

Energy Fluctuations

Among people experiencing long-term spiritual transformation, fluctuations in energy levels and moods are fairly common.

All of the experiencers I have worked with have reported at least some fluctuations in their energy levels that were not brought about by any of the usual physical causes, such as illness or lack of sleep. In different cases—and at different times—these fluctuations range from what is often described as "feeling low in energy" to not having enough energy to carry out daily tasks. These episodes may alternate with periods of increased physical or mental energy. Many experiencers also report periods of increased emotional lability that either are not related to events in their lives or are intensified by events far more than normal.

Common fluctuations associated with energy and mood include:

- Unexplainable fluctuations in physical energy, from highly energetic to lethargic.
- Unexplainable periods of fatigue or increased susceptibility to illness.
- Periods of exceptionally high physical energy that may include strong urges to exercise strenuously or run for long distances.
- Episodes that are sometimes described as feeling "speedy" or "revved up"; sometimes accompanied by dizziness or light-headedness.
- Periods of exceptionally high mental energy, and mental clarity.
- Periods of low mental energy or mental states sometimes described as "mental dullness," often characterized by an inability to think as quickly, efficiently, or clearly as normal.
- Unexplained fluctuations between extremely high and low mental energy.
- Periods of increased irritability or an increase in moodiness or mood swings.

In terms of the modern kundalini model, these unexplainable energy fluctuations and mood swings are related to the body's fluctuating ability to meet the nervous system's and the brain's

need for prana and ojas. When the supply of prana is being con-
sumed more rapidly than it can be replenished, the body feels low
in energy. The various levels of fatigue may well be directly pro-
portional to the level of depletion of prana. When the body is
meeting demands adequately, energy levels are normal or higher
than normal.

Moods may be affected in the same way. When adequate supplies of prana and ojas are reaching the brain, moods are normal
or good. When the supplies are inadequate, moods are propor-
tionally lower. Both high physical energy and hypomanic moods
could be explained by the body's producing very large amounts
of prana.

In my work, I have found—as Gopi Krishna did from his
research and from his correspondence with hundreds of people
around the world—that these fluctuations in energy and swings
in mood are often more pronounced in STE experiencers who
have immoderate, irregular, or stressful lives, who disregard the
importance of regular, well-balanced meals, or who indulge in
smoking, excessive drinking, drugs, or excessive sexual activity.

Some STE experiencers seem to be more prone to fluctuations in
energy and moods than others. Although a certain amount of energy
fluctuation is probably unavoidable during the process of spiritual
transformation, doing the psycho-spiritual housecleaning described
in Chapter Sixteen and living the well-balanced, regulated lifestyle
described in Chapter Fifteen, may be the most effective ways to moderate energy and mood swings. Further research may show that some
individuals may be genetically predisposed to have mood swings
after beginning to have STEs. We know that a genetic predisposition
exists for the more extreme manic-depressive disorder.

Yogic Phenomena

A number of professionals, including Dr. Bonnie Greenwell and
myself, who have been working with people undergoing STEs
and long-term spiritual transformation have noted the emergence of physical symptoms that can be loosely characterized as

yogic phenomena. These include a variety of movements and postures that the experiencer either does spontaneously and without volition or feels an overpowering inner urge to do. Many of these movements are Hatha Yoga postures or mudras—in this case, certain hand movements used in some spiritual rituals, postures, and meditation practices. Other experiencers may spontaneously or involuntarily do yogic breathing techniques. One of the most fascinating things about this phenomenon is that people who have no training in or knowledge of yoga often report doing these yogic activities spontaneously. Some even report spontaneously uttering words or mantras that they believe to be—and, in some cases, are verified to be—Sanskrit, the ancient and sacred language of India.

Although the modern kundalini hypothesis does not offer a specific explanation for these unusual occurrences, they may be the result of a kind of "wisdom of the body" that intuitively urges the experiencers into positions that facilitate the flow of prana throughout the body during periods of kundalini activity. Perhaps some of the many yogic postures, hand movements, and chants were originally developed by yogis who spontaneously did them after awakening kundalini and then, because they were beneficial, continued to do them until they eventually became systematized as part of the yoga teachings.

In *The Energies of Transformation*, Dr. Greenwell postulates that the postures might occur "because of an unconscious force that knows exactly what the body needs to release a block." About the yogic breathing patterns that sometimes occur, often during intense meditation, she writes that perhaps they are "stimulated by physiological needs, or connections with memories in the collective unconscious, or triggered for specific healing purposes unknown to the conscious mind."

Although these experiences are generally not painful—and, in fact, are often quite pleasant—their sudden appearance can be distressing, especially to people who do not understand the important and beneficial role postures, hand movements, chants, and breathing techniques have played over the centuries in the practice of yoga. These phenomena can also be socially inappropriate and embarrassing if they happen in a public place. Fortunately, they usually occur only when the experiencer is meditating or involved in some other spiritual practice. When this happens, it is beneficial to follow the inner urge, relax, and allow the body to move, slowly and gently, into the position, movement, or pattern of breathing. In the same way, spontaneous chants and sounds can be allowed to flow freely rather than being struggled against.

When the urge to begin one of these yogic phenomena occurs in a public place, it can generally be suppressed for a short time until a private or socially appropriate place for flowing with the inner urge can be found.

Distinguishing Physical Illnesses from STE Symptoms

The unusual physical symptoms that appear as part of the process of spiritual transformation often cause a great deal of confusion and leave experiencers wondering whether a particular sensation or symptom is related to their spiritual process or to some unknown physical illness. I cannot emphasize enough how important it is that unusual physical symptoms be investigated by a qualified medical doctor.

Unfortunately, some people have gotten the idea that true spirituality brings with it an immunity to normal physical illness or some sort of paranormal ability for self-healing. In fact, there are countless examples of highly spiritual people who have died from disease. Sri Ramakrishna died of cancer, Krishnamurti of pancreatic cancer, and Gopi Krishna of complications arising from pneumonia. How, then, can those of us who are simply moving at our own pace along the spiritual path expect to have physical invincibility? People who have STEs can develop cancer, diabetes, pneumonia, meningitis, AIDS, and other physical illnesses just like the rest of the human population.

In fact, in my practice I have found that certain physical illnesses actually seem to occur more frequently in people undergoing STEs than in the general population. These include respiratory allergies, skin contact allergies, food allergies and food sensitivities, hypoglycemia, diabetes mellitus, and thyroid disorders.

It also seems that some people undergoing STEs also react differently to treatment than the general population does. Some seem to be more prone to side-effects from drugs, and some seem to be more sensitive to anesthetics and more likely to notice subtle—or even sometimes pronounced—after-effects. These may include temporary mood fluctuations, fatigue, and suppression of the creative impulse. One writer I know noticed that his writing ability and creativity disappeared for almost two years after being under anesthetic for eighteen hours during a complex operation. I suspect that an individual's pranic spectrum is affected by drugs, surgery, or anesthetic, and I hope future research determines whether this is the case. In the meantime, one thing is certain: It is a mistake to presume that intensive spiritual practices, positive thinking, or repeated affirmations make one immune to the biological laws of nature. I have also seen a number of individuals in my practice who tried to deny the physical illnesses they had because they believed that acknowledging the illness would somehow "give it power" and make it worse. This prolonged denial led to unnecessary delay in obtaining much-needed medical treatment.

Like everyone else, people undergoing STEs should find a medical doctor with whom they have good rapport and go for a thorough physical examination at least once a year. STE experiencers should also inform their doctor of any unusual or distressing physical symptoms so that the doctor can investigate these symptoms thoroughly. Only after all the tests and investigations are completed and the doctor feels certain that there is no underlying medical cause can an experiencer assume that the physical symptoms are a normal part of the transformative process.

Although I certainly believe that positive thinking, positive visualization, and affirmations—along with a healthy lifestyle— can optimize the body's ability to fight off disease and heal itself, I also believe that God works through people to bring about better conditions for humanity. And one of the things that some people—from herbalists and shamans to medical researchers, scientists, and doctors—have done is to amass an amazing amount of information that can cure or help cure disease. That information is there for us to use. But we can use it only if we seek out the medical professionals who can show us how.

CHAPTER 11

Psychological Symptoms of STEs

People undergoing long-term spiritual transformation and STEs experience many psychological changes as well as physiological ones. These changes are evidence that something else is going on, and thus they can be thought of as "symptoms" just as the physiological changes can.

The immediate emotional and psychological impact of STEs varies tremendously from individual to individual, depending on such factors as personality, the amount of stress in the person's life, and whether they are in a supportive environment in which their STEs are treated as valid and valuable. Most people undergoing long-term spiritual transformation also notice long-term psychological symptoms. It seems as if the transformation process itself propels them at some point into intense self-reflection (emotional recovery work) or depth psychotherapy (inner healing work). The personality is being purified, morally developed, healed, and polished. Christian mystics refer to this process as "purification" and "purgation." I call it spontaneous psycho-spiritual housecleaning, and will discuss it in more depth in Chapter Sixteen.

Some of the psychological reactions to STEs are positive and demonstrate inner growth or healing. Others are challenging or distressing and indicate that more inner work needs to be done. Almost everyone undergoing STEs has both kinds of reactions. Fortunately, in my work, I have found that, in the long run, for most people, the positive reactions outweigh the negative ones. Further, when negative psychological reactions are treated as challenges they can often be worked through and turned into opportunities for growth. Although I have characterized these reactions generally as "psychological," many of them have to do with our attitudes and spiritual values.

Positive Psychological Symptoms and Reactions

Positive changes are wide-ranging and relate to personality, emotions, attitudes, outlook, and values. Some of these changes occur suddenly; others develop gradually over time. Many STE experiencers have several of these positive symptoms and reactions; others have only a few, and the experiences themselves do not necessarily manifest in exactly the way I described them.

Maturation of the personality. Experiencers may abandon irresponsible and immature behaviors and exhibit new independence, clarity of thought, personal strength, and social responsibility.

Spontaneous abandonment of self-destructive habits. Experiencers may develop a strong inner urge for a healthier lifestyle and give up smoking, excessive alcohol use, non-medical drugs, or a sedentary lifestyle.

Re-evaluation of jobs. Experiencers may decide to modify or leave work situations that are unsatisfactory, stress-producing, or emotionally unfulfilling.

Re-evaluation of relationships. Experiencers may examine relationships with family, friends, and partners and attempt to improve communication and understanding and to resolve conflicts that have been simmering for years. When all else fails, they may finally break off dysfunctional relationships.

Resolution of psychological blocks. Repressed memories of

unresolved psychological issues and conflicts may spontaneously surface in the experiencer's conscious mind, become clear, and eventually be resolved. This resolution sometimes occurs much more rapidly than normal.

Setting healthier interpersonal boundaries. Experiencers may find themselves increasingly aware of their own codependent relationship patterns, and previous denial or minimization of abusive relationships. They may begin to set clearer, healthier boundaries in their relationships and break away from "victim" and "rescuer" roles.

Absolute belief in the existence of a higher power. Experiencers may develop an unshakable conviction concerning the reality of the existence of God, Allah, Brahman, or some type of omnipotent, omnipresent, omniscient, and loving power behind the universe, or an existing belief may become much stronger.

Loss of the fear of death. Experiencers may no longer perceive death as the end of life but as a transition from physical to spiritual form, or perhaps as a "coming home." They may come to believe in reincarnation, and thus view death as a positive transformation, but suicide as unacceptable.

Being inspired by the memory. Experiencers may feel uplifted by the memory of STEPs or profound STEs; these memories seem to act as beacons in times of darkness or as guideposts in the continuing attempt to become a better human being.

Increased humanitarianism, love, and empathy. Experiencers may develop or strengthen any or all of the following: a belief in the oneness of all humankind; a greater capacity to feel unconditional love for friends, family, and humanity in general; a greater love for all living creatures, and a greater capacity for forgiveness; deeper understanding, greater sensitivity to and awareness of others' suffering; less rigid or intolerant thinking; and greater compassion. This often leads to an increase in humanitarian attitudes and actions.

Increased altruism. Experiencers may develop a more selfless nature and a greater desire to be of service to others.

Increased morality. Experiencers may be conscious of a desire to be more honest, truthful, and fair and follow more spiritual ideals and/or live by a moral or ethical code.

Decreased materialism. Experiencers' desire for material possessions, financial success, and fame may lessen. Achievements in business and finance become less important.

Increased spiritual focus and deeper spiritual insights. Experiencers place more importance, and spend more time, on prayer, meditation, reading about spiritual subjects, or participating in spiritual practices. They may desire more and more to live in accordance with the world's great spiritual teachings. When they read or discuss the scriptures of the world's great religions or other spiritual writings, they may have new spiritual insights and far deeper levels of understanding.

Increased intuitiveness. Experiencers may develop or increase the ability to hear an "inner voice," learn from higher, inner guidance, and be intuitive in all aspects of life.

Increased creativity. Experiencers may feel a stronger urge to express the self through writing, music, or art; in some cases, their ability to do so also develops or increases.

A belief in the reality of one's spiritual experiences. Experiencers may be strongly, even unshakably, convinced of the reality of their STEs, and especially their STEPs. This conviction remains firm in the face of opposition and is often a source of inner strength.

The following story was told to me by a forty-eight-year-old gay woman, Pam. Her kundalini awakening, which was brought on by five years of intensive psychotherapy, dream analysis, and regular meditation practice, was marked by dramatic rushes of energy up her body, strong sensations of light, and overwhelming feelings of love and bliss. This STE led to tremendous positive psychological changes.

> *I'm not too proud of the person I used to be. I suppose it was all part of my growing-up process. Before my spiritual awakening, I was a pretty mixed-up person. I used marijuana and hashish regularly. I drank alcohol to excess almost every weekend. But I was most unhappy with my*

personal relationships. I felt powerless and needy of love, so I put up with a lot of emotional abuse.

After my kundalini awakening I found it very easy to quit drinking alcohol, using drugs, and smoking. I suddenly became aware that the physical and sexual abuse I had experienced in my childhood was affecting my behavior today. I started working with my psychotherapist with renewed vigor, to try to work through my childhood traumas and sexual abuse that had helped make me act this unhealthy way.

Now, five years after my kundalini awakening, I feel that I am a different person. I have completely changed my circle of friends. I am in a long-term monogamous relationship which is tender and caring. I have been drug-free for years. I volunteer regularly for a small community service organization which helps sexual abuse survivors. I strive to be as loving and open as possible in all my relationships. My spiritual growth has become the most important thing in my life.

In some people, the most noticeable positive psychological impact of STEs is decreased materialism combined with increased humanitarianism. This was true of Gerald, a sixty-year-old successful businessman.

Prior to my mystical experience, my business was the most important thing in my life. I was the president of a medium-sized publishing house, and I aspired to be a multi-millionaire. I worked hundred-hour weeks, and I had time for little else than my work.

In 1975, while at a conference in the Rocky Mountains, I had a profound mystical vision which changed my life. I saw the face of the man who was to be my future spiritual teacher. With the image of the face came a feeling of profound love, overwhelming compassion, and understanding. I wept. I suddenly felt ashamed of my life, which was so materialistic and devoid of love.

When I returned home, my wife hardly recognized me. She said that my face was beaming with light. She was amazed and delighted when I told her that I was cutting down my work hours and beginning to practice a spiritual discipline. I sought out the teacher who had appeared in my vision. When I found him, I began to study with him, learning yoga and meditation. I began donating at least 10 percent of my income to spiritual causes, and still do so to this day.

My spiritual quest is the most important thing in my life. I have toned down my work. Money is not important to me any more—I give away more of it than I keep.

Challenging or Negative Psychological Symptoms

I have found that many of the psychological reactions to STEs that might be considered negative or difficult to deal with are caused, at least in part, by a lack of information or incorrect information about spiritual transformation. They are also often exaggerated or worsened by the lack of an appropriate framework or perspective in which to place the STEs. Significant unresolved psychological issues can also intensify or increase the difficult reactions. Although most of the following reactions can be thought of as negative, I prefer to regard them as challenging. This underscores the idea that they usually can be dealt with, worked through, or resolved in a variety of ways. Most people undergoing STEs have some temporary challenging reactions from time to time, others a great many. And all of the following reactions can be experienced in different ways and degrees.

Anxiety. A sense of anxiety or general emotional distress which is often due to uncertainty about what the experiences are, what they mean, and why they happened; anxiety is often intensified by not having anyone to talk to who can understand or interpret the experiences in a positive way.

Confusion. A sense of confusion resulting from not understanding the nature or meaning of the STEs; confusion about the nature of reality itself, especially when "reality" as it is perceived during the STEs does not fit with previously held beliefs and assumptions about the universe.

Mental dulling. Difficulty concentrating; feeling that the brain is "overloaded"; feeling incapable of coping with normal mental tasks or emotional stresses—most common immediately after STEPs or intense STEs.

Fixation with experiences. Thinking about or focusing on the STEs or STEPs to the exclusion of all else, so that it interferes with daily functioning and performance.

Despair that a STEP has ended. Despair or deep sadness that a STEP or profound STE has ended and cannot be re-created or re-experienced at will.

Rebound depression and lassitude. Temporary mental exhaustion, lassitude, or depression that occurs immediately after a STEP or intense STE and usually disappears within a few days or weeks; this reaction may be due to a depletion of the stores of prana or ojas.

Decreased capacity to love. Feelings of emotional depletion or of being incapable of feeling affection or love for one's spouse, family members, and friends. This reaction tends to be most common immediately after a STEP or during high STE activity; although it may recur, it is almost always temporary and usually resolves itself in a matter of weeks or, in some cases, months.

Fear of losing control. A sense that one is no longer in control of one's life and actions, and a subsequent attempt to suppress the spiritual experiences; this fear is often aggravated by the fact that, in truth, no one can completely control the spiritual transformation process.

Fear that one is dying. A fear that a STEP or profound STE is a signal that one is going to die soon.

Fear of going insane. A fear that one is going insane or already is insane without realizing it; this reaction is often more common when the STEs conflict with one's view of reality or are completely outside the range of one's life experience.

Fear of possession. A fear that one is being taken over or controlled by evil spirits or entities. This reaction is more common in people who believe strongly in such evil entities, who attempt to "play" with the dark forces, or who have little or no information about the process of spiritual transformation.

Fear of the devil. A fear that STEs are the "work of the devil"; more frequent in individuals who belong to rigid, fundamentalist religious groups and/or are told by the leaders of those groups that the phenomena associated with STEs are brought about by the devil.

Inexplicable mood swings. Unexplainable and sudden temporary changes in mood; waves of anger, guilt, anxiety, or depression which may resolve as suddenly as they appear; uncharacteristic emotional lability or irritability, characterized by bursting into tears, getting upset, or becoming very angry quickly and easily over small things; often more marked directly after STEPs or strong STEs.

Cyclothymia. Recurrent cycles of mild depression or lassitude that alternate with cycles of normal or high-level functioning; sometimes relating to seasons of the year or to lunar cycles but not Seasonal Affective Disorder or Bipolar Disorder.

Intensification of unresolved psychological issues. Spontaneous awareness of unresolved psychological issues, with the associated emotional conflicts becoming more intense; repressed memories of traumatic events may surface spontaneously; relationships with people responsible for childhood trauma or other emotional conflicts may become increasingly dysfunctional; anger, guilt, fear, depression, or anxiety concerning these issues may intensify.

Emotional distress. The surfacing of memories or unresolved issues—and an inability or unwillingness to deal with them—may cause generalized psychological distress, depression, or anxiety; sometimes this reaction is described as feeling "less centered" or "less together."

Gender identity crisis. Uncertainty over sexual orientation sometimes develops, particularly when the experiencer is undergoing the physiological symptom of greatly intensified sexual urges; this reaction is usually temporary and generally resolves itself when the experiencer's sexual drives return to normal.

Poor ability to control increased sexual urges. An inability to cope with or control the physiological symptom of intensified sexual drives, resulting in inappropriate or promiscuous sexual behavior; this reaction is sometimes characterized by feelings of sexual attraction to all persons of the opposite sex (sometimes of the same sex) who come into close proximity and, in some cases, having indiscriminate sexual contact with them; this condition is usually temporary and resolves itself when sexual drives return to normal.

In some cases, challenging psychological reactions can intensify and develop into the types of crises, spiritual emergencies, or psychoses discussed in Chapter Thirteen. One of the signs that this might occur is the experiencer's beginning to have trouble discriminating between inner and outer realities. An experiencer may begin to think that his or her paranormal and spiritual experiences are being shared by everyone.

Delusions of grandeur are another sign that negative psychological reactions may worsen. Experiencers may assume that their experiences have far greater significance than they actually do, or may even begin to think that they are divine messengers or have been given the secret of the universe.

Another sign of potential trouble is paranoid delusions in which experiencers begin to think that others are using special mental powers to control their behavior or to cause the unusual or paranormal phenomena they are experiencing.

Tensions and Conflicts in Relationships

In my clinical work, I have sometimes seen experiencers become uncertain about their relationships after a STEP or in the course of the long-term spiritual transformation process. In cases where incompatibilities already existed, they often become magnified—and conflicts and disagreements tend to increase.

Another very common area of difficulty relates to changes in the experiencer's sex drive. A dramatic increase or decrease in one partner's desire for sex can throw any relationship into turmoil. A decrease in sex drive may be poorly understood by the partner, and may be misinterpreted as a lack of love or a lack of commitment to the relationship. An increase in sex drive may also confuse the partner, or make them feel pressured into having more frequent sex than they desire. Matters are complicated even further when the increase in sex drive is so great that the experiencer begins to desire other sexual partners.

I have also seen cases where the sensation of overflowing love associated with a powerful bliss episode or heart-chakra opening was mistaken for "falling in love" with someone outside the relationship.

Trying to deal with the temporary loss of the ability to feel love and affection that sometimes accompanies spiritual experiences can also be very hard on both partners.

Spiritual pride can cause problems, too, especially when it leads an experiencer to become dissatisfied with a partner who does not have the same spiritual ideas or focus.

Other types of problems may arise, depending on the partner's reaction to what the experiencer is going through. A partner's disbelief in or ridicule of spiritual or paranormal experiences, for instance, can be very difficult for the experiencer to handle. I have also seen partners who were aware of spiritual experiences and became jealous because their own experiences were not as profound or dramatic.

In other cases, I have seen partners who were unable to adjust to the experiencer's changing interests, values, and increasingly spiritual focus. Some are also unable to accept the experiencer's desire to make lifestyle changes or to deal with the changes in personality that accompany long-term spiritual transformation. It can also be difficult for a partner to cope with the challenging reactions experiencers sometimes go through.

Risa, one of my patients, experienced several of these typical difficulties in her relationship with her husband once her experiences began, and she unfortunately responded negatively.

I noticed a tremendous variability in my sex drive during my intense kundalini awakening. I also felt a strong desire to spend large amounts of time each day in meditation, writing in my journal, or practicing yoga. My husband did not support these changes and started to ridicule me about my increasing spiritual focus. My husband also did not understand how my sexual drive could swing from very intense to virtually nonexistent. He was uncomfortable with and resistant to my new sexual exploration during periods of high sex drive. I in turn found myself wanting to have sexual relations outside the marriage, and I began to feel that my husband was not an appropriate partner for me. I eventually started a sexual affair outside the marriage.

Fortunately, Risa and her husband were able to heal the marriage by going for marriage counseling and by their consultation with me which helped them both understand how the kundalini awakening had affected Risa's sex drive and enhanced her urge to do spiritual practices.

Coping with Challenging Psychological Reactions

A great deal can be done to heal and resolve some of the challenging psychological reactions. In many cases, these are the same measures that help one resolve and cope with various degrees of spiritual crises and spiritual emergencies. One of the best is to find a qualified doctor, psychotherapist, or spiritual counselor to help you through the process. Ideally, this person would be familiar with and have an open, positive attitude about spiritual and paranormal experiences. If such a person is not available in your area, an alternative is to find a sensitive, supportive, open-minded doctor or psychotherapist who is willing to accept your reports of your STEs at face value and seems willing to learn more about the whole process of spiritual transformation.

Although a number of strategies for dealing with the varying degrees of challenging psychological reactions and other difficulties sometimes associated with STEs are discussed in detail in Chapters Fifteen, Sixteen, and Seventeen, it's worthwhile to summarize a few of the main ones here for quick reference.

1. Realize that these challenging psychological reactions are experienced by others on the spiritual path and that many of them have been recorded in the yogic literature and in other mystical traditions. This realization can help "normalize" the reactions, make them less frightening, and help put them in better perspective.

2. Remember that these reactions are, in most cases, temporary—even though they might recur from time to time. Knowing that STEs and associated symptoms are temporary is reassuring and helps experiencers cope with them while they are occurring.

3. Focus on the positive aspects of STEs and be grateful for them rather than thinking too much about the negative ones. This helps develop a sense of perspective and prevent the negative cycle in which the experiencer spends more and more time focusing on the negative.

4. Pray, meditate, read spiritual material, and/or repeat positive affirmations for moderate amounts of time each day. Turn your problems over to the divine. Ask for his or her help in your healing, learning, and growth. This can be a tremendous source of strength.

5. Develop a more moderate, healthy, balanced, and regulated lifestyle. This can improve the body's general health, contribute to better mental health in general, provide an outlet for excessive energies, and help regulate and moderate the flow of the spiritually transformative energies within the body.

6. Temporarily relocate to a tranquil, supportive environment—for example, a spiritual retreat or even

a cottage—to get away from daily stresses and to work psychological issues through.

7. Talk to a supportive person—a friend, doctor, spiritual teacher, or counselor.

The following story shows how one of my patients, Arlene, used these strategies to cope with the emotional challenges she faced after her psychic opening in which she started to unblock past-life memories.

Two years ago, I was having bad relationship problems. My common-law boyfriend, Bill, was becoming very rude and verbally abusive. I started suspecting that he was having an affair. This was a phase in my life when I had been meditating for one hour a day. I had been praying for guidance for God to help me understand what was going wrong with my relationship.

Suddenly, one day during my meditation, I got a clear visual memory of a past life that I had seemed to live with Bill. I was the man in that life, and Bill was a woman, my wife. In the past-life memory, I had caught my wife having an affair with another man. I saw myself kill my wife (Bill) in the heat of an argument.

This past-life memory had a devastating impact on me. I suddenly felt very guilty, responsible in some way for the problems I was having with Bill. Further, I had nobody to talk to. I had no friends who believed in past lives, and I certainly couldn't talk to Bill. Our relationship became even more strained than before.

A few weeks later another past-life memory came to me during meditation. In this one, I was a woman and Bill was my husband. This time he was very abusive. He was unfaithful, having numerous affairs, and he also argued with me frequently and hit me during arguments. I could see a real parallel in how Bill was beginning to be abusive towards me in this life.

I felt overwhelmed and confused by these two memo-

ries. I had no idea how to integrate them into my life. I started worrying that they were hallucinations and that I might be going crazy. I was totally preoccupied with them and found it difficult to concentrate on my work. I finally became so anxious that I was unable to concentrate, and I had to take time off work. I heard about Dr. Kason, so I went to her office.

She reassured me that what seem to be past-life memories were common, and were not a sign that I was going crazy. She helped me see them as something positive, a gift from the unconscious mind to help me understand the dynamics of my problems with Bill. I read a book she recommended about other people who have recalled past-life memories. I took Dr. Kason's advice to adopt a more regular lifestyle, with more sleep and more exercise. I went for daily walks out in a local park. I started going for weekly psychotherapy sessions with a psychologist in my area. Within a few weeks I felt much calmer, and I was able to return to work. With the help of psychotherapy, I developed the inner strength to end the abusive relationship with Bill two months later.

The self-help strategies listed above, along with the ones discussed throughout the rest of the book, should reassure anyone who is experiencing negative or challenging psychological reactions. Even though these reactions can be painful while they are occurring, they are usually only temporary, and a great deal can be done to help heal and resolve them. Finally, experiencers can take comfort in the knowledge that the often challenging psychospiritual housecleaning has been recognized for centuries by yogic and other mystical traditions as an essential part of the long-term spiritual transformation process, the "Mystical Path."

CHAPTER 12

Spiritual and Paranormal Symptoms

People undergoing long-term spiritual transformation develop a similar range of spiritual and paranormal symptoms after or between the STE experiences, no matter which type of STE they have had. Many of these symptoms have been touched upon in Chapters Three and Six, which dealt primarily with mystical and psychic STEPs.

In the beginning, spiritual and paranormal symptoms may simply be very subtle shifts in consciousness. They do vary in intensity, however, and over time they tend to increase in strength and frequency until they become a permanent feature of the experiencer's consciousness. In general, the gradual increase in these symptoms can be thought of as a slow opening of the experiencer's "baseline" consciousness to spiritual and paranormal dimensions. These symptoms can be thought of as part of the vast continuum of experiences that characterize the process of long-term spiritual transformation of consciousness.

Sometimes, when I am giving a presentation, I draw an analogy with the development of color vision to illustrate this long-term process. A person having a profound STEP would be like a person living in a color-blind society who, like everyone else, can only see in black and white—until suddenly he or she has an intense experience of full-spectrum color vision. This would radically alter the person's world view and have a definite transformational impact. People who have ongoing or recurrent STE activity can be compared to people with black and white vision having episodes in which they perceive one or two colors—perhaps primary colors like red or blue. This would enrich their lives and change their world view, but would have less transformational impact than a sudden change to full-color vision would have.

The changes in consciousness associated with paranormal symptoms are even more subtle and gradual. To continue the analogy, at first, after their STEP or STE of color vision, people would see only stark black and white, then between episodes of more colorful vision they might gradually start to see shades of gray, then faint hints of red, and then pure, bright red, and so on, coming gradually closer to full-spectrum vision over a long period of time. This gradual change in baseline consciousness and perceptions would not radically alter a person's world view or have any significant transformational impact, but would enrich their normal consciousness.

Most paranormal and spiritual symptoms seem to add to the experiencer's normal conscious functioning. Eventually they may become a permanent feature—and indication—of the transformation that has occurred in consciousness. For example, a woman who has had a profound mystical experience may notice that she is becoming more intuitive, and eventually she may begin to have premonitions or other types of psychic experiences. These experiences may become more frequent until they are an accepted part of her everyday inner life.

While many of these spiritual and paranormal symptoms are nondisruptive or even mildly positive or pleasurable, some may be disturbing or disconcerting in and of themselves. Others are disturbing to certain experiencers simply because they represent an unknown or are quite different, unusual, or even bizarre compared to the type of experience that the person has become accustomed to. For example, a deeply religious man may have experienced prayer-related mystical STEs of bliss and love so often in his life that he thinks of them as a beautiful part of existence. He may, however, be puzzled or distressed if he suddenly begins to have recurrent psychic visions that he can neither comprehend nor explain.

The following list of spiritual and paranormal symptoms associated with long-term spiritual transformation can reassure experiencers and let them know that it is perfectly normal to be having a wide range of experiences and symptoms of varying intensity. In addition, the list contains strategies that I have found helpful to experiencers in dealing with symptoms that are distressful.

I have organized these spiritual and paranormal symptoms into five broad categories: (1) the mystical and spiritual; (2) kundalini; (3) the psychic and paranormal; (4) changes in dream life, and (5) changes in visual perception. Experiencers may have symptoms from any or all of the categories.

Spiritual and paranormal symptoms tend to develop in the same way that other symptoms do: Most frequently, they first occur when the experiencer is actually taking part in a spiritual practice such as meditating, praying, doing yoga, reading spiritual works, or asking for spiritual guidance. They tend to occur more frequently when the experiencer is spending a lot of time in spiritual practice. The symptoms also tend to be more marked just after STEPs or during high STE activity. Later, the symptoms may begin to occur at any time and, eventually, become part of normal conscious functioning. The symptoms come to represent a richer state of consciousness than the one the experiencer had before the spiritual transformation process began.

Symptoms Associated with the Mystical and Spiritual

Symptoms associated with the mystical and spiritual may include subtle or minor experiences of any type listed in Chapter

Two. The following, however, are the ones that tend to cross boundaries and become ongoing, recurrent symptoms of the process of spiritual transformation as a whole.

Positive Spiritual Symptoms

Prayer or meditation related mystical visions. Visions of gurus, saints, or religious figures that appear recurrently during meditation, intense prayer, or spiritual contemplation. This symptom is often reported by long-time meditators who eventually begin to have repeated visions of their guru or of other spiritual figures during deep meditation. These visions can also occur spontaneously and at any time but are more usual during different types of spiritual contemplation. The experience is uplifting and inspiring, but not as transformational in impact as an STE.

Bliss. Recurrent feelings of deep inner happiness or waves of bliss and peace, sometimes experienced as an inexplicable urge to laugh or smile radiantly. Bliss may become a frequent occurence during meditation. Bliss symptoms may last from hours to days.

Union. Recurrently feeling the unity of all things, oneness with God/Brahman/Allah and with all creation; certainty that all is right in the universe; recurrent sensations of merging with a person, a thing such as a tree, or the universe. While unitive experiences are usually STEPs in themselves, milder, much less intense feelings of union may occur, recur, or last for fairly long periods of time—often after a STEP. Feelings of union may also manifest as a mild blurring of personal boundaries, a feeling of melding with nature or others.

Higher guidance. Occasional, ongoing, or recurrent impressions of being able to ask your higher self or the Higher Power for guidance or being able to tap into the divine cosmic intelligence to ask for and receive guidance. The guidance coming from the higher self or divine source may appear in a variety of ways. For instance, it may be experienced in dreams, felt in terms of a sudden, inner urge, heard as a voice inside the head, seen as words flashing across the mind, seen as a clear visual image, or appear as a symbolic visual image in the mind's eye (e.g., seeing a red light that means "no" or a green light that means "yes"). Some people feel surges or rushes of energy through the body; a certain type of sensation, for example, might indicate for a particular person that a decision is correct or that something they have just heard is particularly important.

Divine inspiration. Occasional, ongoing, or recurrent feelings that a higher spiritual source is inspiring you, guiding you, and encouraging you, often to work for the betterment of humankind or to work for humanitarian goals. This divine inspiration may take such forms as innovative ideas for public-service projects; creative compassionate solutions to complex life-problems; ideas for inspirational presentations, workshops, or talks; and ideas for socially minded articles or books.

Expansions of consciousness. Occasional, recurrent, or ongoing sensations of consciousness being expanded beyond the size of the head. This may last for minutes, hours, or even weeks.

Higher guidance is probably the most common spiritual symptom reported by STE experiencers. I have received higher guidance many times, most notably during the airplane crash in which I had my NDE. As I described in Chapter One, a voice inside my head repeatedly urged me, "Swim to shore!" Swimming to shore undoubtedly helped save my life.

A similar episode of higher guidance happened to me a few years ago.

> *I had been diagnosed by my gynecologist as having an ovarian cyst. I chose to not have surgery, hoping that the cyst would slowly resolve on its own. One morning, while I was in the kitchen making a cup of coffee, I was suddenly stabbed with searing lower abdominal pain. I doubled over and grabbed the edge of the counter, close to fainting from the pain. My husband had already left for work, and I was alone in the house with my infant son, who was sleeping*

upstairs in his crib. Overwhelmed by the pain, I collapsed to the floor. I prayed to God for help.

Suddenly a voice in my head said, "Lie on your back!" I could barely find the strength, but somehow I forced myself to roll over. Within seconds the pain began to fade. I remained on my back for several minutes, until the pain went away completely. I realized that the ovarian cyst must have ruptured, and the excruciating pain was due to internal bleeding. Somehow, lying on my back had made the bleeding stop. When I rose a few minutes later to tend to my son, I felt weak but pain-free. Later tests confirmed that my cyst had ruptured.

I can only attribute the inner voice that aided me in both situations to some higher wisdom.

Negative Spiritual Symptoms

The idea that dark forces, demons, and/or the devil might actually exist is a frightening one. And although it is beyond the scope of this book to discuss concepts of evil, it must be recognized that some people undergoing STEs believe absolutely that they have had experiences that involve evil or dark forces. A number of highly credible people have told me they have experienced "negative visions" or "evil presence."

Negative visions. Occasional or recurring visions of such things as Satan, the anti-Christ, devils, demons, evil spirits, or horrible scenarios that feature such personifications of evil. Like classic mystical visions, these sometimes appear before the open eyes of the experiencer, but more frequently they appear on what is sometimes called the "screen of the mind" or simply flash in front of the mind's eye.

Evil presence. Occasional or recurring sensations that the experiencer is in the presence of an evil force, the devil, the forces of darkness, or demonic entities. In some cases the experiencer even feels temporarily taken over or possessed by these dark forces or entities. Sometimes it seems as if for a short period of time negative, fearful, or paranoid thoughts—such as thoughts that God cannot be trusted—are being "put into" the person's mind by some external force.

Two of the cases of negative spiritual episodes that were reported to me were similar and seemed to follow the pattern that many of these episodes take. In both cases, the experiencers were women who suddenly sensed an evil presence in the room with them. The sensation was quite strong and, as it occurred at night, they both instinctively felt a need to turn on the lights. They then asked the presence what it wanted and told it to leave. They felt that it was still there, however, and in both cases typical poltergeist phenomena such as objects falling from shelves and walls occurred throughout the night. They also heard footsteps in their rooms and felt movements across their beds. Both women began to repeat the Lord's Prayer and continued to pray throughout the night. In both cases, the negative presence seemed to vanish near dawn, and both women were able to fall into a peaceful sleep.

Coping with Negative Spiritual Symptoms

From the above two cases and others that I have heard of, it seems clear to me that both dark or demonic visions and the sensations of dark or demonic presences are best coped with through affirmations of the divine.

Focus on God and affirm that God's divine light and love are protecting you. Affirm the presence of divinity in yourself, in humanity, in the world, and in the universe. Hold images of divine white light or visions of a beloved spiritual master in your mind or repeat simple affirmations such as "God is with me." If you feel an inclination to repeat certain prayers or verses from the Bible or other holy books, do so. Pray to God/Brahman/Allah/Buddha to protect you. Repeat your spiritual master's name, and pray for his or her protection. Read the Bible or other holy books. Tell the demonic vision or presence to be gone, that you are God's child, that evil has no hold on you. Visualize divine light pouring down upon you, filling your entire being, and surrounding you in a bubble of divine energy and light. Tell the presence to go to the light and not to be afraid, that God loves it. Visualize yourself protected within a divine light bubble, egg, or crystal bell. Repeat the "Divine Light Invocation" that is found in Swami Sivananda Radha's *Kundalini Yoga for the West*:

> *I am created by divine light*
> *I am sustained by divine light*
> *I am protected by divine light*
> *I am surrounded by divine light*
> *I am ever growing into divine light*

If you do ever have this type of experience keep in mind the often-taught spiritual concept that negativity can have no hold on you as long as you focus on God, love, and light. Darkness cannot exist in the presence of the Light.

Of course, if you have found that a particular meditation technique, psychic exercise, or any other factor triggers negative spiritual episodes, stop doing it. If the episodes seem to be triggered by meditating in a certain place, try meditating elsewhere. If this is impossible, spend some time before you meditate visualizing the place cleansed and filled by all-loving, all-powerful divine white light.

Like many scientists, I approach the question of whether "demonic" entities exist with a healthy skepticism, but I have heard so many reports from credible people about these types of experiences that I have given the matter a great deal of thought. There are many possible interpretations of these experiences. One tentative hypothesis is that experiences of demonic entities or presences may be related to the multi-dimensional nature of our universe. As mentioned in Chapter Six, mystics and seers have reported "seeing" vast numbers of dimensions populated with disembodied spirits and diverse life forms beyond our imagination. Even physicists are now postulating that there are far more than four dimensions. If the life forms and disembodied spirits in other dimensions do indeed exist, they may vary in their levels of spiritual and moral development just as human beings vary in theirs. Some yogic traditions describe the etheric or "astral plane" as having levels, with less spiritually developed entities living on lower astral planes.

As the channels of perception in people who are undergoing spiritual transformation become more open, other types of entities may sometimes try to make contact. Less spiritually developed entities or those from "lower astral planes" may then be perceived as evil or demonic presences. (Sometimes our own unconscious fears may manifest as dark experiences, also.)

Of course, until far more research is done and our understanding of these matters is greatly increased, we have no objective way of knowing exactly what is going on when these types of negative experiences occur. Still, people should never, under any circumstances, attempt to experiment or "play" with dark forces in any way. Fortunately, everyone I have spoken to who has had an experience of a demonic presence—whatever the cause—was able eventually to vanquish it with prayer, faith, and mental focusing on the protection of divine light and love.

Symptoms Associated with Kundalini

Ongoing, mild kundalini-related symptoms commonly occur in people having long-term spiritual transformation. Although these symptoms may take the form of any of the characteristics of Spiritual Energy/Kundalini Episodes, the following seem to be the most common.

Cranial pressures. Sensations of energy pushing outward and upward through the top of the head; sometimes described as feeling as if a cone of energy was pushing up through the crown and sitting on the head or as if the top of the skull was open. In some cases, these sensations may involve an expansion of consciousness like the one associated with mystical states. Like other symptoms, they can last for varying lengths of time. One experiencer reported that she had these types of sensations last for hours, even when doing mundane chores like driving to the cottage or cleaning the house. Following a STEP, varying degrees of cranial pressure or sensations of expansion sometimes remain for months.

Inner sounds. Recurrent or continuous sounds that do not come from external stimuli. They are commonly reported as being like the humming sound of bees, the musical murmur of a distant brook, the chirping of crickets, the low-pitched rumbling of a distant motor, the roaring of a distant waterfall, the rushing sound of wind or large wings beating, the fine tinkling of distant bells or wind chimes, or the ringing of church bells. Like all the symptoms listed in this section, they are more common at first during spiritual practices. In addition, inner sounds are often more marked in the middle of the night. Many people report hearing inner sounds constantly for many years following an initial STEP. The types of sounds tend to change over time. Sometimes one type of sound is superimposed on another. For example, I sometimes hear the fine tinkling of distant bells—the most common sound for me—superimposed on a sound similar to the low-pitched roar of a distant waterfall.

Energies up the spine. Recurrent or ongoing sensations of energy or heat rushing up the spine; vibrating or tickling sensations in the lower back; gentle sensations like a liquid moving up the spine; sensations of sucking in the genital area sometimes followed by the feeling that something is moving upwards toward the brain. These symptoms often occur when one has a deep psychological or spiritual insight, admires a scene of natural beauty, or performs an act of selfless service.

Light experiences. Recurrent or ongoing sensations that one's consciousness is filled with light; the perception that normal external light or lighting is much brighter than it was before; the perception that objects or living things such as plants are radiating light. Observers sometimes report that the experiencer's face seems to radiate with an inner light.

An eighty-two-year-old patient of mine whom I'll call Ivy provides a good example of how light symptoms sometimes manifest. When Ivy was seventy-eight, during a cataract operation, she had an NDE that was a profound STEP.

After the NDE, Ivy began to have STEs in the form of repeated mystical insights and developed a tremendous new depth of insight into the meaning of scriptures. The surgery was not successful, and Ivy was declared legally blind. However, she developed a new type of visual experience. Although her limited physical vision allowed her to see only vague shadows and shades of gray, she began to have experiences of light. At times, she said, the room she was in would suddenly appear to be flooded with light. These episodes became recurrent and could happen at any time of the day or night—even when she was in total darkness.

A fifty-five-year-old businessman from California whom I'll call Richard provides a more general example of how the symptoms related to kundalini can occur or develop over a period of time.

Richard had his first STEP when he was forty; it was a profound mystical experience that changed him from a materialistic businessman to a person devoted to spiritual growth and to working for world peace. After his experience, he began a regular practice of meditation and deep prayer. Over the years he had a number of STEs involving mystical visions and occasional episodes of inspired spiritual insights.

Richard also developed two ongoing kundalini symptoms that were not strong enough to be thought of as STEs, but were still strong indicators that he was undergoing long-term spiritual transformation. One was recurrent, sporadic rushes of energy up his spine. The other was constant inner sounds. Richard describes his experience of sound as varying from the roar of a distant waterfall to the buzzing of bees, to the tinkling of bells. The experience of inner sound is always with Richard, and, over time, has become part of his normal conscious functioning. He recognizes it as part of his personal spiritual process and is very comfortable with it.

Symptoms Associated with the Psychic and Paranormal

Psychic and paranormal symptoms tend to be some of the most commonly experienced by people in long-term transformation. In the KRN Questionnaire pilot project, 90 percent of mystical and kundalini experiencers reported that they eventually began to have recurrent psychic or paranormal experiences. Often experiencers don't know what to call these unusual subtle experiences and, at first, do not think of them as being "psychic" in nature.

When these symptoms occur, they sometimes seem to impart information that the experiencer can use in a positive or helpful way. At other times the psychic symptoms seem to reflect the increased sensitivity of the experiencer to the thoughts and feelings of others. Over time many experiencers go through a kind of trial-and-error learning process in which they gradually learn to interpret with increasing accuracy the meaning of symbolic images or particular sensations and to develop an appropriate perspective concerning the validity of the messages they are receiving.

Positive Psychic Symptoms

Enhanced intuition and psychic messages. Most experiencers notice that their intuition seems to become more enhanced and pronounced over time. Intuitive flashes may become so clear that they appear to the experiencer as messages. These messages may be sensed or felt in any way. They are often perceived with the inner eye or ear as words, sounds, or visual symbols, or they may be felt as strong impulses. They may even become so pronounced that they seem to be physically seen, heard, or felt. For example, many people report that they felt a sudden strong inclination to open a spiritual book, did so, and discovered a passage that had deep significance for them at the time.

This type of experience may also take the form of a direct message. A friend of mine had been wondering about the answer to a specific question when, out of the blue, his inner ear heard the words "Go to the library" and an image of the library flashed in his mind. He felt compelled to go. At the library, he received another message which told him to go to the rear bookshelf. There, he had an urge to grab a certain book off the shelf. He skimmed through the book and suddenly found the answer to the question that had been plaguing him.

Psychic messages may also appear in the form of symbols like a red or green light or the words "yes" or "no" flashing across the screen of the mind. Like other spiritual and paranormal symptoms, increased intuition and psychic messages often initially occur more frequently during activities such as prayer or meditation.

Clairsentience. The ability to feel the emotion or pain that another is feeling seems to be the most common psychic symptom developed by people undergoing STEs. It includes the ability to sense or locate pain in another's body by experiencing it—or perceiving it in some way—in one's own body. For instance, when a woman who is developing clairsentience is near an individual who is in mental turmoil, she might feel a pressure sensation in the third-eye region. When near a person who is very sad, she might feel a pressure in the region of her own heart chakra. When near a person who is in physical pain, she might feel physical pain exactly where the other person is experiencing it. These clairsentient perceptions usually occur spontaneously. Most people developing this symptom do not, at first, understand what it is. Later, they begin to understand that they are becoming increasingly sensitive to the emotions and mental states of others.

Premonitions. Premonitions were mentioned in Chapter Six as being a form of precognition and, of course, they are. However, precognition is a more powerful experience than are premonitions when they first begin to appear as symptoms. At this time, they are often simply strong hunches or quick intuitive flashes that give a hint that something is going to happen. For instance, a woman might, when asked on a date, have a feeling that she shouldn't go, even though the man who has asked her seems to be very nice. But because she has never had a premonition before and was never particularly intuitive before her STEs began, she—

using her rational mind—decides to ignore her hunch. When she does go out with the man, he makes an unsolicited pass at her and, although she isn't harmed, she has a very unpleasant evening. After experiences like this in which premonitions are proven to be correct, most experiencers learn to pay more attention to them. As time goes on they also learn how to better interpret their premonitions and understand more clearly what they mean. Like other symptoms, premonitions may increase in frequency and intensity over time and develop into clear-cut premonitions or powerful instances of psychic precognition. They may also become clearer. Most people undergoing STEs find that, over time, they begin to repeatedly have premonitions concerning significant life events. These often appear in dreams.

In the last few years I have often been given premonitions in my dreams regarding major events in my life. A dramatic instance related to my dear, and now deceased, grandfather.

About four years ago, I was scheduled to make a presentation at a medical conference in Oxford, England. My life was very busy, so I had planned to fly to England the day before the conference and return to Canada the day after. About two weeks before the conference, I had a dream which told me to visit my grandfather (who lived in Switzerland) after the conference. I was told it would be my final visit with him.

At first I tried to put the dream out of my head, but somehow it kept haunting me all day. Finally, late in the day, I phoned my travel agent and asked if she could book me a two-day side-trip from England to Switzerland. (My schedule was very tight and I could not go for more than two days.) The side-trip was inexpensive and very easy to arrange. I then went to the conference, proceeded on to Switzerland and had a wonderful visit with my grandfather. We discussed my near-death experience and other STEs in great detail, and he told me about some of his experiences. When I flew back to Canada I felt a very strong, close bond with my grandfather.

About two months later, I had a clear dream in which my grandfather appeared to me. His face was as I had never seen it—the face of his youth—and he was radiant and beaming me love. There was no verbal communication in this dream, but I somehow knew that my grandfather had died, and that he had come to say a loving goodbye to me. About half an hour later my telephone rang. I knew immediately what the message was that I was about to hear: Grandpa had died.

Frequent synchronicities. The concept of synchronicity was developed largely by Dr. Carl Jung. Synchronistic events are often defined simply as meaningful coincidences. Synchronicities take infinite forms and can have many types and levels of meaning; however, they all seem to suggest to the experiencer that some Higher Power or higher intelligence is guiding them or validating their insights. A Native Canadian spiritual elder undergoing spiritual transformation for many years recently gave me an excellent example of synchronicity.

> *The elder had been invited to a Native community in Nova Scotia and been asked to re-introduce a number of Native spiritual concepts to the adults in the community, since they had all been sent to Roman Catholic boarding schools as children and had received only that religious training. The group was gathered outside to begin the lesson. The elder began by telling the crowd that he had come to teach the way of contact with the Creator through nature. Just as he said these words, four eagles flew overhead and began to circle lower and lower until they were right above the crowd. In the Native spiritual tradition, the eagle is the totem or symbol for connecting with the Great Spirit, the Creator. Many people present were deeply moved by this example of synchronicity.*

A great many experiencers notice synchronicities for the first time after their STEs begin—or notice that this type of event begins to occur much more frequently than before. When it does occur, synchronicity is often delightful and, frequently, deeply enriching. For many people, it is yet another sign that a divine, loving, and unimaginably vast intelligence is running the universe.

Past-life memories. Many people in long-term spiritual transformation find that at some point they begin to experience the spontaneous memory of relationships or events that seem to be from past lives. Often these memories may mirror present life situations and/or help experiencers understand current relationships, reaction patterns, or life problems. These past-life memories may come in dreams or meditations, or be triggered by a location, person, or event. I will discuss this in more depth in Chapter Sixteen. A number of other psychic and paranormal experiences listed in Chapter Six can also appear in milder form as symptoms.

It is important to realize that even subtle paranormal symptoms can be disconcerting—especially when the experiencer doesn't understand what they are. Labeling the symptom is helpful because it defines it, puts it within certain parameters, and helps the experiencer realize it is something he or she can adjust to or deal with.

Psychic Disorders

The idea that psychic disorders might occur to some people undergoing the process of transformation is disconcerting at best and frightening at worst. It is important for STE experiencers to realize that psychic disorders do not occur to the vast majority of people involved in the process of spiritual transformation, and that, if they do occur, there are a number of effective strategies for dealing with them.

Many thoughtful people have difficulty in accepting the idea of psychic disorders—even those who accept the majority of concepts associated with spiritual transformation. This is particularly true in the case of the symptoms labeled here as channeling disorders, psychic assault, and possession. And, while these concepts are difficult for some spiritually open thinkers to accept, they are completely unacceptable to traditionally oriented thinkers. Nevertheless, the people who experience them perceive them as real—and I have found that many of these people are credible and mentally healthy. Further, anyone who experiences any of these symptoms is in pain and needs help.

Painful clairsentience. This symptom can manifest in any of the ways that regular clairsentience does but much more strongly. It is not unusual for a person who is clairsentient to feel some pain or uncomfortable pressure when perceiving another's distress or pain. In painful clairsentience, however, experiencers feel severe pain or pressure and often find it difficult to function when these sensations are occurring. Painful clairsentience often takes the form of an excruciating headache. This was true in the case of Jeneane, the businesswoman whose painful clairsentience I described in Chapter Six. When she was with people experiencing anger or mental turmoil, she developed a severe pain in her mid-forehead. When she was with persons experiencing great sadness, she felt central chest pain.

People with painful clairsentience may become extremely sensitive to negative emotions and emotional turmoil in general. In crowded public places, especially ones that are closed in and do not allow them to get out at will, such as subway cars and transit buses, these people often feel as if they are being bombarded by negative emotions. They also frequently report feeling tremendous discomfort or pain when they are in the presence of people with severe emotional or psychiatric difficulties.

Excessive clairvoyance. This symptom, too, differs in degree from its regular counterpart. The experiencer clairvoyantly receives too much information and is unable to stop or block the input. Some experiencers report being bombarded by visual images or symbols of such things as another person's actions, spiritual conflicts, physical problems, or past-life issues. Such constant bombardment can put a great strain on everything from interpersonal relationships to casual conversations.

Intrusive past-life memories. In this disorder, one's own past-life memories surface too rapidly, too intensely, or too frequently. They may be so distracting that the experiencer has difficulty functioning in daily life. Some experiencers also become confused about how psychological issues from past lives overlap with those from current life situations.

When past-life memories become too overwhelming or when the psychological issues they represent cannot be dealt with, they can precipitate crises or spiritual emergencies (as explained in Chapter Fourteen).

Horrific visions. The visions common to this disorder are recurrent, persistent, and horrific and cause tremendous mental distress. They can be almost unbearable and even at times, as mentioned in Chapter Thirteen, be associated with a temporary psychosis. These visions often include scenes of atrocities humans have committed against other humans, such as torture, mutilation, or nuclear war; or gruesome or evil figures suddenly appearing in buildings, windows, shadows, or trees. Without warning, a lovely visual image may turn into a horrifying one. Sometimes horrific visions can become personal and feature the self or loved ones being tortured, mutilated, or terrorized.

Possession. Although little is known scientifically about possession, and the phenomenon is not yet widely recognized, many respected scholars have documented it. I have hypothesized that it may be related to multi-dimensional phenomena such as UFOs and "evil presences." Some similar ideas have been put forward by Dr. M. Scott Peck in *People of the Lie* and by Adam Crabtree in *Multiple Man: Explorations in Possession and Multiple Personality*—two informative, if controversial, books.

In this psychic disorder, a spirit entity appears to have entered the experiencer's body against his or her will. The intruding spirit seems to struggle to control the experiencer's actions or thoughts. In some cases, a split may occur, with the experiencer's personality and the spirit personality surfacing and controlling at different times. According to Crabtree, the experiencer may be unaware of the invasion, and the condition may be confused with multiple personality disorder.

People who believe they are experiencing possession need to seek help from either a spiritual counselor or a psychotherapist, or perhaps even both. Fortunately, this disorder can be dealt with on a number of psychological and spiritual levels.

Channeling disorders. Characterized by the experiencer's inability to take voluntary, conscious control of a channeling experience, these disorders take several forms:

1. The channeled "entities" may seem to be able to force the experiencer to lapse into trances so that channeling can proceed, even when the experiencer has no desire to channel at that time.

2. More than one entity may appear to be attempting to channel through the experiencer at the same time. The experiencer may hear the different entities and feel the tension and conflict as they vie for the controlling or dominant position.

3. Negative entities may appear to be attempting to channel through the experiencer. These entities are often described as using foul language, being harsh and critical, and communicating concepts that are tormenting to the experiencer.

4. Negative or morally questionable entities appear to masquerade as gurus, angels, divine guardians, beings from "higher dimensions," or even God. Rather than being humbling and uplifting like true contact with the divine, these experiences inflate the ego, make the experiencer feel special, and may even trick him or her into acting inappropriately.

Since channeling disorders may sometimes be confused with and closely mimic schizophrenia or mania, anyone who seems to be suffering from them should seek counseling so that the true source of the problem can be determined.

Psychic assault or telepathic invasion. In this disorder, it seems that the experiencer is not able to block invasive techniques being used by an unscrupulous or immoral person with psychic abilities. Reported experiences of this type include thoughts, visual images, messages, or even physical sensations that intrude on the experiencer's mind or being and clearly seem to come from a specific outside source. Often the experiencer has a very clear sense of the identity of the invader.

Some contemporary spiritual teachers believe that psychic powers cannot, in reality, be used for such evil purposes; others believe that they can. Future research will show which view is correct. In the meantime, however, the fact remains that credible people report having these experiences. One was a highly educated, articulate nurse I'll call Rachel. Rachel's life was dramatically disrupted after a sudden psychic awakening that occurred when she was thirty-one.

I met Karl through some associates at the office. When he asked me out for a date, I decided to go, since I thought there could be no harm in one dinner date. During the date, Karl told me that he was a practicing "wicken" or warlock. I didn't know what to think of this, as he went on to describe his somewhat unbelievable psychic abilities. It seemed to me that he liked to play psychic games.

I was very surprised to find myself very strongly physically attracted to him by the end of the evening. When he kissed me goodnight, I felt what seemed like an electric current run through my body. From that moment onward I started receiving telepathic messages from him. I found this interesting, because I had never previously had any psychic experiences.

Karl had to leave town for business reasons, and I did not see him again for six weeks. Two weeks after he left, however, I had an extremely strange experience that I can only describe as feeling as if I was being psychically sexually assaulted by him. I was lying in bed, about to go to sleep, when I got the sensation that my body was being sexually stimulated. I knew telepathically that it was Karl. I felt my genitals become moist and excited, my abdomen was heaving, as if being stroked, and my breasts were protruding with nipples erect. I felt my back arch repeatedly, and I had the sensation of sexual intercourse. The experience was so vivid that I could actually smell the odor of semen. Initially I found the whole experience intensely pleasurable. Then, I suddenly became overwhelmed with a sense of guilt, anger, and shame. I barely knew Karl, and our relationship was not at a stage where I would consider being sexually intimate. I felt as though I had been raped psychically.

I continued receiving strong telepathic communications from Karl but was able to resist them from this point on. However, I continued to feel so attracted to him that I went out with him again about a month after my psychic encounter with him. I felt very uncomfortable, as if we had actually already had sex together. It seemed natural that the next logical step was to physically have sex, so we did. When I had my climax from our lovemaking, I felt my consciousness slip out of my body. I was floating above our two bodies, looking down at us below. After a few moments, my spirit re-entered my body.

From that instant onward, I had repeated and increasingly dramatic psychic experiences. These experiences were uncontrollable. I would look at a person and know things about them. I would accurately locate pain in other people's bodies by feeling it in my own. I had accurate premonitions about friends and relatives, as well as about world events. I could clearly see auras and people's chakra activity.

I could not seem to turn off the psychic input. Finally I had to take a leave of absence from work until these psychic energies slowed down. I cut off all contact with Karl. I was angry that he had admittedly deliberately tried to stimulate my psychic energies without my consent, and had psychically invaded me sexually that evening against my will.

Rachel found a number of things that helped her get her feet back on the ground after her tumultuous psychic awakening and the period that followed. She took a four-month leave of absence from work. During this period she focused on "grounding" herself, started psychotherapy, and worked on resolving the psychological and spiritual issues that began to surface as part of her process. Although Rachel's psychic gifts have continued to develop, the pace has slowed and she has learned to filter and integrate the input so that it does not interfere with her day-to-day functioning.

I should stress that reports of psychic assault, especially in this degree, are rare. I also believe there are ways we can help prevent psychic disorders of all types.

Causes of Psychic Disorders

Psychic disorders can be very distressing and disruptive to a person's daily functioning. However, I and other psychotherapists working in this field have found that a great deal can be done to alleviate these symptoms.

In my clinical experience I have found a relationship between psychic disorders and excessive or inappropriate types of meditation. For example, painful clairsentience, excessive clairvoyance, and intrusive past-life memories are experienced most commonly, although not exclusively, by people who are meditating excessively. In terms of kundalini theory, this excessive meditation could overstimulate the brahma randhra and activate paranormal channels of perception prematurely or too rapidly or intensively.

When this happens in relation to psychic disorders, an analogy can be drawn between the activation of these paranormal channels and a radio receiver. In the case of painful clairsentience, excessive clairvoyance, and intrusive past-life memories, and perhaps some cases of horrific visions, the radio receiver can be thought of as having a broken volume control. The psychic input comes blaring in so loudly and powerfully that it disrupts the experiencer's normal thought processes or detracts from his or her ability to function in the world.

Channeling disorders and other types of disorders which feature some type of invading or intrusive entity or force seem to be related to inappropriate meditation practices, in particular ones that leave the inner self open to input from anyone or anything in the cosmos. These inappropriate techniques may include such dangerously open affirmations as "I open myself to the universe" when, in fact, one should not open oneself to anything but the divine!

In intrusive channeling disorders, the altered perception might be likened to a radio receiver with a broken fine-tuning control that allows hundreds of different signals to pour in without any means of filtering out the undesirable ones.

From my clinical experience I have come to the conclusion that psychic disorders are real and, consequently, that "playing games" with psychic energies, deliberately opening yourself indiscriminately to other dimensions, or dabbling with occult powers can be very dangerous. This may well be why the religious traditions that have recognized the development of psychic gifts have also emphasized that they are simply a by-product of spiritual development and that they should not be focused upon excessively or striven after.

Coping with Psychic Disorders

The following are some of the strategies I have found effective in dealing with psychic disorders. Although they overlap to some extent with other helpful strategies mentioned throughout the book and detailed in the final three chapters, they are summarized here for easy reference.

Adopt a more grounding lifestyle. Grounding activities are particularly helpful in slowing down the activity of the brahma randhra. As detailed in Chapter Fifteen, they include stopping all forms of meditation, cutting back on concentration, eating more regularly, decreasing activities such as yoga or Tai Chi, participating in physical exercise, and taking a holiday from your work and daily stresses.

Visualize your chakras retracting and closing. For a short time each day, visualize the chakras closing up. Some people like to visualize them first as open roses or lotus blossoms and then visualize the petals gently closing up and the open flowers turning back into buds.

Visualize a protective bubble. Begin every day with a short visualization that affirms the presence of the divine light within you. Then visualize this divine white light expanding outward and forming a protective bubble or egg around you. (Some people find it more effective to visualize a crystal bell or a thick protective wall.) Affirm that the barrier acts like a one-way mirror, allowing your positive energies and love to shine out, but not allowing external negative energies to penetrate. Affirm that the divine light is protecting you.

Prepare yourself for situations you think might be difficult by using this strategy, and repeat it if distressing psychic input begins.

Cleansing negative energy. When you feel negative energy around you or being projected at you, take a moment to visualize it in your mind's eye, perhaps as a gray cloud. See this cloud being cleansed from your aura or subtle body. Some people like to imagine something like a giant sponge that washes over them and removes the negative cloud. Others like to perform something like the yoga "ha" breath that is believed to cleanse the subtle body. Still others like to visualize the gray cloud and see it coalescing into a small ball that can easily be thrown into a flame of love and divine light that destroys it. Some people send the energy back where it came from with wishes of love and light.

Remove yourself from negative environments. If you find that a particular situation, for example a room filled with extremely tense, angry, or hostile people, is causing negative psychic input, remove yourself. If you can't leave for good, go to the washroom or go for a walk in the building for several minutes. While you're out, visualize your protective bubble, affirm the divine presence, and visualize your chakras closing. In future, avoid entering similar settings whenever possible.

Mitigate horrific visions. When these visions occur, turn your thoughts inward and focus on God or spiritual concepts and affirm the divine. Some experiencers also find the visions can be turned around and used in a positive way as an impetus to work towards improving the world situation. In most cases, horrific visions stop on their own after a period of time. If they do not, they can often be helped by many of the strategies used in dealing with crises and spiritual emergencies.

Attune yourself to God only. No matter what images you see, what sensations you feel, or what other psychic input you receive, focus yourself totally and only on the divine. Say familiar prayers, read holy scriptures, focus on uplifting spiritual passages or concepts, and pray that God's divine light will shine on you and cast out the darkness. Affirm that God's voice is the only voice you will hear or listen to. Affirm that God is present in you at all times. Pray for God's direction, guidance, and grace to rid you of all negative psychic input. If you are experiencing intrusive energies, tell them that you are God's child, protected by God, and that they have no hold on you.

Pray for protection. Pray to the Divine to protect you and shield you from negative psychic influences. Repeat your prayers as often as you feel the need during the day. Many people have learned that such simple prayers can be the most powerful of strategies.

Changes in Dream Life

Most STE experiencers notice a gradual and increasing change in their dream life after their spiritual experiences begin that is yet another symptom of the transformation of consciousness. The content of the dreams may change in a number of ways. Experiencers' dreams often contain more premonitions than those of people not undergoing STEs. Common premonitions include warnings that loved ones need medical attention or may soon die, or that something negative—and sometimes preventable—is going to happen. For example, a woman may dream repeatedly that a particular man at work is trying to discredit her in order to make himself look better. When the woman discovers this is, in fact, true she can then begin to take precautions to protect herself and her job. Experiencers' dreams also often seem to contain more messages about major life issues than they did before the STEs began. Although it is thought that everyone's dreams contain this type of information, the dreams of experiencers often seem to be more clear, dramatic, or easily interpreted than they were before the experiences.

Dream content may also become increasingly complex, with intricate, detailed plots and complete story lines. Experiencers sometimes report feeling as if they are living in a movie or a short novel during their dreams. Some experiencers report spontaneously developing lucid dreams—the ability to be consciously aware of the dream while it is going on and to alter or influence the path the dream is taking. Lucid dreaming frequently occurs during twilight sleep, the period just prior to actual sleep, or just before waking.

Also during twilight sleep, unusual visual images may seem to flash rapidly across the screen of the mind. The images are frequently of scenes and—even more often—faces that are unfamiliar to the experiencer. Although they begin spontaneously and seem to flash uncontrollably, they usually stop on their own after a few minutes.

Dreams that deal with spiritual themes often become more frequent. Some of these are inspirational and guide the experiencers into ways of expressing themselves in more spiritual or humanitarian ways. Others receive creative guidance in their dreams. For instance, Ellen, the artist mentioned in Chapter Seven, received all the subject matter for her paintings in her dreams. Synchronicity in dreams often increases. It also becomes more common for experiencers to receive answers or solutions to problems that have been plaguing them. These solutions may come either in a dream or immediately on waking.

The dreams themselves—not just their content—also often begin to change. One of the most common is an increase or change in color perception. People who dreamed in black and white before their STEs often begin to dream in color after them. Sometimes people only realize that they once normally dreamed in black and white after they begin to dream in color. In time, the color in their dreams may become far more intense, vivid, or brilliant. For some, it may even become luminescent. People may also begin to remember more of their dreams.

Many people find it helpful to their personal development and their process of spiritual transformation to begin to pay more attention to their dreams and also begin to remember them more frequently. Keeping a dream journal has long been recognized as an effective tool. Dreams should be recorded in the journal in as much detail as possible immediately on awakening. Once the dreams are written down, they should be reflected upon and possible significance, meanings, and interpretations noted. Sometimes the symbolic meaning of dreams only becomes clear hours or days afterwards. During the process of keeping a dream journal, many people begin to remember far more dreams than they ever did before. They also notice that their dreams seem to contain more guidance and more information that helps them in their growth and spiritual development. The analysis of dreams may be a key factor in the psychological housecleaning that is so much a part of the process of spiritual transformation, and is, in fact, recommended for spiritual seekers in Patanjali's *Yoga-Sutras*.

Changes in Visual Perception

One change in visual perception that accompanies STEs is an increased capacity to perceive beauty and intricacy of detail, particularly in nature. Simple things, such as a flower, an insect, or the ripples on a pond may appear more beautiful than ever before. Such images—or larger ones such as sunsets or mountain vistas—may cause entrancement, awe, rapture, or overwhelming devotion to the divine.

Some experiencers also report that objects in the physical world seem far more vivid or even glow with an inner light. For some the outer world becomes luminescent. Things in the visual field may also seem more whitish in color than before—almost as if they had been dusted with a white or silvery powder.

Other experiencers perceive what appears to be a fine cosmic energy everywhere around them. Experiencers sometimes say they feel as if they are "seeing air" or perceiving prana. One experiencer characterized it as seeing an "energy snow." For some, microscopically minute energy particles seem to vibrate everywhere in the field of vision, while others perceive patterns in this cosmic energy that are specific to different plants, animals, or even other people's emotional states.

These changes in visual perception can be disconcerting, and the experiencer should be given a thorough examination to make sure no medical problems exist. However, once a person adjusts to having these new visual perceptions, they are generally found to be tremendously enriching, serving as a constant reminder of the infinite beauty in the world and the ultimate oneness of all things.

In general, I think the commonality we have seen throughout the last three chapters in types of associated symptoms—no matter what type of STE a person has had predominantly—supports the idea that all STEs have a common biological-psychological-spiritual base. Certainly the preliminary results of the KRN Questionnaire project indicate that this may be the case. I also think that the various patterns of increasing intensity and frequency the symptoms follow over time are the result of the increasing levels of activity in the transforming brahma randhra.

CHAPTER 13

Spiritual Emergencies and Psychoses

Many of the case histories we have examined so far have shown us that the spiritual journey—for all its bliss, joy, and wonder—is not always an easy one. The transformation process itself requires us to examine both our world view and ourselves with piercing honesty and to make changes that may be difficult or painful. And sometimes our friends and family are not always as supportive as we need or want them to be.

Beyond this, the process of spiritual transformation can sometimes lead to emotional and mental turmoil that is extremely difficult to deal with. For some people, the intensity and/or the content of the experiences becomes overwhelming and they have great difficulty in coping. This crisis situation is sometimes called a spiritual emergency. If the difficulties move beyond this level of intensity and a person becomes so disturbed that they lose their ability to function in society or lose their contact with reality, the person becomes, by definition, psychotic. Fortunately, in many cases, the difficulties are only temporary. Still, they involve periods of tremendous turmoil and suffering. For this reason, much of the rest of this book is dedicated to information that can help people adjust to STEs and work harmoniously with the process of spiritual transformation, so that crises and emergencies are minimized or avoided. Let me start by looking in detail at how some of these crises and difficulties manifest themselves and what some of their causes might be.

Spiritual Emergence and Spiritual Emergency

The terms "spiritual emergence," "spiritual emergency," and "Spiritual Emergence Syndrome" have been coined by California psychiatrist Stanislav Grof and his wife Christina. According to the Grofs, spiritual emergence is the process of spiritual transformation and growth, whereas spiritual emergencies are "dramatic experiences and unusual states of mind that traditional psychiatry diagnoses and treats as mental illness that are actually crises of personal transformation." The Spiritual Emergence Syndrome is a cluster of types of "crises of personal transformation" that offer "an opportunity of rising to a new level of [spiritual] awareness." By their definition, the syndrome includes (1) shamanic crisis, (2) awakening of kundalini, (3) episodes of unitive consciousness, (4) psychological renewal through return to center, (5) psychic opening, (6) past life experiences, (7) communications with spirit guides and channeling, (8) near-death experiences, (9) UFO encounters, and (10) possession states.

The Grofs and some of the others involved in the Spiritual Emergence Network tend to think of kundalini awakening as one subtype of the syndrome rather than seeing it as a model to understand all types of Spiritually Transformative Experiences, and most Spiritual Emergence experiences. Future research will clarify these points.

No discussion of the Spiritual Emergence Syndrome is complete without mentioning Emma Bragdon, another California therapist. Her *Sourcebook for Helping People in Spiritual Emergency* and *The Call of Spiritual Emergency* have done a great deal to help people understand the difficulties that are sometimes associated with the process of spiritual transformation. Much of her work is focused on sharing the approaches that she and other therapists at SEN have found most successful in helping people undergoing spiritual emergency.

David Lukoff, a California psychologist, is also doing research on spiritual emergencies. He has written several articles on what he calls "Transient Psychosis with Mystical Features." One of his main goals is to help the psychiatric community recognize that mystical experience is a normal expression of human consciousness that can, in some cases, be associated with transient—or temporary—psychotic features.

A Spectrum of Difficulties

It is helpful to view the range of difficulties that occurs throughout the spiritual process as a spectrum. At one end we have the difficult periods that occur from time to time in every long-term process of spiritual transformation. Then, along the spectrum are various types and degrees of crises, spiritual emergencies, and at the far end, psychoses. Like spiritual crises and emergencies, the different types of psychotic episodes last for varying lengths of time and may be recurrent.

Although almost everyone meets with some challenges on their spiritual journey, not everyone undergoing spiritual transformation will experience a spiritual emergency or psychotic episode. Spiritual emergencies can be a perfectly natural part of the spiritual process. I like to think of them as a "healing crisis." People who experience these phenomena do not have anything "wrong" with them; they are in no way less "normal" than those who don't, and they certainly are no less spiritual. In *The Call of Spiritual Emergency*, Emma Bragdon refers to the extremely difficult periods that Gopi Krishna endured as an example of serious spiritual emergency. He was sometimes unable to either work or attend to the business of daily life—and yet he went on to do ground-breaking kundalini research, write seventeen books, and see them translated into many languages, speak at scores of international conferences, and make a tremendous positive impact on the spiritual lives of thousands of people.

In my work, I have met many people undergoing spiritual transformation who have had extreme spiritual emergencies and who have worked through their difficulties to become more spiritually connected and emotionally adjusted than they were before.

Distinguishing Spiritual Transformation from Spiritual Emergency

Many people ask me how to distinguish between a crisis period in the process of spiritual transformation and a true spiritual emergency. The distinction depends primarily upon the psychological state of the person undergoing the awakening. Although every person's spiritual journey is unique, those people undergoing a relatively smooth process of transformation—punctuated as it may be by difficult periods or crises—share a number of overall attitudes and impressions.

In general, they feel enriched by their experiences and are aware, at some level, of being on a path of spiritual transformation and inner growth. For the most part, dramatic STEs and STEPs are cherished and seen as uplifting, inspiring events. These people function well in society and often hold responsible jobs and positions. They have a firm mental grasp of reality, understand clearly how others view reality, and are aware that their own personal paranormal experiences might be considered odd or "crazy" by many.

Since these people maintain an accurate perspective, they do not develop inflated or grandiose ideas about themselves or their experiences. Their intellectual functioning is generally clear—or even enhanced—and they make logical decisions. Discriminating between their inner and outer realities does not pose a problem. Their emotional responses are appropriate, and they have strong, healthy interpersonal relationships. Those people who are experiencing the traditional signs of kundalini activity find them pleasant or tolerable, or at least not disruptive to their ability to function in their daily lives. As part of the positive process of spiritual transformation, they are embracing their psycho-spiritual housecleaning and they tend to develop even stronger ethical values, humanitarian concerns, and convictions about the spiritual unity of all humanity.

Within this overall positive framework, difficult or crisis periods occur to almost everyone on the spiritual journey. A crisis—even a severe one—is almost always relatively short-lived and does not disrupt the person's ability to function in his or her daily life.

Spiritual emergencies, in contrast, can be extremely disruptive. People who are undergoing them tend to find their paranormal experiences severely challenging rather than uplifting. As long as the spiritual emergency continues, they generally do not welcome STEs and STEPs, for the intensity of these experiences is distracting, disturbing, and/or disorienting.

During a spiritual emergency people find it difficult or impossible to perform their daily duties. At best, they feel emotionally or spiritually off-balance. At worst, they are prone to periods of depression, anxiety, or mood swings. Although people going through spiritual emergencies generally have appropriate emotional responses, they may become extremely sensitive and sometimes have exaggerated emotional reactions. From time to time they may have difficulty judging whether their reactions and behavior are appropriate.

Even though their thought processes are still basically clear, people undergoing a spiritual emergency often have great difficulty integrating their paranormal experiences into their view of reality. They may also develop inflated, grandiose attitudes about themselves. A person might, for example, begin to think he is a prophet or to believe he has reached an extraordinary level of spiritual attainment. In some cases, paranoid tendencies may appear, causing the person to believe, for example, that the disturbing experience has been caused by a malevolent person or force. Inflated ideas and paranoid tendencies are, however, temporary. The person is able to come to grips with them and eventually dismiss them by using logic and rational thinking.

At times people who are going through spiritual emergency may also feel they are close to losing control, live in fear that they are going "crazy," or have difficulty distinguishing between inner and outer realities. Some people in spiritual emergency also see horrific visions or hear outbursts of tormenting inner voices. They usually realize that all these experiences are temporary and not based on physical reality. They are thus able to tolerate them until they pass.

However, people in an emergency episode may have difficulties communicating clearly and maintaining their interpersonal relationships. They are often preoccupied with their inner experiences, and other people may see them as "spaced out." Individuals having the classical signs of kundalini activity sometimes experience them as intense, disruptive, and even painful.

In spite of these difficulties, people in spiritual emergency generally maintain their ethical and moral values.

Distinguishing Spiritual Emergency from Psychosis

A number of differences in thought processes, emotional reactions, and behavior distinguish a person who is in a spiritual emergency from one who is psychotic. Table 5 points out some of the main differences. People who are having intense paranormal experiences often ask me if they are "going crazy." Although no one but a qualified mental health–care professional can make a diagnosis involving mental illness, the following rule of thumb is often helpful: If a person can distinguish between inner and outer experiences, is clearly aware of which inner experiences do not fit into the prevailing world view of reality, is able to function in the world, is able to make discerning judgments, and has appropriate control of his or her emotions, he or she is, by definition, not psychotic. This is true no matter how unusual or bizarre the inner experiences may seem.

Of course, anyone having paranormal experiences who is at all concerned about mental health should see a mental health–care professional—ideally one who has some familiarity with and an accepting attitude towards STEs.

The chart is only a simplistic look at an extremely complex subject. Like spiritual emergencies, psychotic illnesses manifest in a wide variety of ways in different individuals.

Table 5

Spiritual Emergency	Psychosis
Challenged by experiences	Overwhelmed by experiences
Great difficulty functioning	Unable to function
Thought processes clear	Thought processes incoherent or contain loose associations
Transient grandiose ideas	Delusions of grandeur
Difficulty separating inner and outer realities	Unable to distinguish inner and outer realities
Aware at some level that experiences are part of an inner process	Has paranoid delusions and projects cause of experiences onto others
Fears losing control	Is out of control
Exhibits mildly unusual behaviors	Exhibits inappropriate behaviors including outwardly destructive acts, self-destructive acts, disorganized behaviors, fixed obsessions
Able to tolerate negative visions	Overwhelmed by horrific visions
Can ignore voices heard	Overwhelmed by voices heard
Fairly appropriate emotional responses	Inappropriate emotional responses
Difficulty making discerning judgments	Unable to make discerning judgements
Moral and ethical values remain intact	Moral and ethical values may be lost

It is not the purpose of this book to examine the many different types of psychotic illnesses, or to look at the ways they are distinguished from each other. However, I would like to add a few interesting observations drawn from my medical practice. A few of the patients I have seen who have slipped from a very difficult spiritual emergency into psychosis have temporarily developed the symptoms of paranoid schizophrenia. The large majority, however, have developed acute mania. Over the last few years I have seen fifteen such cases. This is an extremely high number given the nature of my practice and the type of patients I see.

The temporarily schizophrenic patients were helped by the major tranquilizers commonly prescribed in cases of schizophrenia and by adopting the grounding techniques that I discuss in detail in Chapter Fifteen. With the patients suffering from mania I have found that the traditional mood-stabilizing drugs prescribed for mania, such as lithium and clonazepam, were effective. They were also helped by grounding techniques and by counseling that focused on distinguishing more clearly between inner and outer realities. As I have seen such a high percentage of people developing acute mania, I have included in Table 6 the major criteria for the diagnosis of manic episodes.

Table 6
Main Diagnostic Criteria for Manic Episodes

In a diagnosis of mania, criteria I, II, and III all need to be present.

I. A distinct period of abnormally and persistently elevated, expansive, or irritable mood, lasting at least one week.
II. During the period of mood disturbance, at least three of the following symptoms have persisted (four if the mood is irritable) and have been present to a significant degree:
    1. Inflated self-esteem or grandiosity.
    2. Decreased need for sleep, e.g., feels rested after only three hours of sleep.
    3. More talkative than usual or pressure to keep talking.

4. Flight of ideas or subjective experience that thoughts are racing.
5. Distractibility, i.e., attention too easily drawn to unimportant or irrelevant external stimuli.
6. Increase in goal-directed activity (either socially, at work or school, or sexually) or psychomotor agitation.
7. Excessive involvement in pleasurable activities which have a high potential for painful consequences, e.g., the person engages in unrestrained buying sprees, sexual indiscretions, or foolish business investments.
III. Mood disturbance is sufficiently severe to cause marked impairment in occupational functioning or in usual social activities or relationships with others, or to necessitate hospitalization to prevent harm to self or others, or there are psychotic features.

The information in Table 6 is taken from the *DSM-IV*, the American Psychiatric Association handbook that contains the criteria for the diagnosis of psychiatric disorders.

A Case History of Acute Mania

One of the people I have seen slip from spiritual emergency into acute mania was a man I'll call Jurgen.

Jurgen was a very successful businessman in his mid thirties. Extremely intelligent, he held a Master's degree and excelled in a number of areas. He was the president of a large corporation that he had founded, and he had accumulated assets worth well over two million dollars.

Jurgen's work required that he read and study almost constantly when he wasn't involved in other activities. While reading late one night, he suddenly began to receive channeled material. Although he was extremely surprised, he began to write down the material, which he perceived as being "dictated" to him inside his head.

Over a three-month period, Jurgen meticulously recorded three entire books. These books described the spiritual shortcomings of humanity and the need for humanity to rediscover its true spiritual nature.

After these books were completed, Jurgen began to develop some inappropriate and inflated ideas about himself and what had happened to him. He believed he had received these works directly from God and thought that these channeled books were proof that he was God's special messenger.

Eventually Jurgen's wife became concerned about these delusions and brought him to my office. When I talked to Jurgen, I found he was unable to put his channeling experience into any rational perspective. He saw his experience as special, even unique. Convinced he was God's special messenger, he believed his message was of utmost importance for the world. Despite these inflated ideas about himself, Jurgen was able, at times, to put his experiences in a more rational perspective; he also continued to function very well at his workplace for several months.

At the end of this period, however, he started to spontaneously channel a number of other books. This time the books had a different theme. They described in great detail the plans for a spiritual retreat in the desert that he should attempt to finance and build, utilizing his accumulated wealth and business talents.

Once again Jurgen thought that the channeled material was being given to him directly by God, and he began to lose the ability to put this in perspective rationally. Gradually, he also lost any ability to judge when and where it was appropriate to discuss his channeling experiences and the material he received. He began to speak about them— and his belief that he was receiving direct communication from God—with business associates, legal advisors, his secretary, cab drivers, and finally with almost everyone he

met. As these changes were occurring, he was also begin-
ning to exhibit the classic signs of mania: he became very
excited and agitated, he developed rapid-fire speech, his
appetite dwindled completely, and he spent his nights writ-
ing, channeling, and walking rather than sleeping. Soon he
became so preoccupied with his inner experiences that he
was no longer able to function at work. Jurgen had clearly
slipped from spiritual emergency into psychosis. He was
admitted to a psychiatric hospital and diagnosed as suf-
fering from a manic psychosis.

Analyzing Jurgen's case in terms of spiritual experiences, spiritual emergency, and psychosis, we can see that he had a spontaneous psychic opening—such as countless people have
had—but, perhaps due to the intensity of the experience, was
unable to put it into any kind of perspective and instead developed extreme delusions about himself and his ability. Eventually,
he lost contact with reality as society views it. Jurgen met the
diagnostic criteria for mania, as his expansive mood lasted for
many weeks, incapacitating him from working, and he demon-
strated grandiosity, a decreased need for sleep, more talkative-
ness than usual, and flight of ideas.

Following his discharge from hospital, I worked with Jurgen
to help him develop a far more balanced perspective on his
psychic experiences. Throughout the process Jurgen remained
convinced that the psychic experiences themselves were real. I
did not challenge the reality of his experiences—only the way in
which he interpreted them. In the course of counseling, I helped
Jurgen to see that a great many people had received channeled
material and produced books. As he familiarized himself with
some of these books, he began to realize that his experiences
were not at all unique. With my urging, Jurgen also re-examined
his assumption that the channeled material came directly from
God. One technique he finally decided to try was to ask the
channeled voice to identify itself. It did—as the spirit of a long-
deceased person. Jurgen was then able to admit, rather sheep-
ishly, that he must not have been channeling God.

Although Jurgen's journey to regain complete mental health will be a long one, his growing ability to keep his experiences in perspective and to let go of his grandiose ideas has enabled him to remain nondelusional and functional for a considerable period.

The Eight Limbs of Yoga

Gopi Krishna described several ways he thought problems with kundalini awakening might be related to some forms of mental illness. He often referred to this as an aberrant or malignant awakening of kundalini. (The risk of mental disorder as the result of a faulty awakening of kundalini is mentioned repeatedly in the yogic tradition.) Based both on his years of study and on his own experiences, Gopi Krishna described a number of problems that could occur: the energy rising, as it did in his own case, through the incorrect nadi; the body being unable to supply the brain with either great enough quantities or pure enough prana; the body not being able to supply the brain with enough nutritive, regenerative ojas; and genetic factors or emotional dysfunctions or physical imbalances in the body or brain that might adversely effect the kundalini mechanism.

In order to understand how these and other difficulties might occur, we need to take a closer look at the Eight Limbs of Yoga—or the eight-fold path—that is described in the Yoga Sutras of Patanjali. The first four limbs represent the physical, psychological, and spiritual disciplines that are needed for success in yoga and, in my opinion, to help ensure a healthy awakening of kundalini. Through them, yoga aspirants learned to purify their psyches, bodies, and prana so that they were physically, emotionally, mentally, and spiritually fit and fully prepared for the gradual development of transcendental states of consciousness. Once this preparation was complete—often after a lifetime of dedication—the aspirant could begin or intensify the practice of the other four limbs that were designed to bring about transcendental states of consciousness.

The eight limbs of yoga are as follows:

1. *Yama (Restraint)*. The development and observances of moral practices, which are the basis of spiritual discipline. The main five listed in the Yoga Sutras
are: not doing harm, truthfulness, not stealing,
chastity, and greedlessness. Other yogic texts also pre-
scribe sympathy, rectitude, patience, steadfastness,
moderation in diet, and cleanliness.

2. *Niyama (Discipline)*. The five practices listed in the
Yoga Sutras are: purity, contentment, asceticism, study,
and devotions to the Lord. Other texts include practices
such as charity, affirmation of the existence of the divine,
listening to scriptures, hospitality, modesty, exertion for
the good of others, the repetition of prayers, and performing spiritually motivated sacrifices.

3. *Asana (Posture)*. Patanjali says simply that "the
posture should be steady and comfortable. It is
accompanied by the relaxation of tension and the
coinciding with the infinite." According to Eliade,
Patanjali goes into so little detail because asana must
properly be learned from a guru. Other references to
asanas are found throughout Hindu and yogic literature and were well systematized in Hatha Yoga.
Hatha Yoga teaches asanas that are designed to keep
the body strong and flexible and to purify it. Many
asanas facilitate keeping the spine straight, the head
and neck in correct alignment, and/or the prana
smoothly flowing through the spine when the kundalini is awakened. Some asanas are believed to stimulate certain chakras, and thereby stimulate the
kundalini mechanism.

4. *Pranayama (Control of prana via the breath)*.
Exercises for controlling the breath and, in this way,
influencing the flow of prana into and throughout the
body. Certain pranayama techniques are believed to
open shushumna and stimulate kundalini.

5. *Pratyahara (Sense withdrawal)*. Withdrawal or
detachment of the senses; withdrawing mind into

itself; developing the ability to enter, at will, a state of intense inner-mindedness.

6. *Dharana (Concentration)*. Developing the mind's capacity for concentration. In the Yoga Sutras, dharana is referred to as binding consciousness to a single locus. Traditionally, yoga aspirants learned to concentrate more and more deeply on a point or image, such as that of a deity, or on an internalized sound.

7. *Dhyana (Meditative absorption)*. Meditation or contemplation; progressively deeper levels of intense, single-pointed concentration, often on the divine.

8. *Samadhi (Ecstasy)*. The final limb of yoga, sometimes described as self-realization. The Yoga Sutras call it the condition in which consciousness shines forth as the intended object; the Upanishads say it leads first to wondrous consciousness and later to liberation. In Vedanta, samadhi is sometimes referred to as the union of the psyche with atman or the transcendental Self.

After examining the eight-fold path one can see how, by mastering the prescribed disciplines, the aspirants would be prepared physically, psychologically, mentally, and spiritually for the activation of kundalini and for the attainment of higher states of consciousness. Unfortunately a great many people are intensely practicing some aspects and certain types of yoga today while ignoring the system as a whole. In North America, vast numbers of people are diligently doing the physical postures, the breathing exercises, and/or intensive meditation, but few are making any attempt at doing the groundwork involved in the moral and psychological observances of yama and niyama. Further, many people are unwittingly mimicking the limb known as dharana (concentration) through the intense levels of concentration that are required for long periods of time in so many of our jobs and activities today.

The result of all this may be that many people are activating kundalini long before they are ready. They may not have the physical strength or mental discipline necessary to handle the energy; their bodily organs may not be able to produce the needed purity or quantities of prana, and they may not have developed the sexual discipline needed to ensure that the essential nutritive ojas is not squandered. Based on my work and my experience with the Kundalini Research Network Questionnaire Project, I have come to the conclusion that these types of situations may indeed result in, or contribute to, some forms of spiritual emergency or even mental illness.

Better Treatment in the Future

As a doctor and transpersonal psychotherapist, one of my main reasons for researching kundalini and STEs has been the hope that greater understanding will aid the medical and psychological communities in their efforts to help people who are having difficulties associated with these types of experiences.

Distinguishing among crises that are part of the spiritual journey, spiritual emergencies, and psychoses is sometimes difficult even for doctors and psychotherapists who are familiar with all of them. Imagine, then, the difficulties that can arise when the professionals treating people having paranormal experiences don't accept the reality of such things as STEs, spiritual emergence, and spiritual emergency.

Dr. David Lukoff is one of the people working to heighten people's awareness. As mentioned in Chapter Nine, he was one of the doctors who suggested the new classifications of religious or spiritual problem for the DSM-IV. He has also put forward the idea that, although some people have mystical experiences that are associated with transient psychosis, these experiences are quite different from other types of psychoses in that they are relatively short-lived and tend to eventually resolve themselves spontaneously as long as the person is simply cared for supportively rather than being hospitalized in a psychiatric ward, labeled as delusional, and automatically medicated with the major tranquilizers used in these settings.

It is my hope that the results of the kundalini research currently being done will help provide much of the impetus for sweeping changes that are needed in the treatment of people undergoing spiritual crisis, spiritual emergency, and the types of psychoses—temporary or otherwise—that seem to be related.

In the next chapter we'll consider some of the factors that seem to precipitate severe difficulties, examine how many of them relate to the eight-fold path, and look at a number of case histories of spiritual emergency and psychosis.

CHAPTER 14

Who Has Spiritual Emergencies and Why?

In my work over the last twenty years, I have found a number of specific factors that seem to predispose people who are undergoing STEs to slip into spiritual emergency or even into psychosis. A number of them relate directly to disregarding or contradicting the teachings of the ancient yogis regarding the physical and psychological preparation that is necessary before one begins the more intensive practices that can lead, ultimately, to expanded states of consciousness. I have noticed that the greater the number of contributing factors present, the greater the likelihood that the person will develop a spiritual emergency or—as the number increases even more—psychosis. As well, the greater the intensity of the factors, the greater the problem.

Spiritual Emergency and Psychosis—Possible Predisposing Factors

Although I have found at least twelve possible predisposing factors, the two most common are an out-of-balance lifestyle and excessive spiritual practices. These two factors have a more wide-ranging effect than the others.

> 1. *Out-of-balance lifestyle.* An out-of-balance lifestyle exacerbates any of the other difficulties that may arise. It includes irregular or skipped meals, an unbalanced, low-nutrition diet, insufficient sleep, excessive indulgence in sex, alcohol or drug abuse, smoking tobacco, a stressful and hectic schedule, and lack of physical exercise, outdoor activity, recreation, or time for reflection or quiet contemplation.

Although this unbalanced lifestyle is quite common in the West today, it is very different from the one that aspirants on the yogic path led centuries ago. They were taught moderation in all things. Their lives were peaceful rather than stressful and hectic, they were moderate in their sexual practices or completely abstinent, and life in an ashram tended to be orderly and regulated. Diet was also considered important. One Hatha Yoga manual says that mita-ahara (moderate diet) was one of the essential prerequisites to beginning pranayama.

The adverse effect of an out-of-balance lifestyle relates to the modern kundalini model in a number of ways. In order to manufacture and supply adequate amounts of potent prana, the body's organs and nervous system need to be strong and in good condition. This cannot occur without an adequate, balanced diet and exercise. Sufficient sleep is very important because it is during sleep that the body regenerates and builds up energy. Drug and alcohol abuse and smoking tobacco may also affect the purity of the prana. It has long been believed in the yogic tradition that excessive sexual release leads to the depletion of ojas. (See Chapter Fifteen for a more thorough discussion of a balanced lifestyle.)

> 2. *Extremely intensive spiritual practices.* Although such practices as yoga, meditation, prayer, contemplation, and Tai Chi are generally positive when practiced in moderation, intensive or excessive practice of any

spiritual discipline for long periods of time may over-stimulate the kundalini mechanism and cause it to awaken before the individual is psychologically and/or physically prepared. This is particularly true with those spiritual disciplines that have been designed specifically to awaken the transformative energy.

This is probably one important reason why many of the ancient yogis—like teachers from many traditions—taught aspirants to proceed gradually along the path and recommended that they have a guru who could monitor their practices and tell them when they were ready to proceed to the next stage.

When kundalini is activated too rapidly or aggressively, the strain on the body, the physiological symptoms, and the massively altered states of consciousness may be too much for the experiencer to bear. Further, when the kundalini mechanism is activated forcefully or suddenly, the body's organs and nervous system may not have had the time needed to adjust to the high level of activity required to produce greater quantities of purer, more potent prana. The much-needed supply of nutritive ojas may also be missing or inadequate. The problems arising from any of these situations can be particularly severe if the kundalini is activated so forcefully that it reaches the crown chakra on its initial awakening and overactivates the brahma randhra.

Continuing to practice intensively, or for long periods of time, the spiritual discipline that has prematurely awakened kundalini makes the problems even more severe.

3. *Extremely intensive concentration.* The long, intense periods of concentration demanded by so many of today's activities, particularly work and study, have a similar effect on the brain as the forms of concentration so assiduously developed by the yogis. The sixth limb of yoga is dharana, or concentration. When carried to extremes, scholarly concentration may have the

same stimulatory effect on the spiritual process as intense or excessive spiritual practices.

In my practice I have seen several people (for example, Gwen, the young medical student) who awakened kundalini when they were studying and reading large amounts of material during difficult, advanced academic programs.

4. *Inadequate psychological "housecleaning."* When kundalini awakens and the spiritual transformation moves into high gear, unresolved psychological conflicts that are held repressed in the unconscious—often those left over from childhood or early adulthood—frequently begin to surface to conscious awareness. This process is very different from the one that occurs during psychotherapy with a competent therapist in which previously repressed memories are encouraged to gradually resurface in a supportive environment. With the sudden awakening of the transformative energy, these repressed memories seem to shoot into the conscious mind with great clarity and intensity and without any prior warning. Sometimes several memories resurface in rapid-fire succession. Since these memories were originally repressed because the conscious mind was not able to deal with them, their rapid resurfacing can be so psychologically overwhelming that it causes the STE experiencer to slip into spiritual emergency or psychosis. This is especially true when the memories are of traumatic childhood events such as sexual abuse or incest. Such horrible memories are difficult to deal with even in carefully moderated, supportive psychotherapy. When they occur without warning, they can be devastating.

The spiritual seeker who has worked gradually over the years on their psychological housecleaning will already have come to terms with many difficult or traumatic memories. And, in the event that other memories do become unblocked, the person who has done a great deal of psychological work is already familiar with how painful this process can be and has probably already developed a number of strategies and skills for facing and resolving the surfacing issues.

> 5. *Unblocking unresolved psychological issues from perceived past lives.* The activity of the transformative energy seems not only to unblock psychological issues from this life but also from what appear to be past lives. I, along with many other psychotherapists, have observed this to be a common and normal part of spiritual transformation. In the yogic tradition, reincarnation and past-life memories are accepted as reality. In fact, Patanjali states that yogis will, at some point in their development, begin to experience past-life memories. In Western culture, however, reincarnation is not widely accepted, and some Western psychologists interpret past-life memories as meaningful symbolic metaphors, created by the subconscious. Whatever the actual origin, when past-life memories occur, they often generate strong emotional reactions. This suggests that some type of residual, unresolved psychological conflict exists and is associated with (or symbolized by) the remembered incident. These conflicts often seem to relate to people with whom the experiencer is currently having difficulties. The memories, and the associated guilt, pain, or anger, may sometimes be so intense and overwhelming, and seem so difficult to resolve, that they trigger a spiritual emergency.

Perceived past-life memories are even more likely to trigger crises if the experiencer does not believe in reincarnation or cannot find supportive persons to talk to about the past-life memory. In these cases, the person who has already done some psycho-spiritual housecleaning is often far better able to deal with these memories and to distinguish and integrate what psychological and spiritual lessons can be learned into his or her daily life. Perceived past-life memories are discussed in more detail in Chapter Sixteen.

Concepts that relate to both psycho-spiritual housecleaning and past-life memories can be found in the ancient yogic teachings. In them, samskaras are described as the imprints left on our subtle body by our past actions, both in this lifetime and in past lives. Western psychologists might conceptualize samskaras as traumatic memories repressed into our unconscious. Understanding samskaras in their proper context requires an explanation of Hindu and yogic philosophy that is beyond the scope of this book. (More information can be found in Mircea Eliade's *Yoga: Immortality and Freedom*.) Still, parallels can be found between the process of self-examination required in psychotherapy and the first two limbs of the eight-fold path, yama (restraints) and niyama (disciplines), which were designed to purify.

> 6. *Excessive greed and desire for wealth*. In my work I have seen a number of people on the spiritual path experience tremendous conflict when they have strong, unresolved desires for wealth and possessions. They almost invariably come to a point in their spiritual journey where they must choose between their materialistic desires and their spiritual goals. When most of a person's time and energy has been tied up with the pursuit of money and possessions, the shift in focus required when one begins the process of spiritual transformation can be so disconcerting—and require so many lifestyle changes—that the person can be thrown into crisis or even spiritual emergency.

I have also seen a few people whose lust for wealth corrupts their spiritual process and causes them to try to use some aspect of their spiritual or paranormal gifts unscrupulously to amass vast personal wealth. This was true of a meditation group leader I once met. After a profound near-death experience and subsequent kundalini awakening, this woman had a psychic awakening as well. Initially, she set up her meditation group on a volunteer basis, to be of service to the community. But in time, she built up the group in a pyramid-sales type of structure, with herself at the top. She quit her job and began to use the meditation courses to generate her personal income. She then started trying to use her new psychic abilities to discern methods to get people to enroll in her courses. Slowly but surely, her gift became corrupted into a money-making venture.

These types of crises are less likely to occur to aspirants following the sequential stages of the eight limbs of yoga, for they would begin striving to overcome greed and detach themselves from material possessions at the very beginning of their spiritual journey.

7. *Excessive ambition and lust for power.* The same type of conflict arises when people cling to the desire for power, status, and position, when they have awakened the transformative energy.

Some people I have met have had STEs but have never gotten their lust for power under control. Some of these people eventually got involved in "psychic games" and tried, for example, to influence or control other people's behavior with their "psychic abilities." People who try such things are certain to experience intense inner conflicts and are likely to experience a difficult spiritual transformation. They may even become delusional.

The eight-fold path of yoga helped prevent these types of situations by developing such characteristics as "greedlessness," "truthfulness," "asceticism," and "nonattachment." Further, many spiritual masters have repeatedly warned aspirants about the dangers inherent in paying too much attention to powers and psychic gifts that undoubtedly develop as one successfully undergoes spiritual transformation.

8. *Fixation on psychic gifts.* In my work I have seen a number of people who have become obsessed with their newly developing psychic gifts. In previous chapters there have been examples of people, like Jurgen,

whose belief in the uniqueness of their gifts contributed to their severe ultimate state of delusion.

One of the reasons the yogic and other spiritual texts warn against the fixation with siddhis, or psychic gifts, is that individuals may begin to focus their energies on striving for greater psychic gifts rather than on attaining higher spiritual states of consciousness. As their focus on the psychic increases, such individuals are in danger of being led even further off the path by the temptations that come with the increased attention, fame, and adulation they may receive and with the impression that they are gaining power over others.

It is my experience that this often leads to ego inflation, grandiosity, an increasing loss of perspective—or even loss of contact with reality—that can, in turn, lead to spiritual emergencies or psychoses.

9. *Unresolved conflicts with the God concept.* I have come across a number of people who had difficulties when they began—intentionally or unintentionally—to undergo the process of spiritual transformation while they still had deep-seated inner conflicts concerning the divine power behind the universe. In some instances, these people harbor a tremendous anger at God. In many cases, the person originally believed deeply in the concept of God they were taught during childhood and then felt let down or abandoned when they believed God allowed some terrible event to happen or did not answer their prayers. In my practice, I have seen people who had this reaction to such events as the death of a child, the suicide of a brother, or the torture or death of their relatives in a concentration camp. Similar conflicts can also arise for people who have turned away from God because they cannot accept the fact that a divine power could exist and yet do nothing to prevent the tremendous suffering they see in the world around them.

When people begin to undergo the process of spiritual transformation while harboring these unresolved attitudes about their God, they may experience intense inner conflict that can contribute to crises and spiritual emergencies. People who are angry with God, or who have turned away from a God they once loved, need to resolve these feelings if they want to minimize the difficulties in their spiritual process.

10. *Turning to the dark side.* Whether one believes in the existence of such things as the dark side, the devil, or Satan, it cannot be denied that many people do believe in this negative concept, and in some cases consciously embrace it. I have spoken with several patients who were severely psychologically traumatized or even physically or sexually abused by persons who claimed to be working with the dark forces.

Leaders of Satanic cults would fall into this category. They may even be striving to awaken kundalini forcefully because they believe it will bring them power that they can use for their own selfish or evil purposes. In the rare event that such a person did activate kundalini, I believe their negativity, ego-involvement, and grandiose ideas would eventually lead to spiritual emergency or psychosis. In extreme cases, the person's efforts may end in madness or self-destruction.

11. *Unresolved spiritual guilt.* Like repressed memories of traumatic events, the memories of events we feel guilty about often resurface during the spiritual process and sometimes become more intense. The feelings themselves can become so strong that the experiencer is pushed into crisis or emergency. In some cases, people who feel they have done something "bad" in the past may suffer from severe conflict when they begin to have positive spiritual experiences, because they feel they don't deserve them. I have seen this happen frequently

in women experiencers who have unresolved spiritual guilt about an abortion earlier in their life.

As you'll see later in this chapter in Minnie's story about abortion and unresolved guilt, examining our past faults and transgressions is an essential part of the spiritual journey, but refusing to forgive ourselves for them can be extremely detrimental.

> 12. *Terminal illness.* Although terminal illnesses are very different from the other types of factors that have been discussed here, they can precipitate spiritual crises and emergencies in a number of ways. Facing a terminal illness often forces people to examine large spiritual questions and look at specific spiritual issues that they have avoided facing for years. Sometimes a feeling of urgency makes the person try to deal with too much too fast.

In some cases, people facing terminal illness begin intense spiritual practices or long periods of highly focused prayer. When these practices inadvertently stimulate the transformative energy, the person's weakened body may have difficulty handling it. Further, if the person is still psychologically troubled about impending death, the other processes often triggered by the energy, such as the unblocking of past memories, can be very difficult to deal with.

> 13. *Hereditary factors.* The fact that heredity plays a role in some types of mental illness is no longer disputed. I feel it also plays a role in predisposing some people to having spiritual emergencies or psychoses— especially when they are undergoing a very rapid spiritual awakening.

Unfortunately, medical science is only beginning to understand the role of genetics in mental illness, and a great deal of research will be needed to determine how it relates to spiritual emergencies. In my practice I have noticed that individuals with family histories that include psychiatric disorders, particularly manic-depressive illness or schizophrenia, have difficulties with their spiritual process far more frequently than those who have no family history of mental illness. This is one more reason why I feel the research on kundalini and its relationship to mental illness is so important.

Inadequate Psycho-Spiritual Housecleaning

When the transformative energy awakens, it is like a bright light that rises in the "house" that is our consciousness and shines on our inner self. The brilliant light illuminates the cobwebs and debris that need to be cleaned away—our unresolved psychological issues and wounding. In general, the less psychological housecleaning a person has done, the greater the number of inner issues and wounds they may discover and the less their supports and coping skills to deal with these will likely be. Therefore, the more distressed they may be to discover that the cobwebs and debris exist at all.

This was true of a medical technologist I'll call Beth who came to see me in my office for the first time when she was in her late forties. Beth told me that she was afraid she was losing her mind. Memories from her childhood kept flooding, unwanted and unbidden, into her conscious mind, and she desperately wanted help in finding a way to stop them. At that time in her life, she felt she simply couldn't bear the distress they were causing.

> I always thought of myself as a very anxious person. When I was in my late twenties, I became interested in meditation and began to hope that it might cure my constant anxiety. I even joined a Buddhist temple and was involved there for several years. Unfortunately, I discovered that my anxiety increased the longer I meditated.
>
> Frustrated, I finally left the temple thinking that I had inherited some type of imbalance in my brain chemistry from my parents and that I was doomed to suffer forever from chronic anxiety.

Matters became worse when I lost my hospital job due to local budget cuts. About the same time, my common-law husband of several years announced that he had found a new girlfriend and was leaving me. Realizing that I could not afford my apartment any longer, I was forced to move in with my parents until I could re-establish myself. Although I was on speaking terms with them, I did not particularly like either of my parents. I found living at home extremely anxiety-provoking and uncomfortable.

During this extremely stressful time, one of my friends convinced me it would be a lot of "fun" to participate in an intense, two-day seminar on "breathwork."

Eager and excited, I signed up for the seminar with my friend, expecting to have a fun and relaxing weekend that would provide a much-needed escape from my mental turmoil and anxiety. My experience at the seminar proved to be dramatically different from my expectations. After doing about two hours of the breathing techniques I had been taught, I suddenly began to experience powerful rushes of energy up my body and spine. Then, quite without warning, I began to unblock a number of horrific memories from my childhood that had been completely repressed. As the first of these memories arose, I began to experience clear, vivid flashbacks of being raped by my uncle in the barn on my grandparents' farm when I was fifteen years old. I then began to unblock memories of being sexually abused by my father for several years during my early childhood. Terrified, overwhelmed, and horrified, I received no help from the seminar instructors when I explained what was happening. Finally, I bolted from the seminar.

At this point in my life, I felt I was incapable of dealing with such memories. I desperately hoped they were not true and was unable to face the fact that they might be. After leaving the seminar, I went into a state of extreme anxiety and agitation.

I had been under a great deal of stress when I began to

experience the energy rushes and was poorly equipped to deal with the unblocked memories. The situation grew worse when I tried to return home and live in the same house with my father, whom I now suspected might have abused me, and the mother who might not have protected me.

By the time Beth came to my office for help she could barely function in her home and was in a severe state of spiritual emergency. She had experienced an intense kundalini awakening during the breathwork, and then unblocked very traumatic repressed memories for which she was totally unprepared. She had never done any prior psychological housecleaning. Thankfully, continued therapy is now helping her sort through and come to terms with her traumatic childhood memories. Also, a number of the techniques discussed in Chapters Fifteen to Seventeen have helped her moderate her energy experiences.

It is my opinion that Beth's system was ripe for a kundalini awakening because of her several years' intense meditation practice in the Buddhist temple. The breathwork taught in such seminars is similar to a type of intense pranayama exercise used by yogis to stimulate the kundalini, and may cause people to remember deeply buried traumatic memories during the breathwork session. The intensive pranayama-like breathwork she did in the seminar triggered the energy before she was psychologically prepared. Unfortunately, in many types of breathwork seminars the instructors themselves may be unfamiliar with pranayama, yoga, or kundalini and they may not have any idea how to deal with a kundalini awakening. Further, the instructors—or breath-workers as they are sometimes called—in many of the courses are usually not fully trained psychotherapists and, consequently, have no idea how to help the participant deal with the traumatic memories or extremely emotional experiences that sometimes occur, nor are they able to provide any psychological follow-up and support.

In my work I have come across a number of people who have had experiences similar to Beth's with breathwork. Another young woman, Jana, had even proceeded to the point of taking an intensive (and expensive) instructor-training course in a type of breathwork that involved swimming with dolphins. She, too, awakened her kundalini during the course and began to spontaneously unblock memories of childhood physical abuse. When she began to cry and sob uncontrollably, the instructor—unlike the one in Beth's case, who did nothing—began to shout at her. She told Jana to "get herself under control" because the class was "not a therapy session." When this pushed Jana even further into crisis, the instructor became increasingly hostile and angry with her.

As I come across more and more cases like Beth's and Jana's, I become increasingly concerned when I hear of "breath-workers" who are not fully trained in dealing with the emotional and psychological upheaval that can result from unblocking deeply buried memories. Many have no idea that they are working with a form of pranayama, and even those who are may not be aware of its potential effect on kundalini. Even those who have some understanding of kundalini often have no awareness of the immense power of the awakened energies—and mistakenly believe that they can "control" or "suppress" the energies. In short, they may have no idea that they are toying with awesome techniques that were designed to awaken a spiritually transformative force—a force whose ultimate power is beyond our control. Intensive breathwork techniques should only be practiced under the supervision of a trained psychotherapist or knowledgable spiritual teacher or counselor who can deal with a possible psycho-spiritual crisis.

The experience of pranayama can, of course, be positive. A man I know whom I'll call Rubindar studied yoga under an excellent teacher in India. He had been doing Yama and Niyama, self-development and inner-growth work for years. One day when he was practicing intense pranayama, he began to experience rushes of energy up his spine, sensations of heat and light, and uncontrollable shaking. The guru he was studying with came to him immediately and sat calmly beside him. Using the same type of techniques a well-trained Western psychotherapist would, the guru began to speak to Rubindar in a calm reassuring manner. As the symptoms continued, the guru told Rubindar that what he was experiencing was called kundalini, and that the experience was not abnormal. The guru then put the experience in context explaining its place in yoga. All the while, he continued to reassure Rubindar, telling him not to be afraid and explaining that kundalini was a powerful but positive energy. No traumatic memories unblocked. Although Rubindar's dramatic kundalini symptoms continued for several hours, the guru did not leave his side until they abated.

The guru's wisdom and understanding helped turn what could have been an overwhelming and terrifying experience into a positive one. It also helped Rubindar begin his journey of accelerated spiritual transformation, triggered by the awakening, on the right foot.

Unresolved Spiritual Guilt

A woman I'll call Minnie came to my office for therapy in a state of extreme depression and severe agitation. She, too, had awakened kundalini through intense meditation practices, and her condition was made worse by deep-seated, unresolved spiritual guilt.

> I began my intense spiritual practices as a means of trying to deal with a tremendous amount of inner pain. For the last four years I had been meditating and chanting for as much as two to three hours a day. However, about two months prior to coming to Dr. Kason's office I had increased the amount of time until I was meditating and chanting during most of my waking hours. My dedication to these practices had become so great that I was no longer able to work. Up until this time I had been fairly successful and had held middle-management–level jobs.
>
> My reason for stepping up the intensity of my spiritual practices was an increasing depression. I felt as if there was a "black hole" in my soul that was trying to surface—and I was struggling desperately to keep it from coming up.
>
> I had had a difficult childhood. My brother died young and my parents were cold and domineering and

had a very unhappy marriage. When I was in high school, I was date-raped and became pregnant.

My parents and the doctors involved pressured me to have an abortion. I believed that abortion was murder. But, feeling powerless against my parents, I went through with the operation. In my mind, however, I made a secret pact with God: if God would forgive me, I would promise to never have another abortion as long as I lived.

Later I married a medical student and, while we were both still in university, I accidentally became pregnant. My husband insisted that I have an abortion and threatened to leave me if I did not, because he believed that having a child at that time would ruin his career. Again feeling trapped and powerless, I broke my promise to God and had the abortion.

This event marked the beginning of my depression. I separated from my husband shortly afterwards, and I left the Christian church I had been raised in. I began to follow yogic spiritual practices, but when my depression persisted after trying this for a few years, I dropped yoga and became a Buddhist.

It was about a year after this that I had an intense kundalini awakening, and afterwards I noticed that the "black hole" I had been trying so desperately to suppress surfaced. I went into a deep depression.

Like many people, Minnie had had no idea that intensive spiritual practices, rather than helping her escape from reality, would eventually force her to face it. It is my opinion that the day-long meditation and chanting Minnie was doing up until the time of her breakdown had stimulated the transformative energy. Instead of blocking out the past, the awakening energy had the opposite effect and illuminated her past so brightly that she could no longer hide from it. Her distress was related to the fact that she had never forgiven herself—or accepted God's forgiveness—for breaking her promise and having the second abortion.

Although Minnie's therapy and treatment may last a long time, she is gradually learning to deal with her traumatic past and let go of her spiritual guilt.

Spiritual Experiences Mislabeled as Psychoses

Fortunately, mislabeling of spiritual experiences as psychotic episodes does not happen as frequently as it once did. Standardized diagnostic criteria for the different types of psychosis now exist, and mental-health professionals who use them correctly are far less likely to create this kind of error.

Still, many people reading this book may have had profound spiritual or paranormal experiences that were labeled delusional by doctors or psychologists. I have seen three separate cases in my practice. All three are deeply spiritual women who are now either middle-aged or elderly. Many years ago, each one was hospitalized and labeled as psychotic after having profound mystical experiences. In each case their families and doctors thought the woman had been hallucinating, and the doctors believed her experiences were symptoms of psychosis. Since these women were in fact mentally healthy, had a good grasp of reality, and had sound judgment, they learned very quickly, in order to avoid psychiatric hospitalization, not to talk about their mystical experiences.

Although all three women went on to lead productive lives, they had to live with the trauma and stigma of being treated for psychiatric illness when they had been, in fact, mentally healthy. Further, they were forced to keep their rich spiritual lives and their mystical experiences a secret from those around them. They all found living this double life a tremendous burden. How much fuller and richer their lives—and the lives of their families—might have been if their experiences had been understood for what they really were.

Some people being treated for psychoses might be better understood and more effectively treated if more doctors and psychologists were aware of the reality of spiritual emergency and the possibility of associated transient psychosis. Of course, I am not trying to claim that all types of mental illness are related to the spiritual process.

Fortunately, most people undergoing spiritual transformation do not have to endure spiritual emergency or psychosis, but most go through some difficult growth periods. It seems to me that this is a necessary part of the mystical path. The most pressing reason I had for writing this book was to help people undergoing STEs and other health-care professionals to become more aware of spiritual and paranormal phenomena and the strategies that can help people integrate these experiences into their daily lives. For this reason, most of the rest of the book is dedicated to providing more information on the long-term, accelerated process of spiritual transformation and on the techniques that can help us survive the difficult periods and come to a fuller understanding of the extraordinarily wonderful experiences that also bless us along the way.

CHAPTER 15

Strategies for Living with Spiritual Transformation

Most of my work over the last ten years has been dedicated to helping persons undergoing STEs, observing, researching, sharing as much information as possible on how one can best survive the process of spiritual transformation, and traveling widely to share ideas and learn from diverse spiritual teachers and other kundalini researchers. As many of the case histories in this book have shown, spiritual transformation is a life-long process of learning, healing, and personal growth, as well as a process of deepening connectedness with spirit. The process can be difficult at times. There are, however, many strategies that can help decrease the number and/or intensity of the difficulties. In this chapter we'll look at a number of the strategies that I have found to be the most effective.

Balance is a key concept. I believe that, if you want to travel as far as possible on your spiritual journey and make this journey as smooth as possible, you need to take the best possible care of your physical, psychological, and spiritual health—and you need to pay equal attention to each.

Since I think that the spiritual transformative energy is in fact a biological-psychological-spiritual energy, it makes sense to me that we need to take care of all the areas in which this energy operates—the body, the mind, and the spirit. It is important not to forsake your body's needs while you are absorbed in the needs of the spirit, or become so intensely involved in psychological issues that you forget to take care of spiritual ones. My clinical experience has shown me that a balanced approach works best.

Promoting Physical Health through a Balanced Lifestyle

The importance of promoting physical health is far too often ignored by those on the spiritual path. Some people get the idea that paying attention to the physical body is somehow "unspiritual." However, references to the importance of maintaining a healthy physical body can be found in many spiritual traditions. Several, such as Judaism, have dietary laws that were originally intended to help maintain physical health. Some traditions, such as Hatha Yoga, are even based on making the physical body a worthy vehicle for self-realization.

Balance and moderation are the best approaches to nurturing physical health. It is essential to have a well-rounded, nutritious diet, drink lots of water, get plenty of sleep, and get regular exercise, while avoiding drugs, tobacco, and other toxins. Physical and medical problems need to be heeded and attended to. As discussed in Chapters Thirteen and Fourteen, ignoring the physical aspects of the spiritual process can lead to an increase in the number and intensity of problems, crises, and even spiritual emergencies. Conversely, clinical experience has shown me that paying attention to physical needs and balanced lifestyle can decrease problems and help stabilize the process of spiritual transformation.

The following is a basic list outlining the features of a balanced lifestyle. As a doctor, I think a balanced lifestyle is important for everyone, but even more so for persons undergoing the spiritual transformation process.

The Basics of a Balanced Lifestyle

1. Develop and stick to a regular daily routine— have regular rising, bed, and meal times and set aside regular periods each week for exercise.

2. Get plenty of sleep and rest and set aside regular times for daily relaxation and weekly recreation.

3. Do not skip meals. Eat a nutritious, well-balanced diet. You don't need to deprive yourself of occasional treats, but avoid junk foods in general.

4. Keep the amount of stress and hectic activity in your life to a minimum.

5. Communicate and share your thoughts and feelings with a supportive person daily, or as often as possible.

6. Keep your sex life moderate, and pay attention to your body if it seems to be telling you to cut down.

7. Spend time in nature; get plenty of natural daylight.

8. Avoid toxins and self-destructive habits such as smoking and drugs; keep alcohol consumption to a minimum.

9. Get regular physical exercise, at least two or three times per week.

10. Spend a moderate amount of time each day in meditation, prayer, and/or a spiritual practice.

Since a healthy diet is central to balanced lifestyle and to this process, I want to discuss it in a little more detail. A great many dietary modifications are promoted today as being necessary for true physical health. Some are even promoted as necessary for spiritual growth. An increasing number of people advocate the vegan diet—one that contains no animal or dairy products of any kind. Others favor lacto-ovo-vegetarianism, which allows eggs and dairy products but no other animal products. Some advocate eating meats, fruits, and vegetables, but no dairy products. Others say you should eat foods only in certain combinations. One well-known diet promotes eating specific types of foods only at certain times of the day. Another advocates eating a vegetarian diet if you are a certain blood type and a nonvegetarian diet if you are another.

These and other diets and food fads indicate that there is absolutely no consensus among health-food advocates or spiritual teachers about exactly what constitutes a healthful or a "spiritual" diet. Therefore, it seems to me that there are two sensible things to do: Avoid any fanatical approach and eat a nutritious, well-balanced diet, and learn to listen to what your own body tells you about your particular needs. My experience has taught me that different people function better on different diets; no one type of diet is right for everybody.

Find a well-balanced, nutritious diet that makes you feel good. If you feel sluggish after eating, lack energy in general, or are having difficulties with the process of spiritual transformation, try gradually changing your diet and see if this helps. You should be all right while you are experimenting as long as your diet still includes lots of fresh fruit and vegetables, whole grains, and adequate protein and keeps fats and sugars to a minimum.

My own family provides a good example of how different people thrive on different diets. My first husband, an extremely athletic man who exercises a great deal, has known for years that he feels sluggish and sleepy after meals that contain meat—especially red meat—and that his energy level is much higher when he sticks to a lacto-ovo-vegetarian diet that is high in carbohydrates. I feel bloated and weighed-down when I eat a meal high in carbohydrates, and my energy level and general well-being are much higher when my diet contains lean meat—both red and white—or fish and lots of fresh vegetables, with a minimum of carbohydrates. Our young son is already showing signs of thriving on the same type of diet that I do. With these facts in mind, I would plan our family's meals so that everyone was getting the type of foods they thrive best on.

Grounding Strategies

The term "grounding" conveys the importance of mentally having one's feet on the ground and of remaining centered and connected to the physical world even when one is undergoing profound inner spiritual and psychological experiences. If one is overwhelmed by the inner experiences of spiritual transformation, the STEs' intensity and frequency can usually be decreased and inner calm can be restored by using grounding strategies. The following are the grounding strategies that have proven most effective.

1. Stop meditating.
2. Decrease all forms of concentration.
3. Keep prayers very brief.
4. Decrease amounts of reading.
5. Decrease stress and the hustle and bustle in your life.
6. Increase your sleep, rest, and relaxation time.
7. Try to follow a fixed daily routine.
8. Try eating smaller, more frequent meals instead of three large ones per day. Never skip meals or fast during periods of intense STE activity, even if you feel an aversion to food. Eating frequent, light meals is essential.
9. Avoid caffeine (be aware that many foods besides coffee and tea contain caffeine—for instance, chocolate and cola); avoid junk foods; avoid excessive and regular intake of refined sugar. (Some people occasionally crave sugar during a STEP or a crisis and, in such cases, a sweet snack sometimes seems to have a positive effect, but more nutritious foods should form the basis of your diet.)
10. Cut out alcohol consumption or occasionally have just one glass of beer or wine per day. Small amounts of alcohol can be very grounding; unfortunately, this can lead to an experiencer's using it instead of techniques that contain no potential harm—some

experiencers have become alcoholics. Reserve alcohol as an emergency grounding measure.

11. Increase your daily intake of protein, such as yogurt and other dairy products, chicken, and fish. For the most grounding effect, eat red meat.

12. Cut out recreational drugs and tobacco if you haven't already.

13. Take some light physical exercise daily, such as walking, cycling, or swimming. Walking in a pleasant environment is a very grounding exercise.

14. Do light manual work, such as gardening, cooking, housecleaning.

15. Increase body awareness by rubbing your body or massaging your legs and feet; for an immediate grounding effect take a hot bath or shower, vigorously scrub your body with a cloth, sponge, or loofah, rub your scalp, and wash your hair.

16. Try having a vigorous massage to increase body awareness, but monitor the effect it has on you, as many types of massages may stimulate the flow of energy.

17. Set aside time for contact with nature; regularly spend some time outdoors in a park or other natural environment.

18. Be exposed to natural light (not direct sun or UV rays) as much as possible.

19. Take time off from work if necessary and spend some time in a peaceful, quiet environment.

20. Pay careful attention to how your sex life correlates with any difficulties you may be having and moderate your behavior accordingly. If your sex drive is very high, having sex and orgasm with your partner may release sexual energy and have a grounding effect; if your sex drive is low, do not have sex or masturbate.

21. Visualize your chakras closing up, like full lotuses closing into buds and withdrawing back into their stem.

22. Visualize your energies withdrawing from your head region, moving down to the base of your spine, and staying there.

23. Visualize your energies traveling down your legs to your feet, and focus on feeling your feet firmly planted on the ground; feel your energies linking you to the ground.

24. Visualize your energies extending down from your body and projecting down to the center of the earth. Feel your energy "hook" into or connect to the center of the earth.

25. Find a creative outlet for your energies, such as art, dance, music, or writing. Observe how these activities affect you and moderate them accordingly.

26. Try to flow with surfacing psychological or spiritual issues rather than trying to resist or struggle against them.

Some of these grounding strategies help slow down or moderate the transformative energy and, thus, lessen the intensity of experiences and the accompanying symptoms. Others allow the process of transformation to flow more smoothly by helping ensure that the body can supply the necessary prana and ojas. Others help ensure that body and psyche are strong and able to function at fullest capacity.

Promoting Psychological Health

Psychological health also needs to be nurtured as much as possible in order to facilitate a healthy process of spiritual transformation. Attitudes are important. We can strive to think positively, practice gratitude daily, and be honest, forgiving, and compassionate—we must also deal with unresolved psychological issues. In order to do this we must strive to be honest, compassionate, and forgiving with ourselves.

Good psychological health enables us to function at our highest potential in our day-to-day life and allows the spiritual energy to function smoothly. Part of being psychologically healthy—even when one is undergoing profound spiritual transformation—involves nurturing healthy relationships, remaining active in society, and continuing to contribute to society in general and serve others in some small way. Ideally, the insights received during spiritual transformations will be translated in our daily life into healthier attitudes, increased responsibility for our actions and our growth, clarity of thought, and greater self-awareness.

When experiencers become reclusive or totally absorbed in the abstract aspects of their inner experiences, they miss out on the grounding—and humbling—effect that our daily interactions with others have. They can become so absorbed in the abstract spiritual aspects of their experiences that they lose perspective; they miss out on opportunities for "reality testing" and begin to lose contact with the here and now. Although some people may want to enter this purely mental and spiritual realm, most of us need to keep functioning in the physical world. We are not sadhus wandering through the woods, nor hermits or spiritual recluses on Himalayan mountaintops. We are regular people with families, jobs, and responsibilities, and we unfortunately live in a society that does not provide many places of sanctuary or have many roles to fulfill for the person who is totally absorbed in the spiritual. I certainly have had to maintain my roles as mother, physician, wife, psychotherapist, medical teacher, and homeowner while I continued to experience spiritual transformation! And although temporary, brief periods of withdrawal from society at a retreat or in a natural setting may be helpful or even essential at some time during the spiritual process, this is very different from becoming reclusive or completely absorbed in abstract spiritual matters.

As we have seen in the chapters dealing with spiritual emergency, when people begin to lose contact with the world around them they can develop serious psychological and emotional problems. And although most people undergoing spiritual transformation are not in danger of losing contact with reality, all of us—like everyone who wants to grow—can improve our level of psychological health. This does not mean that we are psychologically "unhealthy"; it means that our insights into ourselves and our unconscious mental and emotional patterns can continue to develop and improve over time. The process of spiritual transformation is also the journey to greater psychological self-awareness, to the healing of our wounds, and to self-realization.

The key to psychological and emotional growth is to get in touch with our feelings, thought patterns, unconscious, and our shadow or dark side—to discover unresolved psychological issues and unhealthy belief systems—and then to heal and resolve them. And we all have unresolved psychological issues and unhealthy belief patterns. Everyone involved in the process of spiritual transformation eventually discovers this. After many years working in the field it seems increasingly clear to me that what I call psycho-spiritual housecleaning is an absolutely essential—and unavoidable—part of the process of spiritual transformation.

Promoting Spiritual Health

Spiritual health is ultimately the most important aspect of spiritual transformation of consciousness. The goal of this process is, after all, to live perennially in a state of deep and clear mystical union while functioning in the world. The mystic in a unitive state lives as a vessel, manifesting the divine will in the world in whatever small way Heaven designs.

Spiritual deepening moves the experiencer away from a life motivated by the desire to satisfy personal wants, towards a life of surrender, motivated by the spiritual desire to be in union with and an instrument of the divine on the planet. A prayer that many people find helpful during spiritual transformation is derived from the "Grace prayer" of the Unity Church:

> Please heal in me what needs to be healed,
> Please teach me what I need to learn.
> I surrender my life to you.
> Thy will be done.

Spiritual health can be developed by a daily practice of prayer, meditation, gratitude, and surrender to the divine. It can also be developed through reading the holy books of the major faiths and reading other spiritually uplifting books. As so many spiritual masters have said over the ages, those on the spiritual path are being propelled by the transformative energy to strive to develop love, honesty, compassion, humility, and detachment. Further, spirit compels experiencers to use the insights gained from spiritual transformation to help others in some way and to make the world a better place.

It is also essential to keep our spirituality in balance and in perspective. It is not always easy to remember this. Once deep mystical experiences begin, many people begin to focus more and more exclusively on spiritual matters and may forget to take care of their physical and psychological health. As we have seen, this can contribute to a wide range of difficulties, crises, and spiritual emergencies. But mystical experiences are so extraordinary and lift us so far above the everyday, mundane world that some people are drawn towards immersing themselves in this aspect of life to the exclusion of all else. They may begin to strive to have more and deeper spiritual experiences. Frequently, they begin to meditate, pray, or engage in some other spiritual activity almost constantly.

When individuals begin to lose interest in their daily activities and to ignore their worldly responsibilities and focus only on the spiritual, it is called "spiritual intoxication" in some traditions. In such cases, people may forget to take care of the needs of the physical body or even deliberately ignore the physical body's needs because they think that the body is the antithesis of all that is spiritual. Some people in this condition may repeatedly perform some ritual that has come to have deep significance for them. In extreme cases, they may even wish that their spirit could leave the physical body so that they could remain permanently in a mystical state of consciousness. The spiritually intoxicated feel a lack of connection both to the body and to the physical world. In short, they have lost their grounding.

People in this state may also become completely detached from how others react to them. As they lose this awareness, they

286 • Farther Shores

may begin to exhibit inappropriate or completely bizarre behaviors, such as dancing in the street partially clad or even naked, oblivious to external stimuli.

Brief experiences of spiritual intoxication can be a temporary feature of an intense STEP. However, spiritually intoxicated individuals are in danger of being labeled psychotic if they are not able to integrate their spiritual experiences with everyday reality, and to function appropriately in everyday life again after a short period of time.

Even though most people undergoing STEs do not become spiritually intoxicated, it is still essential to keep spirituality in perspective. My clinical experience has shown me that people in spiritual transformation have far fewer difficulties and crises when they maintain a moderate, healthy approach to all aspects of their life, body, mind and spirit. Ignoring any one of the three aspects puts us at risk of undermining the process as a whole.

Helping Someone Else in a Spiritual Transformation

You may well be reading this book not because you are going through the process of spiritual transformation yourself but because someone you love is. Being the friend, companion, lover, partner, or spouse of a person who is involved in this process is not always easy. It is particularly difficult when your friend—or whoever—is going through difficult periods, for instance, experiencing crises or emergencies, unblocking traumatic memories and trying to deal with them, or doing intensive psycho-spiritual housecleaning in general. If you are sexually involved, tremendous stresses can be added to your relationship by your partner's fluctuating sexual desires. Fluctuating energy levels and mood swings can stress any type of relationship. Further, you may be confused by your friend's changes in interest. The number of things you have in common may seem to be decreasing, and you may feel left out or be afraid that you'll be "left behind." You may even feel jealous if you, too, are on the spiritual path and are not having the types of profoundly moving experiences that your partner is. Of course, if you really are dedicated to your own path, you will soon become aware that each of us is moving at our own pace towards a goal that everyone will eventually reach. And, more important, the person who appears to be further along the spiritual path is not necessarily going to reach the goal any faster than you or anyone else. Undergoing STEs does not make a person "better," "more spiritual," or more "worthy" than anyone else in God's eyes.

If the person involved in the process of spiritual transformation is your life partner, you may be shocked by changing needs or values. For instance, your partner's need to take time off work may leave you with added financial responsibilities, or a decision to leave a high-paying job for a more spiritually satisfying one may force you to give up a lifestyle you enjoy. What's more— until you began to read this book—you may not even have believed that your partner's experiences were "real."

Communication is the key to dealing with your feelings about the changes in your relationship—just as it is in dealing with any type of problem in any type of relationship. Although admonitions about communicating openly and honestly have become so common that they sound like platitudes, the fact remains that they are true—especially when it comes to dealing with a life partner. You must begin to tell your partner, without acrimony or accusations, how the changes in your relationship are making you feel. You also can encourage your partner to talk about his or her inner experiences and how they are affecting him or her. If you can do this, you can begin to build a new relationship. And you may have to accept the fact that it will almost certainly be a new relationship. Your partner is involved in a process of transformation and is becoming, to varying degrees, a different person. Of course, all of us change to some degree throughout our lifetimes, and everyone who is "in growth" is changing. If you are willing to accept the fact that your partner may be changing more rapidly than is usual, to accept the changes, and to make positive efforts to grow yourself, your partnership will have a good chance of surviving and emerging as a richer, deeper relationship. It is not necessary for you to have profound spiritual experiences yourself, but it is necessary for you to remain open and accepting.

The following are a few guidelines that are useful for helping those we care about through their transformational journey.

1. Support them by listening in a nonjudgmental way when they talk about their experiences and the meaning of those experiences.

2. Validate their experiences. Help them realize that others have had similar experiences. Accept their experiences as real. If you cannot accept them as real in an absolute sense, accept the fact they are real to someone you love, admire, and respect and, because of this, cannot be discounted or treated lightly.

3. Become better informed and help them do the same. Read—and suggest they read—books about mystical experiences, spiritual emergence, kundalini awakening, NDEs, etc. Do the same with the spiritual books from the major faiths. Suggest that they seek out, talk to, and learn from others who are undergoing similar experiences. Suggest that they go to educational conferences on these subjects. Attend yourself if you desire. However, while you are reading and attending conferences, etc., be discerning. Weigh ideas carefully—and test them against the teachings of the great spiritual teachers—before you accept them as truth.

4. Advise them to go to a qualified doctor for a physical checkup. It is essential to determine that none of the unusual symptoms are actually symptoms of an illness. Reassure them by letting them know that your suggestion doesn't mean you think their experiences are not spiritual; people can have STEs and also have serious medical problems just like anyone else.

5. Focus on the idea that STEs are a positive, growth-promoting experience. Remind them that many authorities think STEs are a normal part of human evolution. Remind them that they are involved

in a long-term transformative process; changes do not occur overnight.

6. Respect their needs to change their lifestyle temporarily or even permanently. Support their desire to decrease their workload and to decrease concentration. If this impinges on your lifestyle, try to be accommodating and understanding. Remember that people going through these experiences are not being difficult "on purpose." They are not able to turn their experiences off and on—they are being propelled by a force so powerful that it is literally beyond human comprehension.

7. Give them some time and space to integrate their experiences; understand that some degree of mental preoccupation with inner experiences is common, especially during periods of high STE activity.

8. Realize that there may be confusing changes in their sex drive and erratic fluctuations in their feelings about family relationships. Strain on relationships of all types is very common. Give them time and space to work through these issues.

9. Help them with self-empowerment. Encourage them to get in touch with their inner voice and to listen to the true higher guidance that they receive. Encourage them to pray and/or meditate about any problems. Encourage them to keep a journal and record any dreams, insights, or visions.

10. Encourage them to face their surfacing memories and to do their psycho-spiritual housecleaning. If they are in great emotional distress over surfacing memories, gently encourage them to seek professional support and help.

11. Support their desire to go for psychotherapy or counseling if they feel the need for help. Encourage them in this regard by helping them see their psycho-spiritual housecleaning process as a positive, growth-promoting step.

12. Reinforce their spirituality. Encourage them to

find spiritual meaning in the experiences that they are going through. Encourage them to read uplifting spiritual books. If they belong to an organized religion, support their desire to attend services, masses, or other events.

Regardless of whether it is you or a loved one who is undergoing the difficulties that are sometimes associated with spiritual transformation, it is helpful to remember that processes such as the surfacing of repressed memories and the accompanying psychological housecleaning usually come in waves. In other words, although psychological housecleaning is a process that may last a lifetime, the difficult periods are temporary—and they lead to successive stages of insight and understanding that can continually enrich our relationships and our lives.

At this point, I would like to say a few words to the doctors, psychotherapists, and counselors who may be reading this book. In my clinical experience, what people undergoing STEs really want is a professional person who will honor and respect their STE as something sacred, and not automatically label them as psychopathology. STE experiencers want to hear that they are not crazy, and that many other healthy, well-functioning people are having similar experiences.

Beyond this, most of the strategies outlined above can be used by therapists in helping patients who are experiencing spiritual transformation. The approach that I have found most useful in helping experiencers integrate their experiences and grow from them is based on the following four strategies:

1. *Support.* Listen to the story of the person's inner experiences in a nonjudgmental way.

2. *Validate.* Verify to the person that their experiences are real and not psychotic.

3. *Educate.* Help inform the person about the nature of STEs and spiritual transformation.

4. *Facilitate.* Promote the psycho-spiritual house-cleaning process by using standard and transpersonal psychotherapeutic techniques.

I sincerely hope that as more doctors, counselors, and therapists become familiar and experienced with helping people undergoing STEs throughout the world, these people will finally find the professional help and guidance that is often necessary to facilitate a healthy spiritual transformation.

CHAPTER 16

Psycho-Spiritual Housecleaning

Richard Bucke, Teilhard de Chardin, and Gopi Krishna all believed that the eventual goal of spiritual transformation was the evolutionary development of a new, spiritually illuminated level of human consciousness. Before reaching this state, the transformative energy remodels and purifies the individual's psyche. Gopi Krishna once wrote that the future illuminati would be "chastened and purified by the fire of kundalini." I think this is a powerful description of what goes on during the process of psychological housecleaning.

Samskaras and Psycho-Spiritual Blocks

To understand this from the yogic perspective, let's look at the concept of samskaras. Samskaras are mentioned in both the yogic and Buddhist traditions. Georg Feuerstein translates the word "samskaras" as "imprints," "tendencies," or "activators." He says they are not just marks or traces of our past actions but dynamic forces in our mental processes. He adds that one form of samskara is thought to activate, or generate, the thought processes that reinforce ego-identity and propel us away from God-realization. Samskaras can also be thought of, more simply, as imprints or scars left on our unconscious by our experiences and actions, from this lifetime or others, as well as imprints related to our past karma.

For our purposes here, however, what is important is that in Yogic and Buddhist traditions samskaras are thought to form blocks in our etheric body to the flow of prana and kundalini. In some ancient texts they are metaphorically depicted as blocks held on the lotus petals at the chakras. In Tibetan Buddhism, they are sometimes described as knots that block the flow of the vital winds through the body.

In Western interpretations, samskaras are sometimes characterized as our unconscious mental and emotional tendencies that are caused by unresolved psychological or spiritual issues. In this sense, I think samskaras do indeed exist and that they may well represent impediments to the transformative energy as it goes about the business of remodeling and purifying consciousness.

Eventually, as our souls evolve, the psycho-spiritual blocks held in our unconscious, or held as samskaras on our chakras, must be and are going to be removed and healed—whether we like it or not. I think this is part of what Gopi Krishna meant when he talked about the purifying and chastening effect of kundalini. I believe that the energies that course through the etheric and physical bodies after a kundalini awakening encounter these blocks in the subtle body. Because the blocks need to be cleared away, the memory of the original traumatic event and any unresolved emotions rise from the unconscious to the surface of our consciousness so that we can resolve them. As the samskaras surface we experience both the memory and the associated feelings. The inner drive to remove these blocks can be so strong that we even unconsciously attract situations to our lives that force us to face and deal with the difficult issues associated with the blocks.

Sometimes when I am making presentations I use the metaphorical image of lotus flowers at the chakras to illustrate how I think this kundalini-driven cleansing process works. It is believed that our samskaras are held on the petals of our lower chakras. After a kundalini awakening, as the energy rises to a chakra, it strives to open it, uncurling and opening the petals of the lotus bud. When a samskara (unconscious block) is encountered, the energy strives to cleanse it from the petal, so that the petal can unfurl and the lotus flower can open further. When the kundalini meets the block and begins to loosen it from the petal, it causes the associated memories and feelings to surface from the unconscious into conscious awareness, so that the related spiritual issues can be faced, the lessons learned, and the issues healed. This kundalini-driven cleansing is ongoing; it continues through the process of spiritual transformation until, ultimately (over many lifetimes), all our chakras are cleansed and our unconscious issues cleared. Our consciousness becomes like a vast, clear, and still ocean.

Our individual psyches and prana are gradually being cleansed and freed of impediments as we progress in the spiritual journey. I believe this is one reason why all of us must go through some degree of suffering in our lifetimes. This is the chastening effect of kundalini: suffering for the purpose of learning moral and spiritual lessons. When the psycho-spiritual lesson is learned by the soul, the suffering ends.

When some people suffer in life, they believe that they are being punished by God for their transgressions. I do not believe an all-loving God punishes people. But I do believe the purpose of our life journey is to learn spiritual lessons and grow—and we often feel pain in order to learn them. God is not punishing us. But it may well be that God, like an incredibly wise, loving, and patient parent, has structured the world in a way that allows us to learn and grow from our mistakes.

When we begin to "know the self," we don't always like what we see. Taking personal responsibility or discovering—and then healing—the buried guilt we feel over things we have done and the anger and resentment we feel over things that have been done to us is not an easy process. Unblocking psycho-spiritual issues and learning our lessons is often very painful regardless of whether the issue comes from this lifetime or a previous one. In my experience, real healing of deep emotional wounds can only be done by turning our wounds over to God, by surrendering the feelings to the Higher Power and asking for help. Experiencing inner healing and learning spiritual lessons brings great joy and psychological release, develops inner strength and inner peace, and ultimately deepens our faith in the love and healing power of the divine.

Spontaneous Surfacing of Memories

When the process of spiritual transformation accelerates, we sometimes begin to learn our spiritual lessons a little more quickly than we expect. As was discussed in the chapters on spiritual emergency, unresolved psychological issues and repressed traumatic memories often begin to surface spontaneously, intensely, and rapidly for people undergoing STEs.

Many other people involved in this field, including Dr. Bonnie Greenwell, have noticed this phenomenon. NDE researchers such as Kenneth Ring, Bruce Greyson, and Barbara Harris, author of *Full Circle: The Near-Death Experience and Beyond*, have collected data showing that a high percentage of NDE experiencers unblock memories of childhood abuse. Based on this data, they speculate that early sufferers of abuse could have a higher predisposition for NDE and kundalini awakening than the general population. I think, however, they may eventually discover that their data actually indicates that people who have NDEs—like people who have all types of STEs—are simply more likely to unblock repressed memories of childhood trauma and were not necessarily more frequently abused.

Regardless, the spontaneous unblocking of repressed memories seems to arise in a variety of ways. They sometimes burst into a person's conscious mind with no warning and without any obvious trigger. At other times they are triggered by a particular event or experience that relates in some way to the repressed memory.

Sometimes the memories surface after we have offered a sincere prayer for help in understanding a problem that is troubling us. This happened to a woman in her mid-thirties whom I'll call Sally.

> *I had been undergoing STEs for about four years when I came home from working out at the health club one afternoon and found that my husband was not home. Instead of accepting this as a normal occurrence, I suddenly began to get very upset and became overwhelmed by the suspicion that my husband was having an affair. I frantically began to look around the house for evidence of an affair, checking beside the phone for any scraps of paper that might reveal a number or some other incriminating evidence.*
>
> *Suddenly I stopped myself; I realized that I was behaving ridiculously. My husband had never done anything to give me reason to believe he was having an affair. I sat down and said a prayer asking God to help me understand why I was having such negative suspicions about my husband. Without warning, a memory that I had suppressed for years unblocked and flooded into my consciousness. I vividly recalled an instance ten years earlier in which I had been unfaithful to my steady boyfriend. Although I had managed to block the memory of the event, I realized I still felt a great deal of guilt about my actions that I had never resolved. It also became immediately clear to me that, because the issue was unresolved, I was projecting my own infidelity onto my husband.*
>
> *After meditating and praying on the matter, I was finally able to accept God's forgiveness and to forgive myself for my actions. Afterwards, my groundless suspicions about my husband's possible infidelity disappeared.*

Blocked memories of unresolved psychological issues do not always float up as easily or as completely into consciousness as this one of Sally's did. Partial memories sometimes surface during the daytime as brief glimpses or "flashbacks" and a good deal of energy and effort is required before the pieces can all be pulled into place. Sometimes the flashes are not at first recognized as memories at all; until a moment of recognition occurs, they are thought to be the product of an overactive imagination. In some cases, blocked memories begin to surface—either completely or in bits and pieces—in vivid dreams or recurrent nightmares. Blocked memories are sometimes held not only in our minds but also in our physical bodies. These are sometimes referred to as "body memories." They may begin to surface in the form of unusual sensations, sensitivities, or pains in different areas of the body—often an area that was traumatized during the original event. Body therapy on that specific region of the body may also trigger these body memories. A thirty-year-old patient of mine whom I'll call Betty provides a classic example of this.

> *I have always been a devoutly spiritual woman. I have prayed and meditated daily since my teens. At the age of twelve or thirteen, I had been sexually abused by my older sister's husband. I knew the abuse had occurred but I had no memory of what had actually happened and held no conscious anger towards my former brother-in-law.*
>
> *When I came to see Dr. Kason, I was complaining of recurrent symptoms, including outbreaks of herpes around my mouth, unpleasant gagging sensations, and sensations of pressure in my lower abdomen and pelvis.*
>
> *When meditating, I unblocked the memory of my abuse. I recalled being vaginally raped and being forced to have oral sex on another occasion. During the hypnosis, my abdominal and pelvic pressures flared when I remembered the vaginal rape, and my gagging sensations became vivid as I recalled the oral assault. I also remembered that I first developed herpes soon after the oral assault.*

Soon after this, the physical symptoms of pressure and gagging associated with the repressed memories rapidly decreased, and her herpes outbreaks became far less frequent. Betty was also able to begin the process of psychological healing through releasing and resolving her blocked rage with the help of prayer, meditation, and psychotherapy. As this healing occurred, Betty's process of spiritual transformation accelerated.

When either flashes of memories or complete memories begin to surface, they are sometimes accompanied by anxiety or other distressing emotions. Because these emotions are unpleasant or even frightening, people sometimes struggle to force the memory back down. Often they are not consciously aware that they are doing this and are puzzled by seemingly inexplicable attacks of anxiety, panic, rage, or depression. In some cases, the strong negative emotions that were associated with the original event are the feelings that surface along with the memories, and they, too, may cause the experiencer to struggle unconsciously to suppress the memory again. A good example of this was Beth whose story of childhood sexual abuse was told in Chapter Fourteen. Beth felt a great deal of low-level anxiety most of the time. Each time she came close to unblocking the memory of her abuse, she felt increased anxiety, fear, and attacks of panic, and she tried to push the memories back down. She was even diagnosed by another doctor as suffering from panic attacks. Eventually she reached the point where she was ready to deal with the memories, and she allowed them to surface. With psychotherapeutic help she was then able to deal with the memories and begin the process of healing. Her "panic attacks" decreased dramatically and eventually stopped completely.

Once a memory surfaces, it must be dealt with and resolved. If it is not it will continue to cause psychological stress. Using the samskara analogy, we would say it continues to be a block to the flow of the transformative energy.

The resolution of surfacing issues is often accomplished only with a good deal of effort. The memories would never have been repressed originally if we had been able to deal effectively with and resolve the event and the associated emotions when they first occurred. For this and other reasons, many people undergoing the process of transformation decide to seek out counseling or to begin psychotherapy when memories begin to unblock.

Unfortunately, a surprising number of people are reluctant to ask for this kind of help. Even in this enlightened day and age, some people still think a stigma is attached to going for psychological help or to undergoing psychotherapy. They think it means something is "wrong" with them. Of course, nothing could be further from the truth. Seeking professional help is a sign that you are actively and enthusiastically involved in the growth process. Often it is the person who is the most "together" who seeks professional help first.

Whether you resolve traumatic memories alone or with a therapist, virtually all psychologists agree that you have to face the trauma and fully unblock the memory before you can begin to acknowledge, express, and eventually let go of the emotions associated with the original event. Only then can the psychological scars be healed—and the blocks be cleared away.

Strategies to Help Unblock Memories

If you feel that memories are trying to surface but are having difficulty making their way completely into your conscious mind, there are a number of techniques that can help. Before doing these or any other techniques, I recommend that you get under the care of a qualified psychotherapist or counselor who can assist you in dealing with any memories that may surface.

1. First, make a conscious decision that you want the memories to surface and that, as part of your spiritual growth, you are willing to face any painful issues they bring up.

2. Pray to the divine for help in unblocking the memories that you are ready for and that you need to face at this time to further your spiritual growth. Repeat this prayer occasionally throughout the day and again before falling asleep at night. You may receive help in flashes of intuition that occur during or right after a prayer. You may be led, for instance, to

re-read a passage from a certain book and, when you do, find it provides new, relevant insight.

3. Whenever you feel a memory begin to surface, focus on it. Don't push it away. If possible, take some time then and there to focus on the memory fragment and let it, and the associated emotions, flow into your consciousness. Try to re-experience the memory as fully as possible.

4. Write down dreams that have an unusual impact, that are recurrent, or that are associated with childhood.

5. Have some bodywork done—massage, shiatsu, or acupuncture, etc. Enter a meditative state during the process and pray to unblock memories that are now necessary for your spiritual growth.

6. Visualize and focus on your inner child. See her or him as clearly as you can—your inner child often looks as you did in the full bloom of childhood. Alternatively, your inner child's appearance may bear clues as to your unresolved issues. Embrace your inner child with love. Ask if there are any memories that are causing pain or blocking his or her full expression in your daily life. Ask for help in bringing up these memories so that your inner child can finally be healed and free.

7. Meditate and visualize your heart chakra. Focus on any pain or area of darkness you feel or see in this area. Then, visualize light rising gently up from the base of your spine—or pouring down on you from above—and illuminating the darkness at your heart chakra. See the light flushing away at the dark areas, lifting the dark spots up, bringing them up to your conscious mind, and then flushing them away. Then focus on any images or memories that come to your mind. Some people like to visualize the divine power as a liquid light that flushes the spots of darkness out through the front of the heart chakra.

If, after trying these strategies, you feel you have memories that still will not surface but that you feel ready to face, do not force yourself! Wait a few months. There may be a good reason why these memories are staying repressed at this time.

Whenever a memory does surface, concentrate on it, and try to re-experience the incident in your mind. Try to expand upon the memory, and recall as many details about the event and surrounding circumstances as possible. Try to recall how you felt during and after the incident. Allow yourself to feel the emotions related to the incident. Try to clarify exactly how the incident made you feel, and allow yourself to feel those emotions. Give yourself permission to feel angry, enraged, sad, hurt, jealous, betrayed, or guilty or to experience any other emotion you might be holding about the event. Then, in time, you can work towards forgiving yourself and/or the others involved and, finally, releasing the hold this event has had on you.

After repressed memories begin to surface, psychotherapy and a number of psychotherapeutic techniques can facilitate the healing of the painful emotions and scars left from earlier traumatic events. I have also found a number of techniques and strategies you can use to help resolve some of the psycho-spiritual issues that arise. However, many people find they need psycho-therapeutic help in dealing with surfacing memories at some point in their spiritual journey—especially when the memories are surfacing very rapidly or are related to traumatic incidents such as violence or childhood sexual abuse. If the memories become overwhelming or if you simply decide you'd like to have some help dealing with them, don't hesitate to get it. In the meantime you may find the following self-help strategies helpful.

Dealing with Unblocking Traumatic Memories

1. *Keep a daily journal.* Set aside some time each day to write your insights, thoughts, and feelings in your journal. Include any upsetting incidents that may have occurred or traumatic memories that may have surfaced since the last time you wrote. Make

note of your reflections on these and any other memories or on any other psychological issues you are working with and record insights gained during your meditations. Also, write down your dreams, especially those that recur, seem to have a message, provoke strong emotions, or are particularly vivid or "real." Sometimes the "dream before waking" is particularly significant.

People who regularly keep a journal find that writing down thoughts, feelings, and reflections often helps clarify them and put them into perspective. It also can help people gain personal insights and speed the process of resolving psychological issues or, at least, keep it moving along.

2. *Use inner dialogue.* Sit in a quiet place where you will not be disturbed for a while. Close your eyes, relax, and focus your mind on a memory that has come unblocked. Allow yourself to re-experience some of the emotions involved in the original event, try to visualize the face of the person involved or simply "imagine" that the person is sitting in front of you. Begin an inner dialogue with that person. If the person is someone who hurt you, tell them how what they said or did affected you, how it made you feel, and how it still hurts or affects you. Allow yourself to express the emotions you have about the original incident and its consequences. Don't be afraid to express all of the emotions—anger, rage, resentment, sorrow—you have felt or may have been holding back over the years. And don't be surprised if you actually re-experience some of these emotions quite strongly. When you have finished expressing your feelings, ask the other person why they did what they did. Then wait, and listen for the reply. Often this reply will give you a new insight and bring you to a new level of understanding regarding the incident. Respond to the reply, and continue this inner mental dialogue with the other person as long as you feel you need to and until you feel you have come to a level of understanding that allows you to put the incident more to rest and let go of some or all of the anger and pain. You can repeat this technique as often as you like.

If the memory you have unblocked is of your hurting someone, follow the same process but explain your reasons for doing what you did, apologize, and ask for forgiveness. Give the person a chance to respond, listen, and then continue with the inner dialogue until you feel it has reached a conclusion. Pray to be forgiven for your past hurtful action. Finally, pray for help to forgive yourself for having hurt the other person.

When using this technique, pray and meditate for help in healing the anger, pain, and/or guilt associated with the original incident or the aftermath—and for help in learning your spiritual lessons from this experience.

Ricky, one of my psychotherapy patients, used inner dialogue to resolve anger. Ricky felt deeply hurt by her deceased mother. On the day before Ricky was to be married, her mother had told Ricky's fiancé that he should consider putting off the marriage, because Ricky would be such a difficult person to be married to. After this, Ricky had always felt that her mother disapproved of her husband and that her mother felt Ricky was "bad" and unworthy of a good marriage.

When Ricky used the inner dialogue technique, she told the image of her mother how hurt she had been by the remark made before her wedding. When asked why she had said such a thing, the image of Ricky's mother replied that she had always felt misunderstood in her own marriage to Ricky's father. He had often been cold and insensitive, in contrast to her emotional sensitivity. In the visualization, Ricky's mother went on to tell her that she thought Ricky was a very special, gifted person with deep emotional sensitivity. She explained that she had wanted to protect Ricky from the kind of unhappy marriage she had had and admitted that she had projected her feelings about her own husband onto Ricky's prospective husband.

This answer so surprised and moved Ricky that she began to cry and was able to resolve much of her anger with her mother about the event. She also began to come to a deeper realization of how much her mother had cared for her.

3. *Surrender your problems to the divine*. Remember that the healing power of the divine is far greater than the problems related to the memory—no matter how immense they may seem. Take a moment to reflect on the stupendous power which drives the universe, how it fires the infernos of the sun and other stars and breathes life into the amazingly diverse plants and animals that populate our planet. Reflecting on this often helps us realize that the power of the divine is immensely and unimaginably greater than the power any problem in our lives might have. With this in mind, surrender your problem to the divine and pray for healing and guidance in resolving it. One image that I find helpful is that of putting your problems "at the feet of the Master."

4. *Focus on learning the spiritual lesson*. Instead of focusing your mental energies on the problem and your pain and suffering, focus your energy on discovering the spiritual lessons that you can learn from this experience. Remind yourself that life's hardships provide opportunities for learning and growth. Actively look for the lesson inherent in the problem you are facing. Pray, contemplate, and meditate and ask for help in discovering what the lesson is. Once you truly perceive and process this spiritual lesson, the trauma's negative impact will lessen in this light.

5. *Read inspirational and other self-help books*. Reading about others who have overcome traumas similar to the ones you have suffered can be a great help. Ask someone in the field to recommend a book or go through the self-help section of your library or bookstore and look for one or two books that seem to present a balanced view. Reading generally inspirational books can also be a big help. A few of the authors that I recommend and that represent a wide range of views include Og Mandino, Leo Buscaglia, Marion Woodman, John Bradshaw, and Emmet Fox. And, of course, the holy books of the major faiths can provide great inspiration. The Psalms of the Old Testament have often provided me with tremendous comfort.

6. *Practice Gratitude*. The old adage is that a half a cup of water looks half empty to the pessimist and half full to the optimist! Be a grateful optimist. Rather than focusing on things you dislike or desire, practice expressing gratitude to the divine for things you do

have. During challenging periods, I recommend daily gratitude journalling—writing down five to ten things for which you are grateful every single day. The days it is difficult to feel grateful are probably the most important days to practice gratitude.

7. *Keep your problems in perspective.* Whenever you are feeling overwhelmed by your surfacing memories and problems, try to re-establish a realistic perspective. Reflect briefly on the terrible suffering and horrendous conditions other people have had to endure, such as war, torture, starvation, discrimination, unjust imprisonment, and concentration camps. Sometimes thinking of the hardships others are facing helps us see that our problems are far from being the worst in the universe and that we are more fortunate than many others.

8. *Talk to friends about your traumas.* The psychological burden of past trauma can be greatly lessened by telling a deeply trusted friend or relative about the traumatic memories you have unblocked. Those who know you and really care about you can give tremendous support and can often provide you with new and deeper insights. Sharing the burden does help speed the healing. In time, you may even be able to laugh with your confidante about yourself or certain aspects of your memories—and laughter, being such a powerful healer, can speed your emotional recovery even more.

9. *Join a support group.* Support groups are powerful because they allow you to share your experiences with people who can empathize and understand because they have gone through the same trauma themselves. Listening to these people can remove your sense of isolation and help you learn the strategies they have used for healing and growth.

Learning from Past-Life Memories

As discussed in Chapter Fourteen, I have found in my work that many people undergoing spiritual transformation begin to spontaneously unblock traumatic memories from what appear to be past lives. You might be having similar experiences and be concerned about them because some people think such things are "strange" or "crazy." But let me reassure you that many highly intelligent, mentally healthy people have described this phenomenon to me, and I, along with many other psychotherapists, am convinced that it is real. I have even experienced glimpses of past-life memories myself. The ones that have come to me have all been related to people I am close to in this lifetime—relatives and friends. The scenarios in the past-life memories, whether symbolic or actual, usually helped me understand at a deeper level some of the dynamics and difficult issues within my relationships. I have found the apparent past-life memories, when they occur, to be very insightful, aiding my understanding of complex interpersonal relationships.

During the process of my own spiritual journey, I have become very comfortable with the concept of reincarnation and have come to believe that we return to life on this plane again and again in order to learn spiritual lessons. People who find this concept difficult to accept should keep in mind the fact that Hindus, Buddhists, Native Indians, and members of a number of other religions accept the reality of reincarnation as a matter of course—and these people make up a huge percentage of the world's population. Jewish Kabbalistic teachings accept reincarnation, and some historians believe certain early Christians did too. Further, a 1981 Gallup poll showed that nearly a quarter of all Americans believed in reincarnation, and a more recent one showed that almost a third of all Canadians did too.

Still, many people cannot accept the concept of reincarnation and, consequently, the reality of past-life memories. Some psychologists believe that what seem to be past-life memories are in reality historical images of others' lives that come from tapping into what Jung called the collective unconscious. Yet another theory is that apparent past-life memories are metaphors, symbolic images that are meant to make us aware of psychological or spiritual issues. According to this interpretation, apparent past-life memories can be seen as symbolic messages from our unconscious to our conscious minds, like many of the images in dreams.

Regardless, the fact remains that a great many people unblock traumatic memories from what they perceive to be—or suspect might be—past lives during the process of spiritual transformation. Usually the memories are traumatic, and the psychological issues associated with them need to be dealt with and healed just as with other unblocked traumatic memories.

In my work as a psychotherapist, I have noticed that there are several similarities between unblocking traumatic past-life memories and unblocking ones from this life. First, the experiencers are usually ready, at some level, to face the memory—even if they are not consciously aware of it. Second, unblocking past-life memories often has the same—if sometimes less intense—impact on the experiencer as unblocking present-life memories does. Third, and most important, experiencers can gain great insight and undergo tremendous psychological healing when they try to work with the memory, re-experience the event, release the emotions associated with it, heal the unresolved emotions, and learn the spiritual lessons related to it.

Sometimes past-life memories that surface spontaneously actually warn us, or help us understand another person's behavior towards us. It may seem as if the individuals involved in the memory are actually repeating the same type of unhealthy interaction that they had in a past life. When this awareness surfaces in a person in spiritual transformation, it often prompts them to react differently to the situation this time, or even to walk away from it in peace. This was true for Tom, a 45-year-old business consultant.

> *Tom had a Near-Death Experience when he fell into a severe drinking relapse during his recovery from alcoholism. After the NDE, Tom fully embraced his recovery, went into a spiritually based AA treatment program, and began intensive personal psychotherapy. He also found he now had ongoing kundalini symptoms, energy rushes up the spine, heat experiences, and light experiences. He underwent a profound spiritual transformation of his personality.*
>
> *Tom had many unresolved issues relating to a relationship that had ended a year earlier. He was unhappy*

being single, and he longed to reconcile with his former girlfriend, Alice. Alice blamed Tom and his alcoholism for ruining her aspiration to achieve a high-income marriage. She was angry at his efforts to recover from his alcoholism, and abruptly ended the relationship when he insisted that he could no longer pretend there was no problem and drink alcohol with her at dinner parties. She felt humiliated and said that Tom made her look bad by his admission that he was an alcoholic. Alice expressed rage at how he had not lived up to her standards and expectations, how he did not help her fulfill her dreams. Tom felt profoundly guilty about this whole situation.

Tom had started praying to the divine to help him heal this situation with Alice. About four months after the NDE, Tom started to get glimpses of what seemed to be a past life, coming to him in his meditations, in dreams, and then, finally, in his waking state. Within ten days the pieces of the past-life memory came together. The memory showed Tom that he had been an artist living in the 1700s, supported by a patron, a wealthy married woman—who seemed similar to Alice. An attraction and a clandestine affair developed between the two. The woman had plans for them to run away to Europe together and start a new life with her parents' wealth.

The memory went on to show that Tom had also been married, to another woman who lived in a town distant from the patron. Tom remembered a life-long friend coming to see him at the patron's studio, telling him to come home, that his wife had had a baby and needed his help and support. In the memory, Tom realized his responsibility to his wife and decided to return home. His patron became enraged. She had no compassion for Tom's need to return home to care for his wife and child. She raged at him for shattering her dream of their happy life together in Europe. She complained that his leaving would humiliate her in her social circle. He pleaded for understanding, but she threw him out.

With the insights gained from the memory, Tom was finally able to make sense of his unresolved feelings about Alice. He believed he had been so attracted to her because he unconsciously felt he "owed her something" from their past life together. He also saw that her behavior towards him in both lifetimes was very similar. Alice was not supportive or understanding, and she was very angry when he did not fulfill her dreams and expectations. He also understood Alice's intense anger towards him—she had the anger of two lifetimes inside her.

With this understanding and with the help of prayer and psychotherapy, Tom was finally able to let go of his guilt over the ending of this relationship. Tom now realized that Alice would not be a healthy life partner for him, and that he needed a partner who would be supportive of his path of healing. Some time later, Tom met a woman who was also on a path of recovery, and they now have a stable and happy relationship.

Tom's story shows how past-life memories usually relate to problems that are causing a great deal of pain and distress in this life. In cases like this, it is helpful to focus on learning the spiritual lessons involved. This is particularly true when the apparent past-life memories involve people with whom you are currently having emotional difficulties. As we saw in the story of Tom, the unblocking of the past-life memory often yields new insights and a new perspective on the problems you are struggling to understand.

In my clinical experience I have found that many of the lessons associated with past-life memories seem to be connected to our interpersonal relationships. Some people believe the reasons for this lie in the fact that a certain degree of continuity exists from life to life and that we encounter some individuals again and again. If this is the case, it is plausible that deep unconscious memories concerning an individual and an associated traumatic event might well affect the way we relate to that person in this life—and might also be a factor in some dysfunctional relationships. I have come across a number of people who, after unblocking and dealing with traumatic past-life memories, were better able to understand the unconscious dynamics of a particular relationship and then either improve the relationship or find the strength to leave it.

One of the best ways to discover the unconscious dynamics is to compare the emotional patterns of the past-life situation to those in your present life. Try to discover the parallels between the two situations. The common denominator between the two will often provide a powerful clue to exactly what the spiritual lesson is.

This was certainly true for Denise, the nurse whose story about a past-life memory of being accused of being a witch in Salem was first told in Chapter Six.

> *After unblocking the past-life memory, I came to the conclusion that my brother from the past life—the one who had failed to be at my side when I had been falsely accused of witchcraft—was my husband in my present life. Once I realized this, I became aware of a startling parallel between the two situations.*
>
> *One of the main problems troubling my present marriage to him was my persistent fear that he was going to abandon me. In spite of the fact that my husband was deeply devoted, I was convinced that he would not stand by me as my process of spiritual transformation continued. I constantly found myself questioning his loyalty and, as a defense mechanism, being overly critical and untrusting of him.*
>
> *As the past-life memory became clearer, I recalled that I had been a highly spiritual person in that life and that my strong convictions had led to my being falsely accused of witchcraft. I also recalled that my brother had not understood my spirituality at all. After realizing this, I could see the correlation between what had happened then and what was happening in the present.*

> *After examining my present situation honestly and doing a good deal of psychological work, I eventually came to the conclusion that most of the distrust I felt for my husband was based on my residual feelings about the past life together. Once I was certain this was true, I strove to resolve my past-life anger and feelings of betrayal. I then slowly became able to trust the loyalty my husband was exhibiting in this lifetime.*

Denise's story is also interesting because it shows how—in a therapeutic sense—it makes little difference whether the memory was a real event from a past life or a symbolic message from the unconscious. In either case, the issue was the same: Denise's inability to trust her husband. And the solution was the same: Denise had to examine her distrust and decide whether it was a projection coming from inside her own unconscious or from the fact that she, in reality, had reason to distrust her husband.

When dealing with apparent past-life memories, you might also want to consider the possibility of a karmic link between yourself and a person who has harmed you. It may be that this person's actions in this life are his or her response to your actions in a past life. It may even be that this cycle of action and reaction between the two of you has been repeated many times. If this is so, the realization may give you greater insight into exactly what your role in the situation is, and, with prayer and meditation, you may learn how you can resolve the karmic link and move on, or perhaps even restore harmony and balance between yourself and the other person.

In general, I believe that examining and reflecting on the psychological and spiritual issues related to what seem to be past-life memories has tremendous potential for promoting growth. This is true whether these memories are, in actual fact, from past lives or not. When the memory surfaces, don't waste time and energy debating the reality of reincarnation. Whether these memories are actually from previous incarnations or are symbolic representations of psychological issues surfacing from your unconscious, they are making you aware of valuable psychological and spiritual lessons. These memories—or powerful images, if you will—can be used as tools to assist in your psychological and spiritual growth. However, it should be kept in mind that these images are often extremely powerful. Occasionally images involving abuse or injustice are so powerful and seem so real that experiencers have to be reminded to keep the memory in perspective. Treating the person who apparently carried out an injustice in a past life as if he or she had actually done it in this life, or retaliating against or acting out in anger towards him or her, would be completely inappropriate. It would also ruin the potential for forgiveness, reconciliation, healing, and spiritual growth that the unblocking of past-life memories brings.

Resolution, Transcendence, and Forgiveness

In order to achieve resolution, any unfinished business relating to the unblocked traumatic memory needs to be dealt with. This may be done in a number of ways. Sometimes it can all be resolved in therapy. However, some people find they need to speak face-to-face with the person involved in the original incident, either to express their feelings or ask the person why they did what they did. Others need to ask for forgiveness for their own actions. Some people, for instance those who were abused as children, feel they need to press criminal charges. Of course, the means of resolving unfinished business in an appropriate way are as individual as the people and situations involved. Once it is resolved, the next step is to transcend the experience.

To me, transcendence means rising above the negativity of the experience and using the energy generated by the trauma for a positive purpose. For instance, the anger and outrage you feel about a trauma you suffered might motivate you and give you the energy to use what you've learned from the experience in a positive way. You might decide to start a support group in your area or begin volunteering at a local crisis center. You might speak at churches or schools about your experiences in order to help others. You might write an article about avoiding or dealing with the type of trauma you suffered. Some people write a book about their experience and healing in order to help others. Many find that this is a worthwhile, therapeutic, and cathartic process even if the book is never published. Regardless of the specific action you decide to take, the important element in transcendence is to rise above the negative emotions and to channel your activated emotional energy—along with what you have learned—into something positive.

Forgiveness is the final step in resolving psychological traumas. Many people try to forgive someone too soon, before they have even begun to come to terms with what the other person has done. They then find they haven't forgiven the person at all and wonder why they failed to do so. You can truly forgive only after you have faced the memory, felt and honored the repressed emotions, and begun to strive to transcend those emotions. Once you have accomplished this, you can attempt to forgive and get on with your life.

Pauline, a twenty-seven-year-old singer, prematurely tried to forgive her mother.

When I was in high school, at around age fifteen, while sleeping over at my older sister's apartment in another town, I was raped by my sister's live-in boyfriend. I was horrified, and afraid to tell anybody. Finally, a few days later I told my mom. My mom told me not to tell anybody else, and this rape was never acknowledged by my family.

Four years later, my sister married the boyfriend. When I refused to dance with the groom at the reception, my father insisted to know why, so I finally told my dad the story of the rape. My father was furious that I had never told him at the time. My mother did not remember that she had told me not to tell anyone. My whole family was in an uproar. My sister got very angry at me, claiming that I had made the whole thing up in order to ruin her marriage.

I was furious at my mom. I felt that she was not

standing up for me against my sister or my father. I hated Mom for this!

When I was about twenty-five, I rediscovered my faith, Christianity. I started to pray and read the Bible daily. I made a conscious decision to forgive my mom for siding with my dad and sister at the wedding. I convinced myself that she had to side with her husband.

I really thought I had forgiven Mom, until I started psychotherapy. Suddenly I found myself feeling tremendous rage and resentment towards her. With psychotherapeutic help, I realized that I had not yet faced the real issue that I was angry about. I realized that I was angry at Mom for silencing me and for not having helped me more at the time of the rape. Once this rage had surfaced, I finally felt as if I could really work to forgive Mom.

CHAPTER 17

Stimulating Healthy Spiritual Transformation

People frequently want to know how they can best stimulate the process of spiritual transformation. It should be clear by now that I believe moderation and balance are the essential ingredients in any attempt to further spiritual progress. With this in mind, I am providing a list of stimulants to kundalini. Be aware of them, use appropriate ones only in a balanced and moderate way, and avoid overstimulating the transformative energy. If you are in the least tempted to begin the excessive practice of many of the stimulants, turn back to Chapters Thirteen and Fourteen, read about the importance of balanced living, and consider the tragic consequences of throwing yourself into spiritual emergency—or worse. I do not say this lightly. In my work over the last fifteen years, I have seen people who, in their overeagerness to have spiritual experiences, did themselves great harm. One was a man I met at a conference a few years ago. I'll call him Jerrit.

I was a university professor in a town in the midwestern United States. When I was in my thirties I had a profound mystical experience and decided I would do anything to have the experience again.

Both the university I taught in and the community I lived in were very traditional in their approach. At the time when I had my mystical experience, topics such as Eastern religion and meditation were considered strange. Even the practice of yoga was looked at askance. After my experience, however, I did find someone who recommended Gopi Krishna's books. I managed to obtain them and pored over them, absorbing as much as I could. I noticed that Gopi Krishna repeatedly urged moderation and balance and warned against the dangers of excessive spiritual practices. However, in my intense desire to stimulate another spiritual experience, I decided not only to not follow this advice but to even go so far as to find everything that might overstimulate kundalini and then begin to practice it. I threw myself into intensive yoga, meditation, and Tantric practices. And I did eventually stimulate the awakening of kundalini.

My body and mind were totally unprepared for the tremendous shock to my system. I was thrown into spiritual emergency, and then psychosis. Unable to function, I lost my job. I felt as if I were on fire or burning alive, and I endured sensations of light so bright that they were excruciatingly painful. I suffered through horrific visions and the blackest pits of despair and depression. Unfortunately, I was forced to endure this suffering alone for almost three years, because I couldn't find anyone who understood what I was going through. Finally, I found a sympathetic therapist in a nearby city through the Spiritual Emergence Network. I began to practice grounding techniques and to follow the moderate approach to life and spirituality I had first read about in Gopi Krishna's books. But even then I continued to suffer periodically for some time. Finally, after years of effort, I come close to full recovery.

Jerrit's story serves as a powerful warning, as do the case histories of others who have brought on spiritual emergency by intensive, excessive spiritual practices. At the conference where we met, he spoke openly about his experiences and his suffering and literally begged people not to do as he had done.

Before going on to discuss some of the balanced, moderate approaches that might facilitate progress on the spiritual journey, I here present the list of energy stimulants. The effect that any one stimulant has will, of course, vary from individual to individual, and some individuals will be far more susceptible to each of them than other people would be. In general, the longer each activity is done and the greater the intensity of the practice, the greater the stimulating effect. Most of the practices are not harmful in and of themselves, and many are beneficial when used in moderation. It is intensiveness or excessiveness that can make most of them harmful.

Although it will take extensive research to determine exactly which activities are the most stimulating, I have tried to list them—based on my research and experience—with the strongest stimulants first.

Stimulants to the Transformative Energy

1. Intensely focused kundalini meditation—a type of meditation that involves visualizing and focusing on an image of the kundalini rising from the base of the spine, piercing the chakras, and opening at the crown. Often the image at the crown is one of a lotus bud opening into full bloom.

2. Intensely focused meditation on the divine—meditation that focuses on contemplation of a particular aspect of the divine, for instance, omnipresence, omnipotence, omniscience, or the silence.

3. Intensely focused meditation on chakra points—a meditation in which energy, divine light, sacred images, or opening lotus blossoms are visualized at certain

chakra points. Each chakra may be visualized in sequence, beginning with the first (root) and moving upward to the crown chakra—or a particular chakra may be focused upon exclusively, for instance the heart chakra, the third-eye chakra, or the crown chakra.

4. Intense prayer and devotion.

5. Intense self-reflection, depth psychotherapy, or recovery work.

6. Intense practice of Hatha Yoga.

7. Pranayama.

8. Tantric sexual practices.

9. Receiving shaktipat from a person with a highly active kundalini.

10. Intensive, prolonged concentration or focus on spiritual topics—for example, reading spiritual material, discussing and debating spiritual topics, contemplating spiritual questions, or attending spiritual conferences.

11. Intensive, prolonged concentration or focus on any subject without breaks.

12. Intensive, prolonged periods of reading.

13. Tai Chi, and Chi Kung.

14. Bodywork, massage, shiatsu, etc., that is aimed at increasing or stimulating the flow of life energy.

15. Chanting.

16. Sexual relations with a person who has an active kundalini.

17. Being in the prolonged presence of others who have an active kundalini.

18. Being in a state of emotional and spiritual openness; surrendering to the divine, hitting bottom in addictions and recovery.

19. Being close to death.

20. Being close to someone who dies.

Although most of these activities are self-explanatory, I have provided additional information below on those that some readers might not be familiar with. More detailed quick references for some can be found in *The Encyclopedic Dictionary of Yoga* and far more thorough explanations in Eliade's *Yoga: Immortality and Freedom*.

Hatha Yoga. An important aspect of the Tantric tradition, Hatha Yoga is geared to self-realization through the perfection of the body. According to Feuerstein, the main goal of the student of Hatha Yoga is to intercept the flow of prana and redirect it along the sushumna to arouse the serpent power, or kundalini. In my experience, Hatha Yoga postures or asanas tend to balance and harmonize the healthy flow of prana through the body when practiced in moderation. However, people whose energy is already highly active may find some or any type of yogic practice overstimulating. This is particularly true of practices such as kundalini yoga—a branch of Tantrism specifically aimed at awakening the serpent power—and of some Hatha Yoga postures, such as the cobra, that are specifically meant to stimulate kundalini.

Pranayama. In Hatha Yoga, pranayama—a specific breath control technique—is believed to have a number of purifying, rejuvenating, and curative effects. It is also a primary technique used to force the serpent power into the sushumna to begin its ascent to the crown. The fourteenth-century *Hatha-yoga-pradipika*, the most widely used manual on Hatha Yoga, urges caution in using pranayama, saying "Just as a lion, an elephant, or a tiger is tamed gradually, so should the life-force be controlled: else it will kill the practitioner."

Tantric sexual practices. Although Tantrism contains many divergent schools, most are centered around the concept of shakti—another name for kundalini. According to Feuerstein, one of the three main approaches in Tantrism can be roughly equated with kundalini yoga; the other two are known as the right-handed, or conservative, path and the left-handed path. The latter contains the practices, such as ones involving sexual intercourse, that have tended to tarnish the reputation of Tantrism in general.

Some Tantric sexual practices use spiritual visualizations to encourage the upward release of energy at the time of orgasm (urdhava-retas). Successful upward release at the time of orgasm results in a blast of prana and ojas to the brahma randhra, causing a marked mystical experience. Lack of understanding and misunderstanding have led some untrained Westerners to adopt these techniques to try to experiment with and manipulate the sexual energy during intercourse, thinking it will bring about intensely powerful sexual experiences. People who are doing this are attempting to "play" not just with fire but with the fiery power behind the universe. It can be extremely dangerous. I do not recommend attempting to force the upward flow of energy—it begins to occur spontaneously when the body has been properly prepared and is finally ready.

Shaktipat. More properly "shakti pata," this practice refers to the transmission of spiritual energy from a spiritual adept to another person, usually a student or a disciple. Usually done with a touch, but sometimes a glance, shakti pata is reported to activate kundalini and send the recipient into expanded states of consciousness or even samadhi for a period of time.

Prolonged contact with others who have an active kundalini. This is one of the most interesting phenomena currently being observed but, unfortunately, one we know little about. One of the places this phenomenon has recently been observed is at conferences on subjects such as kundalini and spiritual emergence. A significant number of people report having increased kundalini activity during and immediately after these types of events. Although this effect could be caused by intense focus on spiritual topics, it seems likely that the high concentration of people with active kundalini who are drawn to such events may also be a factor.

Although this phenomenon might seem inexplicable or even unbelievable to some, related phenomena are recognized in the yogic tradition. For instance, sat sanga is the practice of associating with enlightened spiritual masters and sadhus, or saintly people. Such association is believed, in and of itself, to purify, uplift, and stimulate the spiritual process.

It is my opinion that a scientific explanation for this may one day be found. I have speculated that the phenomenon might even be a kind of "tuning fork" effect in which a type of "resonance" that is created by kundalini activity and that emanates from the experiencer might begin to stimulate similar activity in an individual in whom the transformative energy is ready to become more active. Future research might also find that this provides an explanation for the way in which shakti pata manifests.

The Moderate Path to the Evolution of Consciousness

Many people accept the fact that there is far too much risk involved in trying to rush their spiritual progress, but they still want to know how they can accelerate their progress as much as possible in a safe and healthy way. Many also want to know, more specifically, how they can stimulate the awakening of kundalini to some degree and still avoid the pitfalls inherent in trying to force the transformative energy into too much activity too soon. We all need to remember that the science of stimulating kundalini was the work of a lifetime according to the ancient Indian yogis, and that the true practice of yoga affects virtually every aspect of life. You need to be prepared physically, psychologically, and spiritually before taking up those practices that are most stimulating to the transformative energy. Further, you need to remember that the amount of focused concentration most people do in their daily lives today may already be providing more than enough stimulation. With all this in mind, I think the safest route to awakening kundalini might be summarized in this way:

1. Follow a balanced, regular lifestyle. Eat a nutritious diet; have regular meals; get regular exercise; get adequate and regular sleep; avoid drugs, tobacco, and alcohol; avoid excessive stress.

2. Do a light practice of yoga or Tai Chi.

3. Pray briefly several times a day, and/or do a light practice of meditation.

4. Attempt to resolve any psychological conflicts or negative feelings that you harbor relating to your family and other interpersonal relationships. Don't hesitate

to enter into psychotherapy if needed to help resolve deeply rooted conflicts.

5. Conceptualize yourself and all beings as divine children, here in earthly form to express our innate divinity; surrender to the divine plan; pray to be worthy to be an instrument of light in this plan.

6. Participate in the world, but in a manner that is detached from ambitions for power, status, or material possessions; focus your efforts instead on making the world a better place by contributing in whatever way you can; spend some time each week being of service to humankind.

7. Work towards developing the characteristics of unitive consciousness: compassion, humility, gratitude, and surrender to the divine.

Gopi Krishna, when asked "How can the average person achieve higher consciousness and help in the evolution of the race?" gave the following reply:

The surest way should be to voluntarily develop the characteristics of higher consciousness. For instance, to always keep in mind that there is no barrier, no distinction, no wall between man and man. Whenever we see another person, though we may act in the normal way towards him, at the back of our minds should be the thought that the same consciousness, the same Divine substance, that is talking, hearing and listening in me, is also talking, hearing and listening in him; that it is one substance, one cosmic medium, that is expressing itself in all human beings.

This will be in accordance even with the saying of the Christ, "Treat thy neighbors as thyself." And it is also the teaching of the Bhagavad Gita, to treat all fellow human beings as your own self. This would be, perhaps, the most effective way to melt the barriers which are created by the ego—to always put oneself in the shoes of another. . . .

Another very powerful exercise is to keep before the mind's eye an image of Cosmic Consciousness. Or, if one believes in a God, to imagine that it is a Divine Consciousness, a presence, an immanence, an ethereal eye spread all over the universe—omniscient, omnipresent, and omnipotent.

The third would also be a corollary to the first: that since you now think—and you believe—that all men are yourself, having all the same feelings and emotions, and are also expressions of the same energy, you should act in ways that will help them, either by advice or by teaching, or by backing their prospects or by raising them up if they are fallen. Or by advising them where they are mistaken, trying to help them in the same way we would like to be helped when we are in distress. This would be an effective method.

A fourth exercise would be in the morning and evening or at any convenient time—to sit in contemplation of Divinity, Cosmic Consciousness, God, Brahma, or by whatever name you call it, and continue thinking and meditating on it, reflecting on it as you would think, meditate or reflect on a very stubborn problem that needed to be solved. Try to build up the image in the mind, an image of an infinite extension, of an endless duration in time. And then dwell on these thoughts, and never allow the mind to become quiescent or to go into sleep. This exercise is given in many Yoga manuals.

The mind should remain alert, just as it remains alert when we are solving a problem, when we are concentrating on a mathematical proposition, or when we are studying a subject. We should keep the mind alert and reflect on the attributes of God—once, twice or thrice a day—in a devout mood, and offer this contemplation as a prayer to the Almighty to help us raise our consciousness.

The fifth would be to live a life in harmony with one's relatives, friends, and even strangers, in harmony with one's conscience and in harmony with the teachings of great religious prophets—not to be sanctimonious or prudish, but to have healthy instincts, to practice moderation and always to behave in a manner that is noble. High moral caliber goes side by side with an elevated state of consciousness, so all these disciplines are necessary, because the stage we are reaching for is composed of all these attributes. If we voluntarily cultivate them we help the evolutionary forces to build up the consciousness that will be the heritage of the future man.

Throughout history countless people have awakened the transformative energy. But only a few rare individuals have successfully navigated the journey and achieved the transformation of consciousness that leads to the state known as perennial cosmic consciousness, perennial mystical consciousness, Christ-consciousness, Buddha-consciousness, or the Sahaja state.

As we have seen from the stories told throughout this book, the spiritual journey can be fraught with obstacles that range from the distraction of developing psychic gifts to delusions about the importance of one's role in the cosmic plan, to lust for money, status, or power; and from inadequate cleansing of the unconscious to unbridled egotism. When walking the spiritual path one needs to step carefully, pay great attention, and make decisions using intellectual discernment, while always heeding the higher guidance from the divine—which comes to us in our inner voice, prayers, dreams, and meditations.

As you've read through this book, you have become familiar with the wide variety of types and degrees of Spiritually Transformative Experiences. You may have compared them to your own Experiences or those of people you know, learned about the difficulties that can occur during the transformative process, considered the tremendous importance of psychological housecleaning, and discovered how critical a balanced lifestyle is. Beyond all this, you may have wondered about the particular path that you have chosen and whether it is leading you in the right direction. Although no one can make that judgment for you, there are a number of signs that can act as guideposts. If the path you are following is, overall, positive and well-balanced and is helping you progress along the spiritual path, you will eventually begin to notice positive changes in your self and in your outlook. The following are some of the most important:

Signs of Healthy Spiritual Transformation

1. You will find yourself developing more noble traits of character, such as compassion, universal love, gratitude, charity, truth, honesty, and humility.

2. Your desire to be of service to humanity will grow and may become a primary focus as your feelings of unity with all humankind and all creation grow.

3. You will have an intense inner yearning for the divine.

4. You may experience a spontaneous flow of tears and overwhelming emotion at the mention or thought of the divine.

5. You will find yourself developing a more clear, discerning intellect and deeper psychological insights, along with a higher moral fiber.

6. You may find yourself developing new gifts of inspired creativity.

7. You will find yourself repeatedly experiencing mystical states of consciousness.

If you can honestly say that you are passing some of these guideposts along the way, you can be confident that you are moving in the right direction. But, of course, even the best of paths can be traveled too quickly or too intensively. If you find you are having more difficulties than you can easily bear or are having crises or spiritual emergencies, take stock of your practices, your lifestyle, and your need for assistance and make the necessary changes. Perhaps, eventually, you may be one of the rare and blessed individuals who reach the crown of perennial cosmic consciousness in this lifetime. Most yogic traditions contend that many lifetimes of active spiritual transformation are necessary before a soul completes its spiritual growth and purification. But wherever we are on the mystical path, the divine blesses us with many glimpses of union along the way!

If unitive consciousness is indeed the goal of human evolution we will all eventually reach this goal. This fact helps us keep our spiritual experiences in perspective. No matter how profound our experiences are, they do not make us better than anyone else. And they do not mean we are necessarily going to reach cosmic consciousness any faster than anyone else. Ultimately, I believe that this crown is a gift of grace from the divine and that all of us are equally part of this divine cosmic presence.

Right now thousands, perhaps millions, of persons around the world are undergoing the process of spiritual transformation. Within this planetary scheme, each one of us has our own small role. By working together we can change our society to one that is more conducive to and more in keeping with the needs of spiritual evolution. By embracing the part we have to play in making the world a better place and by joining forces we can bring the human race as a whole closer to the divine vision of a planet blossoming in mystical consciousness. For me, and for many, many others, this is the true meaning of the coming of the cosmic Christ—the coming of generations of humans who exist in a perennial state of Christ consciousness. The process of spiritual transformation that we are individually experiencing now is but the first step through a door that leads to a bright and glorious future for us all.

Appendix

The Kundalini Research Network (KRN) was founded in March 1990 at the home of Bonnie Greenwell, Ph.D., by an international group of doctors, scientists, and scholars which included me, Kenneth Ring, Ph.D., of the International Association for Near Death Studies; Francesca McCartney, Ph.D., from the Institute for Intuitive Studies; Russell Park, Ph.D. and Megan Nolan, Ph.D., board members of the Spiritual Emergence Network; George Tompkins, board member of the Kundalini Research Association International; Paul Pond, Ph.D., and Michael Bradford, B.Sc., board members of the Institute for Consciousness Research; Teri Degler, M.A.; and several other individuals interested in kundalini research. The founding members shared an interest in promoting and collaborating on research into spiritual states of human consciousness and their relationship to the phenomenon known in the yogic tradition as kundalini. The KRN is currently undertaking this research and is attempting to bring the existence of kundalini and the symptoms that often occur with its arousal to the attention of the Western world, especially the scientific and medical communities, therapists, and people undergoing kundalini experiences.

The KRN holds international symposia on kundalini and welcomes interested individuals from around the world. It is not restricted to any religious tradition or spiritual discipline. The common thread is an interest in the scientific verification of the kundalini phenomenon.

If you would like to be on the mailing list of the Kundalini Research Network, check the KRN website at www.kundalininet.org. To contact Dr. Kason directly, you can write:

Dr. Yvonne Kason
P.O. Box 88058
2975 Kingston Road
Scarborough, Ontario
Canada   M1M 1N0

The Spiritual Emergence Network is an international information service, which can provide referrals to therapists and doctors experienced in counselling persons having psycho-spiritual crises. Readers wishing a referral to a therapist in their area can call SEN in San Francisco, CA, at (415) 648-2610.

Bibliography

The following bibliographic references that I've drawn on are listed in the order of appearance in each chapter.

CHAPTER 1

Waller, Adrian. "Down in Devil's Gap," in *Reader's Digest*, February 1981, pp 25-30.

CHAPTER 2

Kieffer, Gene, ed. *Kundalini for the New Age: Selected Writings by Gopi Krishna*. New York: Bantam, 1988.

St. Teresa of Avila. *The Interior Castle*. Quoted in Rosemary Ellen Guiley, *Harper's Encyclopedia of Mystical and Paranormal Experience*, San Francisco: Harper, 1991.

Harpur, Tom. *Life After Death*, Toronto: McClelland & Stewart, 1991.

Evans-Wentz, W.Y. *The Tibetan Book of the Dead, or The After-Death Experiences on the Bardo Plane*, according to Lama Kazi Dawa-Samdup's English rendering. London: Oxford University Press, 1960.

Rinpoche, Sogyal. *The Tibetan Book of Living and Dying*, San Francisco: Harper, 1992.

Budge, A.E. Wallis. *The Book of the Dead: The Papyrus of Ani.* New York: Dover, 1967.

Newman, Barbara. *Sister of Wisdom: St. Hildegaard's Theology of the Feminine.* Berkeley and Los Angeles: University of California Press, 1987.

Jung, Carl. *The Psychology of Kundalini Yoga: Notes of the Seminar given in 1932 by C.G. Jung,* ed. Sonu Shamdasani. Princeton: Bollingen Series, Princeton University Press, 1996.

Barton, Chayim Douglas. "Jungian Psychology and the Mahamudra in Vajrayana Buddhism." Dissertation thesis for the degree of Doctor of Philosophy in Transpersonal Psychology, Institute of Transpersonal Psychology, Menlo Park CA, May 8, 1990.

Blofeld, John. *The Tantric Mysticism of Tibet.* New York: E.P. Dutton & Co. Inc., 1970. Cited in Chayim Douglas Barton. "Jungian Psychology and the Mahamudra in Vajrayana Buddhism."

Evans-Wentz, W.Y. *Tibetan Yoga and Secret Doctrines.* London: Oxford University Press, 1935. Cited in Chayim Douglas Barton. "Jungian Psychology and the Mahamudra in Vajrayana Buddhism."

Lansky, Phillip, and Shen Yu. "Bone Marrow Chi Kung: By infusing the bones with vital energy, the ancient Chinese learned how to bolster the immune system and develop their spiritual essence." *Yoga Journal,* July/August 1990, pp. 21-25.

Greenwell, Bonnie. *Energies of Transformation: A Guide to the Kundalini Process.* CA: Shakti River Press, 1990.

Tweedie, Irina. *The Chasm of Fire: A woman's experience of liberation through the teachings of a Sufi Master.* England: Element Books Ltd., 1979.

Kripananda, Swami. "Kundalini: The Energy of Transformation," in *Ancient Wisdom and Modern Science*, ed. Stanislav Grof. Albany: State University of New York Press, 1984.

St. Romain, Philip. *Kundalini Energy and Christian Spirituality: A Pathway to Growth and Healing.* New York: Crossroad Publishers, 1994.

Prayer Department, Unity School of Religious Studies. *Holy Spirit Regeneration.* Unity Village, MO: Unity School of Christianity, 1993.

Guiley, Rosemary Ellen. *Harper's Encyclopedia of Mystical and Paranormal Experience.* San Francisco: Harper, 1991. p 385.

Feuerstein, Georg. *The Encyclopedic Dictionary of Yoga.* New York: Paragon, 1990.

Feuerstein, Georg. *The Yoga-sutra of Patanjali: A New Translation and Commentary.* Rochester, Vermont: Inner Traditions, 1989.

Baba, Bangali. *The Yogasutra of Patanjali, with Commentary of Vyasa.* Delhi: Motilal Banarsidass Publishers, 1976.

Eliade, Mircea. *Yoga: Immortality and Freedom.* New York: Bollington Foundation, 1958.

Krishna, Gopi. *Secrets of Kundalini in Panchastavi.* New Delhi: Kundalini Research and Publication Trust, 1978.

Underhill, Evelyn. *Mysticism.* New York: New American Library, 1974.

Harrigan, Joan Shivarpita. *Kundalini Vidya: A Comprehensive System for Understanding and Guiding Spiritual Development.* Oak Ridge, Tennessee: Pantanjali Kundalini Yoga Care, 1996.

CHAPTER 3

James, William. *The Varieties of Mystical Experience.* New York: New American Library, 1958.

Maslow, Abraham. *Toward a Psychology of Being.* New York: Van Nostrand, 1962.

Bucke, Richard Maurice. *Cosmic Consciousness.* New York: E.P. Dutton and Company, 1969.

Jung, Carl G. *Memories, Dreams, Reflections.* New York: Vintage Books, 1989.

CHAPTER 4

Krishna, Gopi. *Kundalini: The Evolutionary Energy in Man.* Colorado: Shambhala, 1967, 1970.

Jung, Carl. *The Psychology of Kundalini Yoga: Notes of the Seminar given in 1932 by C.G. Jung.* ed. Sonu Shamdasani. Princeton: Bollingen Series, Princeton University Press, 1996.

Avalon, Arthur. *The Serpent Power: The Secrets of Tantric and Shaktic Yoga.* New York: Dover (1919), 1974.

Eliade, Mircea. *Yoga: Immortality and Freedom.* New York: Bollington Foundation, 1958.

Sannella, Lee. *Kundalini: Psychosis or Transcendence?* San Francisco: H.S. Dakin, 1976.

Sannella, Lee. *The Kundalini Experience.* Lower Lake, California: Integral Publishing, 1987.

Grof, Stanislav, and Christina Grof, eds. *Spiritual Emergency: When Personal Transformation Becomes a Crisis.* Los Angeles: Tarcher, 1989.

Greenwell, Bonnie. *Energies of Transformation: A Guide to the Kundalini Process.* Cupertino, California: Shakti River Press, 1990.

Grof, Christina, and Grof, Stanislav. *The Stormy Search for Self.* Los Angeles: Tarcher, 1990.

Grof, Stanislav. *Beyond the Brain.* Albany State University of New York: 1985.

Krishna, Gopi. *The Biological Basis of Religion and Genius.* New York: Harper and Row, 1972.

Krishna, Gopi. *Higher Consciousness: The Evolutionary Thrust of Kundalini.* New York: Julian Press, 1974.

Kieffer, Gene, ed. *Kundalini for the New Age: Selected Writings by Gopi Krishna.* New York: Bantam, 1988.

Kieffer, Gene, ed. *Kundalini, Empowering Human Evolution: Selected Writings of Gopi Krishna.* New York: Paragon House, 1996.

Harrigan, Joan Shivarpita. *Kundalini Vidya: A Comprehensive System for Understanding and Guiding Spiritual Development.* Oak Ridge, Tennessee: Pantanjali Kundalini Yoga Care, 1996.

Jyoti. *An Angel Called my Name: A Story of a Transformational Energy That Lives in the Body.* Prague: DharmaGaia, 1998, pp. 22-24.

Alcoholics Anonymous World Service. *Pass It On: The story of Bill Wilson and how the A.A. message reached the world.*

New York: Alcoholics Anonymous World Services Inc., 1984, pp. 120-121.

Joy, W. Brugh. *Joy's Way: A Map for the Transformational Journey*. Los Angeles: Tarcher, 1979.

CHAPTER 5

Moody, Raymond A., Jr. *Life after Life: The Investigation of a Phenomenon—Survival of Bodily Death*. New York: Bantam, 1975.

Moody, Raymond A., Jr. *The Light Beyond*. New York: Bantam, 1988.

Ring, Kenneth. *Heading Toward Omega: In Search of the Meaning of Near Death Experiences*. New York: William Morrow, 1984.

Morse, Melvin, with Paul Perry. *Closer to the Light*. New York: Ivy Books, 1990.

Morse, Melvin, with Paul Perry. *Transformed by the Light: The Powerful Effect of Near-death Experiences on People's Lives*. New York: Villard Books, 1992.

Harpur, Tom. *Life After Death*. Toronto: McClelland & Stewart, 1991.

The Philadelphia Enquirer, Philadelphia, Pennsylvania, December 1988 (as quoted by Tom Harpur in *Life After Death*).

Bach, M. Taylor. *A Message of Hope: The Near Death Experience—Accounts and Perspectives*. Video. Ft. Thomas, Kentucky: The Counselling Institute, 1987.

Kason, Yvonne. "NDE-Variants and Kundalini: Exploring Death-Watch and Death-Bed Experiences." Presented at Kundalini Research Network Conference, 1995, Philadelphia, 1995.

Kason, Yvonne. "Near-Death and Death-Watch Experiences: Openings onto the Mystic Path." Presented at International Association for Near Death Studies 1999 Conference, Vancouver, 1999.

Brinkley, Dannion, and Paul Perry. *Saved by the Light: The true story of a man who died twice and the profound revelations he received*. New York: Harper Paperbacks, 1994.

Eadie, Betty and Curtis Taylor. *Embraced by the Light*. Placerville, CA: Gold Leaf Press, 1992.

Kason, Yvonne. "Near-Death Experiences and Kundalini Awakening: Exploring the Links." *Journal of Near-Death Studies*, Spring 1994.

CHAPTER 6

McCartney, Francesca. *Personal Communication*, Mill Valley, CA: Academy of Intuitive Studies, 1990.

Ring, Kenneth. *The Omega Project*. New York: William Morrow, 1992.

Fowler, Raymond E. *The Andreasson Affair*. Englewood Cliffs, New Jersey: Prentice-Hall, 1979.

Steiger, Brad. *The Fellowship*. New York: Ballantine, 1988.

Thompson, Keith. "The UFO Encounter Experience as a Crisis of Transformation," in *Spiritual Emergency: When Personal Transformation Becomes a Crisis*, ed. Stanislav Grof and Christina Grof. Los Angeles: Tarcher, 1989.

CHAPTER 7

Newman, Barbara. *Sister of Wisdom: St. Hildegaard's Theology of the Feminine*, Berkeley and Los Angeles: University of California Press, 1987.

Hildegaard, St. "A letter from Hildegaard of Bingen to Guibert of Gembloux." Excerpted in Barbara Newman, *Sister of Wisdom: St. Hildegaard's Theology of the Feminine*. Berkeley and Los Angeles: University of California Press, 1987.

Abell, Arthur. *Talks with Great Composers*. Garmisch-Partenkirschen: G.E. Schroeder, 1964.

Einstein, Albert. *Living Philosophies*. New York: Simon & Schuster, 1931.

Einstein, Albert. *The World as I See It*. New York: Citadel Press, 1979.

Saraswati, Swami Satyananda. *Kundalini Tantra*. India: Bihar School of Yoga, 1992.

CHAPTER 8

Krishna, Gopi. *Kundalini: The Evolutionary Energy in Man*. Boulder, Colorado: Shambhala, 1967, 1970.

Krishna, Gopi. *Higher Consciousness: The Evolutionary Thrust of Kundalini*. New York: Julian Press, 1974.

Krishna, Gopi. *The Biological Basis of Religion and Genius*. Kundalini New Delhi: Research and Publication Trust, 1978.

Saraswati, Swami Satyananda. *Kundalini Tantra*. India: Bihar School of Yoga, 1992.

Harrigan, Joan Shivarpita. *Kundalini Vidya: A Comprehensive System for Understanding and Guiding Spiritual Development.* Tennessee: Pantanjali Kundalini Yoga Care, 1996.

Kason, Yvonne. "Kundalini, the Forefront of Consciousness Research: Evolving Paradigms for the New Millennium." Presented at Kundalini Research Network's 1997 Conference, Watsonville, CA, 1997.

Guiley, Rosemary Ellen. *Harper's Encyclopedia of Mystical and Paranormal Experiences.* San Francisco: Harper, 1991.
Eliade, Mircea. *Yoga: Immortality and Freedom.* New York: Bollington Foundation, 1958.

Krishna, Gopi, *Living with Kundalini.* Rev. by Leslie Shepard. Boulder, Colorado: Shambhala, 1993.

Krishna, Gopi. *The Dawn of a New Science.* New Delhi: Kundalini Research and Publication Trust, 1978.

Feuerstein, Georg. *The Encyclopedic Dictionary of Yoga.* New York: Paragon House, 1990.

Feuerstein, Georg. *The Yoga-sutra of Patanjali: A New Translation and Commentary.* Rochester: Inner Traditions, 1989.

Krishna, Gopi. *Kundalini: The Evolutionary Energy in Man.* Boulder, Colorado: Shambhala, 1967, 1970.

Krishna, Gopi. *The Secret of Yoga.* London: Turnstone, 1972.

Krishna, Gopi. *The Awakening of Kundalini.* Toronto: Find Research Trust, 1989.

CHAPTER 9

Greenwell, Bonnie. *Energies of Transformation: A Guide to the Kundalini Process.* Cupertino, California: Shakti River Press, 1990.

Kason, Yvonne, Michael Bradford, Paul Pond, and Bonnie Greenwell. "Spiritual Emergence Syndrome and Kundalini Awakening—How Are They Related? The Kundalini Research Questionnaire Pilot Project Results, 1991." Academy of Religion and Psychical Research Annual Proceedings, Philadelphia 1992.

Krishna, Gopi. *Living with Kundalini*. Rev. by Leslie Shepard, Boulder, Colorado: Shambhala, 1993.

Lukoff, David, Frances Lu, and Robert Turner. "Towards a More Culturally Sensitive DSM-IV: Psychoreligious and Psychospiritual Problems," *Journal of Nervous and Mental Disease* 180, 11 (November 1992).

American Psychiatric Association. *Diagnostic and Statistical Manual of Mental Disorders*, 4th ed. Washington, D.C.: American Psychiatric Association, 1994.

CHAPTER 10

Kason, Yvonne. "The Modern Kundalini Hypothesis: A Bio-Psycho-Spiritual Model of Transformation of Consciousness." Proceedings of the Sixth Conference on Treatment and Research of Experienced Anomalous Trauma, Virginia Beach, 1994.

Kieffer, Gene, ed. *Kundalini for the New Age: Selected Writings by Gopi Krishna*. New York: Bantam, 1988.

Underhill, Evelyn. *Mysticism*. New York: New American Library, 1974, p. 81.

Greenwell, Bonnie. *Energies of Transformation: A Guide to the Kundalini Process*. Cupertino, California: Shakti River Press, 1990.

Krishna, Gopi. *Living with Kundalini*. Rev. by Leslie Shepard. Boulder, Colorado: Shambhala, 1993.

Kason, Yvonne. "Counselling Clients with Spiritual or Religious Experiences." Presented at Centre for Addiction and Mental Health, Queen Street Site, Toronto, June 23, 1999.

CHAPTER 11

Kason, Yvonne. "Deepening Connection to Spirit: The Kundalini Process and Spiritual Transformation." Presented at the Life Enrichment Centre, Edmonton, April 24, 1999.

Bragdon, Emma. *The Call of Spiritual Emergency: From Person Crisis to Personal Transformation*. San Francisco: Harper and Row, 1990.

Greenwell, Bonnie. *Energies of Transformation: A Guide to the Kundalini Process*. Cupertino, California: Shakti River Press, 1990.

CHAPTER 12

Radha, Swami Sivananda. *Kundalini Yoga for the West*. Boston: Shambhala, 1978.

Besant, Annie. *The Ancient Wisdom: An Outline of Theosophical Teachings*. Adyar, India: Theosophical Publishing House, 1939.

Crabtree, Adam. *Multiple Man: Explorations in Possession and Multiple Personality*. Don Mills, Ontario: Grafton Books, 1985.

Peck, M. Scott. *People of the Lie: The Hope for Healing Human Evil*. New York: Touchstone, 1983.

CHAPTER 13

Grof, Stanislav, and Christina Grof, eds. *Spiritual Emergency: When Personal Transformation Becomes a Crisis*. Los Angeles: Tarcher, 1989.

Bragdon, Emma. *A Sourcebook for Helping People in Spiritual Emergency*. Los Altos, California: Lightening Up Press, 1988.
Bragdon, Emma. *The Call of Spiritual Emergency: From Person Crisis to Personal Transformation*. San Francisco: Harper and Row, 1990.

American Psychiatric Association. *Diagnostic and Statistical Manual of Mental Disorders*, 4th ed., Washington, DC: American Psychiatric Association, 1994.

Lukoff, David. "Diagnosis of Mystical Experiences with Psychotic Features," *The Journal of Transpersonal Psychology* 17 (1985).

Sannella, Lee. *Kundalini: Psychosis or Transcendence?* San Francisco: H.S. Dakin, 1976.

CHAPTER 14

Krishna, Gopi. *Living with Kundalini*. Rev. by Leslie Shepard. Boulder, Colorado: Shambhala, 1993.

Feuerstein, Georg. *The Yoga-sutra of Patanjali: A New Translation and Commentary*. Rochester, Vermont: Inner Traditions, 1989.

CHAPTER 15

Harris, Barbara, and Lionel C. Bascom. *Full Circle: The Near-death Experience and Beyond*. New York: Pocket Books/Simon and Schuster, 1990.

Kason, Yvonne. "EHEs, Spiritual Transformation, and Kundalini Awakening: A Clinical Perspective." Academy of Religion and Psychical Research Annual Proceedings, Philadelphia 1993.

Krishna, Gopi. "Religion, Science, and Illumination." In *Gopi Krishna: Selected Interviews and Discourses, 1979–1983.* Transcription by Michael Bradford. Flesherton, Ontario: Find Research Trust, 1992.

Breaux, Charles. *Journey into Consciousness: The Chakras, Tantra, and Jungian Psychology.* Maine: Nicolas Hayes, 1989.

CHAPTER 16

Kason, Yvonne. "Counselling Persons with Kundalini and Other Spiritually Transformative Experiences." Presented at Kundalini Research Network's 1997 Conference, Watsonville, CA, 1997.

Kason, Yvonne. "Understanding NDEs and their After-Effects: Learning from the Kundalini and Chakra Model." Presented at International Association for Near Death Studies 1999 Conference, Vancouver, 1999.

Bragdon, Emma. *The Call of Spiritual Emergency: From Person Crisis to Personal Transformation.* San Francisco: Harper and Row, 1990.

Greenwell, Bonnie. *Energies of Transformation: A Guide to the Kundalini Process.* Cupertino, California: Shakti River Press, 1990.

Saraswati, Swami Satyananda. *Kundalini Tantra.* India: Bihar School of Yoga, 1992.

Kripananda, Swami. "Kundalini: The Energy of Transformation," in *Ancient Wisdom and Modern Science*, ed. Stanislav Grof. Albany, NY: State University of New York Press, 1984.

Woolger, Roger J. *Other Lives, Other Selves: A Jungian Psychotherpist Discovers Past Lives*. New York: Bantam, 1988.

Jung, Carl. *The Psychology of Kundalini Yoga: Notes of the Seminar given in 1932 by C.G. Jung*. Edited by Sonu Shamdasani, Princeton, New Jersey: Bollingen Series, Princeton University Press, 1996.

Barton, Chayim Douglas. "Jungian Psychology and the Mahamudra in Vajrayana Buddhism." Dissertation thesis for the degree of Doctor of Philosophy in Transpersonal Psychology, Institute of Transpersonal Psychology, Menlo Park CA, May 8, 1990.

CHAPTER 17

Feuerstein, Georg. *The Encyclopedic Dictionary of Yoga*. New York: Paragon House, 1990.

Eliade, Mircea. *Yoga: Immortality and Freedom*. New York: Bollington Foundation, 1958.

Krishna, Gopi. *Higher Consciousness*. New York: Julian Press, 1974.

RELATED WORKS ON KUNDALINI AND OTHER SUBJECTS

Arundale, G.S. *Kundalini: An occult experience*. India: The Theosophical Publishing House, 1974.

Aurobindo, Sri. *Lights on Yoga*. 9th ed. India: Sri Aurobindo Ashram Press, 1981.

Berman, Phillip. *The Journey Home: What Near-Death Experiences and Mysticism Teach Us About the Gift of Life*. New York: Pocket Books, 1996.

Bruyere, Rosalyn. *Wheels of Light: Chakras, Auras, and the Healing Energy of the Body*. New York: Fireside Books, 1994.

Chaney, Earlyne, and William Messick. *Kundalini and the Third Eye*. CA: Astara, 1980.

Chinmoy, Sri. *Kundalini: The Mother Power*. Agni N.Y.: Agni Press, 1974.

Colton, Ann Ree. *Kundalini West*. CA: Arc Publishing Company, 1978.

Condron, Barbara. *Kundalini Rising: Mastering Creative Energies*. MI: School of Metaphysics Publishing, 1994.

Da Avabhasa. *Easy Death*. Clearlake, California: Dawn Horse Press, 1983.

Danielou, Alain. *Yoga: Mastering the Secrets of Matter and the Universe*. Rochester, VT: Inner Traditions International, 1991.

Devananda, Swami Vishnu. *Meditation and Mantras*. New York: OM Lotus Publishing Co., 1981.

Edwards, Lawrence. *The Soul's Journey: Guidance from the Goddess Within*. Putnam Valley, New York: Lawrence Edwards, 1996.

Fraser, Sylvia. *The Book of Strange: A thinking person's guide to psychic phenomena*. Toronto: Doubleday Canada Ltd., 1992.

Frawley, David. *Tantric Yoga and the Wisdom Goddesses: Spiritual Secrets in Ayurveda*. Salt Lake City, Utah: Passages Press,1994.

Goswami, Amit. *The Self-Aware Universe: How Consciousness Creates the Material World*. New York: Jeremy P. Tarcher/ Putnam Books, 1993.

Greyson, Bruce. "The physio-kundalini syndrome and mental illness." *Journal of Transpersonal Psychology*, 25 (1993). pp. 43-58.

Greyson, Bruce, and Nancy Bush. "Distressing near-death experiences." *Psychiatry*, 55 (1992). pp. 95-110.

Grof, Stanislav, ed. *Ancient Wisdom and Modern Science*. Albany, NY: State University of New York Press, 1984.

Harris, Barbara. *Spiritual Awakenings: A Guidebook for Experiencers and Those Who Care about Them*. Baltimore, Maryland: Stage 3 Books, 1993.

Irving, Darrel. *Serpent of Fire: A Modern View of Kundalini*. Introduction by Gene Kieffer: "Two Interviews with Gopi Krishna." York Beach, ME: Samuel Weiser Inc., 1995.

Khalsa, Rama Kirn Singh. *Sadhana Guidelines for Kundalini Yoga Daily Practice*. Los Angeles: Archline Publications, 1988.

Kripaluanand, Swami. *Science of Meditation*. Bombay, India: New Darnodaya Press, 1977.

Kripananda, Swami. *The Sacred Power: A seeker's guide to Kundalini*. South Fallsberg, NY: SYDA Foundation, 1995.

Krishna, Gopi. *The Riddle of Consciousness*. New York: Central Institute for Kundalini Research and Kundalini Research Foundation, 1976.

Krishna, Gopi. *Yoga: A Vision of Its Future*. New Delhi: Kundalini Research and Publication Trust, 1978.

Krishna, Gopi. *The Real Nature of Mystical Experience*. Toronto: New Age Publishing, 1979.

Krishna, Gopi. *Kundalini in Time and Space*. New Delhi: Kundalini Research and Publication Trust, 1979.

Krishna, Gopi. *The Shape of Events to Come*. New Delhi: Kundalini Research and Publication Trust, 1979.

Krishna, Gopi. *Reason and Revelation*. Toronto: New Age Publishing, 1979.

Krishna, Gopi. *The Present Crisis*. New York: New Concepts Publishing, 1981.

Krishna, Gopi. *The Way to Self-knowledge*. New York: New Concepts Publishing, 1985.

Krishna, Gopi. *From the Unseen*. Toronto: Find Research Trust, 1985.

Krishna, Gopi. *The Wonder of the Brain*. Toronto: Find Research Trust, 1987.

Lutyens, Mary. *Krishnamurti: The Years of Awakening*. New York: Avon, 1975.

Malik, Arjan Dass. *Kundalini and Meditation*. New Delhi, India: Manohar, 1994.

Moody, Raymond, and Paul Perry. *Coming Back: A psychiatrist explores past-life journeys*. New York: Bantam Books, 1991.

Mookerjee, Ajit. *Kundalini: The Arousal of the Inner Energy*. Rochester, VT: Destiny Books, 1991.

Muktananda, Swami. *Kundalini: The Secret of Life*. South Falls-berg, New York: SYDA Foundation,1979.

Mumford, Jonn. *A Chakra and Kundalini Workbook: Psycho-spiritual techniques for health, rejuvination, psychic pow-ers and spiritual realization*. St. Paul, MN: Llewellyn Publications, 1994.

Narayanananda, Swami. *The Primal Power In Man, or The Kundalini Shakti*. 4th rev. ed. Rishikesh, India: Shri Narayana Press, 1975.

Paulson, Genevieve Lewis. *Kundalini and the Chakras: A prac-tical Manual Evolution in this Lifetime*. St. Paul, MN: Llewellyn Publications Inc, 1993.

Rai, Dina Nath. *Kundalini Awakening: A Practical Guide*. Luc-know, India: Kundalini Yoga Research Institute, 1997.

Scott, Mary. *Kundalini in the Physical World*. London, England: Arkana, 1983.

Shivananda, Swami. *Kundalini Yoga*. Himalayas, India: Yoga-vedanta Forest Academy Press, 1994.

Svoboda, Robert. *Aghora II: Kundalini*. Albuquerque, NM: Brotherhood of Life, 1993.

Targ, Russel, and Jane Katra. *Miracles of Mind: Exploring non-local consciousness and spiritual healing*. Novato, CA: New World Library, 1998.

Tirtha, Swami Vishnu. *Devatma Shakti: Kundalini—Divine Power*. 6th ed. Delhi, India: Kumar Brothers Printing Press, 1993.

White, John, ed. *Kundalini, Evolution and Enlightenment*. New York: Paragon House, 1990.

Whitfield, Barbara Harris. *Spiritual Awakenings: Insights of the Near-Death Experience and Other Doorways to Our Soul.* Deerfield Beach Florida: Health Communications, 1995.

Whitton, Joel, and Joe Fisher. *Life between Life: Scientific explorations into the void separating one incarnation from the next.* New York: Warner Books, 1986.

Wilber, Ken, Jack Engler, and Daniel Brown. *Transformations of Consciousness: Conventional and Contemplative Perspectives on Development.* Boston, MA: Shambhala Publications, 1986.

Yogananda, Paramahansa. *An Autobiography of a Yogi.* Los Angeles: Self Realization Press, 1946.

About the Author

DR. YVONNE KASON, MD, is a family physician, transpersonal therapist, and an assistant professor in the Faculty of Medicine at the University of Toronto. She was the founder of the Spiritual Emergence Research and Referral Clinic and a founder and board member of the Kundalini Research Network. Dr. Kason is a media resource and has been a guest on numerous radio and television shows across Canada and in the U.S. Her near-death experience has been re-enacted on "Sightings," as well as in two television documentaries. A recognized medical expert on near-death, kundalini, and mystical experiences, she is in demand as a lecturer to professional and public groups internationally.

AUTHOR UPDATE – 2008 EDITION

DR. YVONNE KASON M.D. was the co-founder of the Spirituality in Health-Care Network in 2000. In 2002, she chaired the University of Toronto's first international conference on Spirituality and Health-Care. A goal of both was to promote multi-faith and multi-professional dialogue relating to spirituality and healing. Dr. Kason retired from medical practice in 2006.

CPSIA information can be obtained at www.ICGtesting.com
Printed in the USA
LVOW07s1051170515

438804LV00003B/600/P